AF361397

An Introduction to Relational Network Theory

Equinox Textbooks and Surveys in Linguistics
Series Editor: Robin Fawcett, Cardiff University

Published titles in the series:
An Introduction to English Sentence Structure: Clauses, Markers, Missing Elements
Jon Jonz
An Introduction to Irish English
Carolina P. Amador Moreno
An Introduction to Linguistics and Language Studies
Anne McCabe
Analysing Casual Conversation
Suzanne Eggins and Diana Slade
Genre Relations: Mapping Culture
J.R. Martin and David Rose
Intonation in the Grammar of English
M.A.K. Halliday and William S. Greaves
Invitation to Systemic Functional Linguistics through the Cardiff Grammar: An Extension and Simplification of Halliday's Systemic Functional Grammar (Third edition)
Robin Fawcett
Language in Psychiatry: A Handbook of Clinical Practice
Jonathan Fine
Learning to Write/Reading to Learn: Genre, Knowledge and Pedagogy in the Sydney School
David Rose and J. R. Martin
Meaning-Centered Grammar: An Introductory Text
Craig Hancock
Multimodal Transcription and Text Analysis: A Multimodal Toolkit and Coursebook with Associated On-line Course
Anthony Baldry and Paul J. Thibault
Text Linguistics: The How and Why of Meaning
M.A.K. Halliday and Jonathan Webster
The Power of Language: How Discourse Influences Society (Second edition)
Lynne Young, Michael Fitzgerald and Saira Fitzgerald
The Western Classical Tradition in Linguistics (Second edition)
Keith Allan
Writing Readable Research: A Guide for Students of Social Science
Beverly A. Lewin

Forthcoming titles in the series:
Corpora and Meaning
Steven Jones and Howard Jackson
Functional Syntax Handbook: Analysing English at the Level of Form
Robin Fawcett
Multimodal Corpus-Based Approaches to Website Analysis
Anthony Baldry and Kay O'Halloran

An Introduction to Relational Network Theory

History, Principles, and Descriptive Applications

Adolfo M. García, William J. Sullivan, and Sarah Tsiang

Foreword by M. A. K. Halliday

SHEFFIELD UK   BRISTOL CT

Published by Equinox Publishing Ltd.

UK: Office 415, The Workstation, 15 Paternoster Row, Sheffield, South Yorkshire S1 2BX

USA: ISD, 70 Enterprise Drive, Bristol, CT 06010

www.equinoxpub.com

First published 2017

British Library Cataloguing-in-Publication Data

A catalogue record for this book is available from the British Library.

ISBN-13 978 1 78179 260 5   (hardback)
ISBN-13 978 1 78179 261 2   (paperback)

Library of Congress Cataloging-in-Publication Data

Names: García, Adolfo Martín, editor. | Sullivan, William J. (Linguist)
    editor. | Tsiang, Sarah, 1978- editor.
Title: An introduction to Relational Network Theory : History, principles, and
    descriptive applications / Adolfo M. García, William J. Sullivan, and Sarah
    Tsiang.
Description: Sheffield, UK ; Bristol, CT : Equinox Publishing Ltd, [2017] |
    Series: Equinox textbooks and surveys in linguistics | Includes
    bibliographical references and index.
Identifiers: LCCN 2016041919| ISBN 9781781792605 (hb) | ISBN 9781781792612
    (pb)
Subjects: LCSH: Relational grammar--Methodology | Neuropsychology--methods |
    Neurolinguistics--History. | Psycholinguistics--History.
Classification: LCC P158.6 .A6 2017 | DDC 415.01/825--dc23
LC record available at https://lccn.loc.gov/2016041919

Typeset by ISB Typesetting, Sheffield, UK
Printed and bound by Lightning Source Inc. (La Vergne, TN), Lighting Source UK Ltd.
(Milton Keynes), Lightning Source AU Pty. (Scoresby, Victoria)

Notes on Previous Works

This book represents an original compilation, targeted for newcomers to Relational Network Theory. Some of the contents are elaborations or reproductions of previous material, as indicated below.

Chapter 4 contains a completely rewritten and reoriented version of: Sullivan, W. J. (1998a). Underspecification and feature geometry: Theorems of a reticular theory of language. *LACUS Forum*, 24, 53–65.

Chapter 5 is an original text, but an earlier version was presented by Sullivan as a talk to the linguistic faculty of Maria Curie-Skłodowska University, Lublin, for their working papers series.

Chapter 6 is a modified version of: García, A. M. (2015). A connectionist approach to functional-cognitive linguistics: Spanish pronominal clitics and verb endings in relational-network terms. *Signos*, 48 (88), 197–222.

Chapter 7 is an original text, but draws on examples from the previously published article: Sullivan, W. J. (2004). Participant realization in English narrative. In H. Kardela, W. J. Sullivan, & A. Głaz (eds.), *Perspectives on language: Papers from the 11th annual PASE Conference, 2001* (pp. 273–280). Lublin: Wydawnictwo UMCS; and the conference paper: Sullivan, W. J. & Tsiang, S. (2015). Noun, pronoun, or zero: Who was that masked participant? *LACUS Forum*, XLII, Molloy College, NY.

Chapter 8 is a new presentation but draws on examples from previously published or in-press analyses of Sullivan and Tsiang's speech errors corpus: Sullivan, W. J. (2011). Input, output, and (de)linearization: What we owe to Sydney M. Lamb. *LACUS Forum*, 36, 279–289; Sullivan, W. J. & Tsiang, S. (in press b). Tactic pattern errors and the architecture of stratificational theory. *LACUS Forum*, 37; Tsiang, S. & Sulllivan, W. J. (in press). Unintended blends and the stratification of language. *LACUS Forum*, 38; Sullivan, W. J. & Tsiang, S. (in press d). Substitution errors and the architecture of the linguistic system. *LACUS Forum*, 40.

The appendix is an authorized reproduction of: García, A. M. (2013). Relational Network Theory as a bridge between linguistics and neuroscience: An interview with Professor Sydney Lamb. *Linguistics and the Human Sciences*, 8 (1), 3–27, © Equinox Publishing Ltd [2013].

Figures 2.6 and 2.8 are authorized reproductions of Figures 6.13 and 9.3 from: Lamb, S. M. (1999). *Pathways of the brain: The neurocognitive basis of language*. Amsterdam: John Benjamins. Used by permission of John Benjamins Publishing and Sydney Lamb.

Figure 2.13 is an authorized reproduction of Figure 17.6 from: Lamb, S. M. (2004 j). In J. J. Webster (ed.) *Language & reality: Selected writings of*

Sydney Lamb. New York: Continuum. Used by permission of Bloomsbury Publishing Plc.

Figures 3.1 through 3.6 are free media from Wikimedia Commons. All these images were labeled for commercial reuse with modifications. Due credits for these figures are as follows:

- Figure 3.1. Patrick J. Lynch, medical illustrator; C. Carl Jaffe, MD, cardiologist (licensed under Creative Commons Attribution 2.5, License 2006).
- Figure 3.2. John Henkel, from the Food and Drug Administration (Public Domain).
- Figure 3.3. Anonymous (Public Domain).
- Figure 3.4. Henry Vandyke Carter and Henry Gray (1918). *Anatomy of the Human Body* (Public Domain).
- Figure 3.5. Blausen.com staff. 'Blausen gallery 2014'. *Wikiversity Journal of Medicine*. DOI:10.15347/wjm/2014.010. ISSN 20018762.
- Figure 3.6. Thomas Splettstoesser (licensed under Creative Commons Attribution-Share Alike 4.0 International license).

Contents

List of Figures and Tables   ix

Acknowledgments   xiii

Foreword: On the creation, and the creator, of RNT
(by M. A. K. Halliday)   xv

Introduction   1

Part I: Convergences: Linguistic, operational, and neurological
       considerations

1.   The Origins of Relational Network Theory   11

2.   From Language Structure to Language Processing   27

3.   From Neurological Structures to Language Processing   57

Part II: Descriptive applications

4.   An RNT Approach to Russian Obstruent Onsets   79

5.   An RNT Approach to the Polish Genitive   103

6.   An RNT Approach to Spanish Pronominal Clitics and
Verb Endings   117

7.   An RNT Approach to Participants in English Texts   135

8.   An RNT Approach to Speech Errors in English and Polish   157

Afterword   175

Appendix: An interview with Sydney Lamb   181

Glossary of Terms   205

References   213

Indexes   225

List of Figures and Tables

Figures

1.1.	The three main systems in Stratificational Grammar.	15
1.2.	A five-strata model of the linguistic system, relative to embodied/conceptual/executive cognition.	16
1.3.	Six kinds of realizational discrepancies.	18
1.4.	Some of the main nodes in RNT.	21
1.5.	Some examples of nections.	21
1.6.	Two wrong conceptions of relational networks.	22
1.7.	The appropriate conception of relational networks.	22
1.8.	The lexeme *undergo* as a network of relationships.	24
2.1.	Two abstract notation nodes translated into narrow notation.	32
2.2.	Inhibitory connections acting on output lines of an ordered OR node: The case of a portmanteau realization.	33
2.3.	An inhibitory connection acting directly on a node.	33
2.4.	Handling timing in the ordered AND node via feedback timing.	35
2.5.	A simplified portion of English lexotactics for unmarked, affirmative, active clauses.	36
2.6.	A simplified lexotactic network for English yes/no questions.	37
2.7.	The seven varieties of diamond nodes and four types of non-nodes.	40
2.8.	The locus of the linguistic system in the stratified cognitive arch.	43
2.9.	A simplified diagram of the connections involved in the conceptual category DOG.	44
2.10.	Interacting phonological subsystems.	45
2.11.	Examples of threshold nodes.	47
2.12.	Three states in the strengthening of connections.	48
2.13.	Complex associations in slang lexeme formation.	54
2.14.	Network representation of a mutable lexeme.	55
3.1.	Midsagittal section of the brain.	58
3.2.	Some subcortical structures involved in language processing.	59
3.3.	Lateral section of the left hemisphere.	60
3.4.	A depiction of some Brodmann areas.	62
3.5.	Structural components of a neuron.	63
3.6.	A rough illustration of a synapse.	64
3.7.	Reciprocal connections between areas depend on separate neural circuits.	70
3.8.	Connections with different strengths linked to the concept BIRD.	71
3.9.	A type of inhibitory connection in RNT corresponding to an axoaxonic inhibitory connection.	73
3.10.	A type of inhibitory connection in RNT corresponding to an axosomatic inhibitory connection.	74
4.1.	A_1 / P, T, K and A_2 / F, S, Š, X.	91

4.2. A_3 / A_1, A_2.   91
4.3.   ObOnset / F, B, G.   91
4.4.   F / A_3 and G / A_3, c, č.   92
4.5.   F / A_3 and B / A_2 and G / A_3, c, č.   92
4.6.   ObOnset / [F] [B] (G[Y]).   92
4.7.   The realization of the p,b archiphoneme P and its relation to voice.   93
4.8.   Russian obstruent onsets generalized.   94
4.9.   (Archi)phonemes to hypophonemes: Preliminary (a) and simplified (b).   96
4.10.   (Archi)phonemes to hypophonemes: Fricatives (a), and affricates (b).   97
4.11.   Russian obstruent onsets: Morphemes to hypophonemes.   97
5.1.   Functional relations of the Polish genitive.   109
5.2.   Formal relations of the Polish genitive.   110
5.3.   Lexotactic relations of the Polish genitive.   110
5.4.   The genitive case in Polish.   111
5.5.   The morphological network for the a-stem declension.   113
6.1.   Network account of *me le regalo* in terms of Castel (2012).   120
6.2.   Semantic systems involved in Spanish pronominal clitics and verb endings.   122
6.3.   Semantic and morphemic representations of the Spanish pronominal clitic and verb-ending systems with active connections for *se lo lanzo* indicated.   125
6.4.   Semantic and morphemic representations of the Spanish pronominal clitic and verb-ending systems with active connections for *se lo lanzo* only indicated.   126
6.5.   Relational distinction between meanings and messages.   127
6.6.   A morphotactic network for Spanish pronominal clitics and verb endings with active connections for *se lo lanzo* indicated.   128
6.7.   An integrative RNT model of clitic *se* in the context of *se lo lanzo*.   129
7.1.   Cognition to semotactics for three participants.   150
7.2.   Semotactic network for *Fanta ... gave Ruth's laminated cheek a pat* in discourse context (paragraph-initial).   151
7.3.   Lexotactic network for participant realization.   154
8.1.   A five-strata model of the linguistic system, relative to embodied/ conceptual/executive cognition.   158
8.2.   Anataxis in Russian number phrases.   162

Tables

3.1.   Brodmann areas and neuroanatomical loci implicated in key linguistic functions.   62
4.1.   Segmental obstruent phonemes of Russian per Trager (1934).   80
4.2.   Preliminary inventory of Russian obstruent phonemes.   84
4.3.   Russian obstruents: Factoring out voice.   85
4.4.   Russian obstruents: Factoring out voice and softness.   86
4.5.   Some three-place onset clusters.   86

4.6.   Typical two-place onset clusters.   87
4.7.   Russian obstruents: Factoring out voice and softness.   95
5.1   Distinctive features of Polish cases per Schenker (1964).   105
5.2.   Forms, frames, and functions of the Polish genitive.   107
6.1.   Semantic features of PERSON and THEMATIC STATUS realized by Spanish
        clitics and verb endings.   122
6.2.   Semantic features of PERSON and NUMBER realized by Spanish clitics
        and verb endings.   122
6.3.   Semantic features of PERSON and GENDER realized by Spanish clitics and
        verb endings.   123
6.4.   Semantic features of PERSON and DEIXIS realized by Spanish clitics and
        verb endings.   123
6.5.   Semantic features of PERSON and CASE realized by Spanish clitics and
        verb endings.   123
7.1.   Third-person personal pronouns in English and their communicative
        uses.   138
7.2.   An algorithm for encoding participant reference.   138
7.3.   The participant mentions analyzed according to the algorithm.   142
7.4.   Realizations of participants 1 and 2.   148
8.1.   Spoonerisms in Polish and English.   163
8.2.   Tactic pattern errors in Polish and English.   165
8.3.   Unintended blends in Polish and English.   167
8.4.   Substitutions in Polish and English.   170
8.5.   Error types and linguistic subsystems.   172

Acknowledgments

While we had never collaborated as a trio before writing this book, we knew about each other's work and our shared interest in Relational Network Theory (RNT). In our careers as linguists, the three of us were at some point inspired by this approach as we searched for alternatives to what we considered insurmountable shortcomings in mainstream traditions. On a given day we may pursue different questions, use different tools, and aim at different journals, but we all recognize our debt to RNT for showing us that there was more to linguistics than isolationist speculations which reduce the mind to formal, domain-specific algorithms. We reasoned that it would be good to disseminate the theory and give others the same opportunity.

The present book reflects our deep esteem for the eminent scholars whose ideas prompted this revelation. First and foremost, we would like to thank Syd Lamb for erecting the conceptual edifice of RNT, guiding us through its corridors, and, in the process, granting us the privilege of his friendship. Our gratitude also goes out to Michael Halliday, whose early insights provided the foundations for the theory's notational system. No less important have been the contributions of outstanding predecessors of relational network approaches, including Jan Baudouin de Courtenay, Louis Hjelmslev, and Roman Jakobson. We say thank you to all these giants on whose shoulders we stand.

We are appreciative of other lessons learned from teachers and mentors such as H. A. Gleason, Jr., and Charles Hockett, and from colleagues like David Lockwood, David Bennett, and Peter A. Reich. Additionally, we thank our colleagues in the Linguistic Association of Canada and the United States (LACUS) for their yearly offering of theoretically diverse (and RNT-friendly) conferences – it was actually during one of these conferences, held in Vancouver in 2014, that the three of us first met in person. We also acknowledge the kind disposition from Bloomsbury Publishing, John Benjamins, and the editors of *Linguistics and the Human Sciences*, *Signos*, and *LACUS Forum*, who granted us permission to use and update previously published material. And we thank our current editors at Equinox Publishing for their assistance in producing this book.

On a personal note, Adolfo M. García recognizes the enduring support of the National Scientific and Technical Research Council (CONICET), the Institute of Cognitive Neurology (INECO), and the Faculty of Education at the National University of Cuyo (UNCuyo), his long-standing affiliations in Argentina. He reserves special thanks for Syd Lamb, Michael Halliday, Ruqaiya Hasan, Michel Paradis, Víctor Castel, and Agustín Ibáñez, who have offered him invaluable guidance, encouragement, and friendship. Finally, he dedicates this book to his parents, Raúl and Elba; his brother, Francisco; his grandmother, Dora; and his wife, María. Without them there would be nothing to work for.

Bill Sullivan gives special recognition to Henryk Kardela of Maria Curie-Skłodowska University in Lublin, with whom he spent many hours of discussion: if Henryk is still unconvinced that a purely relational network theory can be constructed without presupposed emes and can answer the questions posed to date, the fault lies more with Sullivan than with him. Additional thanks go to David R. Bogdan and Douglas W. Coleman, his students of stratificational theory at University of Florida, who themselves have published research in the field and never ceased asking pointed questions; and to Mary Sullivan, his wife and primary support, who never lost faith, even when he was confronted by an audience of hostile Chomskyans.

Sarah Tsiang thanks Eastern Kentucky University, which helped fund her conference participation and granted her sabbatical leave to work on this book. She is grateful to her dissertation advisor at the University of Illinois, Prof. Hans Henrich Hock, for his guidance and personal example that continues to inspire her thinking and her work. She is grateful to LACUS, whose conferences and members have been pivotal in developing her career. Finally, she expresses heartfelt appreciation to friends and family who provided encouragement and support for this book, in particular, Patti Costello, John Stephen Hockensmith, and Katarina Starčević.

This volume took more than two years of hard work from the three of us. In completing it, we have become not only coauthors, but also friends. While we will refrain from forcing this argument into the contents, therein lies another merit of RNT.

Adolfo M. García
William J. Sullivan
Sarah Tsiang
March 17, 2016

Foreword

On the creation, and the creator, of RNT

About two years ago I was invited to take part in a three-day symposium entitled 'Reconnecting Paths', convened by Jonathan Webster at the City University of Hong Kong and Huang Guowen at Sun Yat-sen University, Guangzhou. The subtitle of the symposium featured the names of Sydney Lamb, Ruqaiya Hasan and me; the three of us were of course well known to each other – and also to the convenors: Professor Webster was the editor responsible for bringing out collections of our written works. In other words, the occasion was, as a symposium is meant to be, a gathering of people known to each other and sharing enough common ground to take each other's credentials for granted, but working along different lines, perhaps in different fields of academic study.

I was excited at the prospect of reconnecting paths with Sydney Lamb. He and I had come to know each other in the 1960s and had worked together on several occasions. We first met at Georgetown University, at one of their 'round tables'; Syd then invited me to spend a short time working on his machine translation project at Berkeley (Linguistic Automation Project), and then, after he returned in 1967 to Yale, where he had first studied as an undergraduate, he arranged for me to come and stay for a longer period. On that occasion I was able to follow his thinking in much greater detail, and to collaborate with him in exploring some aspects of English grammar in stratificational terms.

Syd Lamb and I shared – as I think we have continued to do – the same perspective on language; the same sense of what language is, of what it achieves (or rather, what people achieve with it) and of how it has evolved to where it is. We share, perhaps, the same cognitive style, as Syd himself has described it; seeing reality in terms of 'probable' rather than 'absolute', and more at home among the 'lumpers' than among the 'splitters' – recognizing that we need 'both the broad strokes and the finer details' if we want to get a rounded picture of language (as, we might add, of anything else).

From the start Syd had followed up a broad and varied range of interests, including description of language based on field studies (his doctoral research was on Monachi, a Uto-Aztecan language of California), historical and prehistorical relationship and comparison of languages, natural language processing by computer (the machine translation project involving both Russian and Chinese), and phonological theory (as distinct from the current 'phonemics'). But all of these were integrated in his overriding concern with a general theory of language, fostered by some of the leading

American linguists with whom he had studied, and reinforced by his own intensive reading of Saussure and of Hjelmslev.

The Georgetown edition of the *Outline of Stratificational Grammar* presented what I take to be a fair, if rather brief, account of Syd's thinking about the description of language at that time. It suggests the influence of Hockett and Gleason, with the underlying theoretical model being closer to that of Hjelmslev. But as early as 1963 he had first encountered the possibility of relating 'the abstract constructions of linguistic theorists' to actual structures and actual processes operating in the human brain; and over the next few years that endeavour came to predominate and to guide the main direction of his work.

This was a change of emphasis, a realigning of Syd's research priorities. It was encapsulated in the replacement of the name Stratificational Theory by Relational Network Theory. The stratificational model seemed to him to focus too much attention on the structural relationships within one stratum, with a distinct realizational component handling the relationship between one stratum and another. The angle of vision was 'horizontal', whereas he needed to adopt a vertical perspective which would bring out the essential continuity in the relational networks across all the subsystems that made up the system of language. The theoretical representation should be consonant with what was known about the operation of the human brain.

At that point, however, Syd and I parted company. Not that we never saw each other; Syd was a valued personal friend, warm, generous, and always good company, and an honorary Uncle Syd to our small son Neil. But the occasions grew rarer. In 1975 I moved to Australia, and although I tried several times to get Syd invited to Sydney I never managed it. Our working lives had also diverged. Syd moved out of academia for a few years, developing a piece of specialized software based on his theoretical research; when he retuned to the academic world it was to Rice University in Houston, at the invitation of Jim Copeland, to head a department of linguistics and semiotics. Ruqaiya and I went to the inaugural conference of that department, at Rice in 1982 or 1983. Meanwhile, while I was flitting about from one topic to another, in pursuit of what I later came to call an 'appliable' theory and description of language, Syd was extending the scope, and the power, of relational network theory, strengthening its foundations and its resonance with neural science (which can't have been easy, given his administrative duties as a head of department).

I have often been asked how I see the connection between relational network theory and systemic functional theory. It seems to me that the two are fully compatible one with the other; and in fact that they are complementary, in the sense that they are concerned with different 'modes of being' of language as a semiotic system, the former with its biological and intra-organism manifestation, the latter with its manifestation as a social, inter-organism phenomenon. At first sight these might seem contradictory, but of course they are not; language has to be understood both as a biological system and as a social system. Representations in these two modes are not, or need not be, commensurate, except perhaps at the very concrete level of the instance: the dimensions of system and structure are not equivalent to 'or' nodes and 'and' nodes; our system networks are analytic tools and make no claim to neurological 'reality'. This does not mean that the organizing concepts of systemic functional theory could not be interpreted in relational network terms; but the relationship would be indirect and complex.

Since we cannot observe language as it evolved, we might think of this in relation to child language development. I was impressed, in my study of the language of early childhood, by the way in which meaning and moving co-developed during the earliest months of life: how each stage in the baby's physical development (agitating limbs, reaching and grasping, rolling over, sitting up, crawling and walking, each one bringing with it a shift in visual perspective) was partnered with some extension of the child's meaning potential. The final moment when the child stood up and walked on two legs was also the moment when he embarked on the mother tongue – language in its usual sense, the human post-infancy semiotic – gradually giving up the remnants of his protolanguage as he gave up crawling or other form of non-bipedal locomotion. Now he could not only look at things from every angle, under his own control; he could walk around them and see what they looked like from behind. This ability to switch the angle of vision has always been a notable characteristic of Syd's approach as a scholar. But it is also the developmental analogue to the 'moment' in the evolution of the human brain as it co-evolved, along with the organs of articulation, in producing what we know as language – a moment that no doubt lasted several thousands of generations.

Syd is entirely at home in the digital age. He is a natural with computers (whereas I can't cope with them at all). This meant not only that he could survive on his skills as a software designer in the unforgiving world of capitalist enterprise but also, more importantly, that he can engage with computer scientists and knows just how misleading the computer is as a metaphor for the human brain. His work, as he has said himself, needs to be evaluated for its plausibility in terms of three areas of enquiry: the system of language, the development of children, and what is now known about the workings of the brain. Up till today, as far as I am aware, relational network theory has not been examined in detail from the point of view of current scholarship in neuroscience. The reason the present book is so timely is that it will provide another mode of access to his theory, for those who would be able to approach it with the required specialist knowledge. It is time that such people let Syd (and the rest of us) know how it shapes up, as an account of the linguistic system, and of the processes of learning and using language, in the light of current research into precisely that phenomenal realm that Syd has been investigating with the knowledge and experience of a theoretical linguist.

Whatever the eventual outcome, Syd Lamb has consistently maintained, and in his own working practice reinforced, the scientific nature of linguistic theory, and of the processes and practices on which such theory depends. He grounded linguistics in scientific method, instead of in the mode of argumentation, in which one supposed counterexample required you to jettison an entire body of theoretical insight (a variant of the structuralist notion of linguistic theory as procedure). Syd is a wise and learned man, who, luckily for those who know him and share his commitment to the study of language, never suppressed the 'roving and adventurous side' of his mentality. It is good to see his work being followed up and made more widely known.

M. A. K. Halliday
November 28, 2013

Introduction

I.   Of Mainstreamers and Bad Guys

This book was completed in 2017, but its genesis dates back to 1957. That year, at University of California, Berkeley, Sydney Lamb completed his Ph.D. dissertation and laid the foundations for Stratificational Grammar. And it was in 1957, too, that Vernon Mountcastle first introduced his hypothesis that cortical columns function as information processing modules within the neocortex. The two lines of research would eventually converge into Relational Network Theory (RNT), the insightful conception of language presented in this volume.

Despite its numerous merits, this interdisciplinary framework has largely escaped the radar of the linguistic community, arguably because of another scholarly event that occurred in 1957: the publication of Noam Chomsky's *Syntactic Structures*. Since the release of that pivotal work, generative models have come to dominate linguistics journals and departments, reducing the visibility of opposing theories – some of which still preserve generative assumptions.[1] As a non-generativist approach, RNT was kept away from mainstream circles for over half a century. Lamb explains the separation as follows:

> [...] back in the 1960s, after I pointed out some mistakes in Chomsky's thinking [...] I became a bad guy. Students of that period were discouraged from paying attention to my work (so I have heard from the lips of one of them, now a leading professor in the field). Later, after obtaining a safe tenured position, when they came to the conclusion on their own that Chomsky had indeed been mistaken, they nevertheless retained the belief that I was a bad guy, whose writings should be disregarded. (2004a, pp. 14–15)

Lamb's early critiques, described further in Chapter 1, dealt with analytical (non-neurological) aspects of linguistic theory. With the passing of time, the conceptual, epistemological, and methodological differences between RNT and Generative Grammar would also pervade their stances on the relationship between linguistics and neuroscience. In the mid-1990s, for instance, Chomsky maintained that 'biology and the brain sciences [...] as currently understood, do not provide any basis for what appear to be fairly well established conclusions about language' (1995, p. 2). Then, in his 2003 Berkeley lectures, he claimed that '[w]e don't know nearly enough about the brain for cognitive science to take it seriously' (cited in Feldman, 2006, p. xi). On the contrary, RNT is committed to proposing neurocognitively plausible constructs. Thus, if certain hypotheses are found to be inconsistent with brain structure and functioning, they must be rectified accordingly. From this viewpoint, a realistic theory of language 'has to be compatible with what is known about the brain from neurology and from cognitive neuroscience' (Lamb, 1999, p. 293).

A full discussion of the implications of Chomsky's position is beyond the scope of the present book, and, in any case, these have been treated elsewhere in the linguistics and neurolinguistics literature.[2] Here we will tell the other side of the story, tracing the successive theoretical steps whereby RNT has tried to model language processes in structurally, cognitively, and neurologically plausible terms. But before we do so, a few introductory remarks are in order.

II.   Preliminary Notions

As a linguistic theory, RNT might be presumed to be concerned with 'language'. But what is language? Defining this term is no trivial endeavor, for it has been variously understood throughout the history of linguistics. For instance, Ferdinand de Saussure conceived of it as a socially-anchored system of signs (pairings of meanings and phonemic sequences), while American structuralists defined it as the collection of utterances produced within a speech community. However, Lamb (2004b, 2006) contends that such conceptions are misleading, as they do not correspond to any discrete, physical phenomenon in the world:

> A language is not a concrete object: it is not tangible or perceivable (hence observable) in any way. Of course we can hear the sound waves produced in speech and read the symbols that make up written texts, but surely no collection of these ephemeral manifestations is equivalent to the structural system behind them. On the contrary, the linguistic system of the individual is tangible and measurable. (Lamb, 2006, pp. 201–202)

As a first step, substantial evidence about such a system can be garnered from the actual (non-idealized) linguistic processes that people engage in and all the verbal messages they produce – no matter how 'abnormal' or 'ill-formed' they are. By characterizing the nature and interrelations of linguistic productions, it is possible to discover the structure of their underlying system, albeit indirectly.

To such an end, language[3] must then be conceptualized within a cognitive framework capable of handling the observed processes in real time. These include producing, understanding, remembering, and learning language in all its forms – even processes leading to slips of the tongue. At this second stage of the exploration, constructs would still be postulated at an abstract level, without concern for their biological basis.

Yet, RNT takes neurological data as a further source of constraints to model language systems plausibly. The examination of how the ensuing theory tallies with such evidence comes in at the third phase of inquiry. This method of successive approximations, from structural to cognitive to neural modeling, calls for an interdisciplinary linguistics.

Hence, RNT is concerned with at least these three basic dimensions: the linguistic, the cognitive, and the biological. Intimately related to their comprehension are the three requirements that Lamb (1999) establishes for a realistic theory of language, namely: (a) *operational plausibility* (the model must describe how people use their linguistic systems in real time, given actual processing constraints); (b) *developmental plausibility* (it must explain how the system expands and restructures itself, not just at its initial stage, but also throughout life); and (c) *neurological plausibility* (it must be consistent with what is known about brain structure and functioning). This book focuses on how RNT pursues these requirements, with special emphasis on the first and the third.

For RNT, then, the linguistic system is preliminarily conceived as a mental system – or, more precisely, a complex of subsystems. To be realistic, a model of such a domain must avoid introjection. That is, analytical characterizations of verbal outputs must not be assumed to belong to the system proper. According to Lamb (1999), introjection can be circumvented by acknowledging 'the transparency illusion', namely, the misconception that our minds comprise the very objects we perceive around us. Far from being a passive reflection of external stimuli, the human mind intervenes with reality, shaping it, distorting it, imposing symmetry and discrete categories where there are none. Our mind, in brief, construes and organizes reality. In this sense, RNT incarnates the following oft-quoted lines of Benjamin Lee Whorf:

> We dissect nature along lines laid down by our native languages. The categories and types that we isolate from the world of phenomena we do not find there because they stare every observer in the face; on the contrary, the world is presented in a kaleidoscopic flux of impressions which has to be organized by our minds – and this means largely by the linguistic systems in our minds. (1956 [1940], p. 213)

Accordingly, mental systems can be seen as mediators between the 'real world' and the 'projected world' (Lamb, 1999). In this conception, the real world corresponds to external phenomena, access to which may perhaps be largely direct – though necessarily limited[4] – at the level of sensory organs, prior to transduction and cognitive processing. On the other hand, the projected world comprises the subjective universe each of us construes, which results from cognitive processing of perceptual input and projection of the ensuing categories onto the real world.

The transparency illusion assumes a correspondence between 'both worlds': led astray by the elusive, self-deceiving nature of our minds, we tend to assume that the real world includes categorically organized objects, which are separated by discrete boundaries, capable of enduring through time, and essentially distinct from the processes performed on or with them. To further complicate matters, the individual's linguistic system is part of that real world which escapes direct apprehension. Yet, the search for mental structures is not doomed to failure, provided one is aware of the influence that the transparency illusion may exert on the process. As shown in Chapter 1, this has been a key concern in the development of RNT since the early days.

RNT first aimed to describe linguistic structure without incurring intro-jection, and then proceeded to integrate the resulting model within a larger theory of mind. All postulates were then framed as a body of hypotheses which needed to pass one further test before being (transitorily) accepted: the test of neurological plausibility. Unlike Generative Grammar, RNT does not leave neurological justification outside of its scope of interest. In fact, it assumes that hypotheses posited in non-neural models must be abandoned if they prove incompatible with neuroscientific data. Linguistic and mental constructs must be neurologically plausible, at both the macro-cerebral and micro-cerebral levels. At the macro-cerebral level, the components of the hypothesized linguistic and mental systems must be correlated with crit-ical brain areas subserving them; at the micro-cerebral level, the types of relationships postulated for the different components of the system(s) must find support in the details of neurons and their connectivity.

Despite being pregnant with descriptive and explanatory possibilities, RNT has seldom been used to characterize particular languages. Although Lamb himself has expressed reservations regarding the usefulness of the theory for such an end (see Appendix), we aim to show that valuable insights can be gained thereof. Crucially, our relational network accounts of various phenomena in structurally diverse languages (Russian, Polish, Spanish, and English) make explicit key organizational and functional properties of language systems across all levels of grammar (from phonol-ogy and hypophonology to semantics and semology). As will be shown in this book, the overall utility of RNT descriptions is that they show not how the brain works, but what the brain must be capable of in the process of communication. Given the theory's broad compatibility with extant neuro-scientific findings (see Chapter 3), the ensuing interdisciplinary bridge is very ample and potentially fruitful.

Overall, this book introduces RNT by showing how it has pursued the above theoretical milestones and by illustrating its potential to characterize various linguistic phenomena. To achieve the first goal, we adopted a historical perspective and highlighted key breakthroughs spanning over half a century. Thereupon, we used the theory's conceptual apparatus to describe specific features and systems of a variety of languages. In sum, we hope to disseminate what is a most engaging (if unorthodox) approach to linguistics.

III.   Plan of the Book

The book comprises two parts and an appendix, as described below.

Part I

Convergences: Linguistic, Operational, and Neurological Considerations

This first part maps the evolution of RNT from the 1960s to the present, highlighting its systemic and stratificational roots and identifying successive theoretical milestones. It considers properties of language structure taken into account in the formation of the theory, and properties of neurological structures compatible with the type of processing RNT assumes.

Chapter 1 traces the origin and first developments of RNT, from related ideas of Baudouin de Courtenay, Saussure, Jakobson, Whorf, and Hjelmslev, to Sydney Lamb's early assumptions and formalizations. The descriptive tenets of RNT are set against the backdrop of contemporary trends in linguistics. Crucially, RNT deviated from mainstream accounts of the 1950s and 1960s and avoided their undermining principles. By the second half of the 1960s, the linguistic bases of Stratificational Grammar, RNT's forerunner, had been solidified, and the theory could now be harnessed to different languages for descriptive purposes. A bidirectional model with a corresponding notation system could now be developed to meet cognitive requirements for real-time processing.

Chapter 2 considers how properties of language structure and related processing assumptions correspond to the formalizations of RNT. Specifically, it introduces the terminology, notational conventions, and diagrammatic representations used in the theory. Relational networks are presented as dynamic systems of nodes which constantly exchange information. Various node types and details of their interconnection are explained with reference to processes of speech production and comprehension. Considerations of the cognitive needs for real-time processing led to the development of narrow notation, wherein each bidirectional line is more accurately represented by two unidirectional lines, with parallel modifications of each node.

Chapter 3 considers the stratificational model from a neurological point of view, beginning with an overview of basic principles of neurology. At the macroanatomical level, key distinctions are introduced at successive levels of precision, with emphasis on structures implicated in language processing. At the microscopic level, neurons, synapses, cortical columns, and functional webs are presented as the bases of coordinated cognitive activity. Next we consider the evidence and rationale through which relational networks can be interpreted in neurological terms.

PART II

DESCRIPTIVE APPLICATIONS

This second part features several case studies showing descriptive applications of RNT.

Chapter 4 illustrates an RNT approach to phonology through a description of Russian obstruent onsets. Russian has an intricate syllable structure, the obstruent portion of the onset being its most complex part. A relational characterization circumvents limitations of structuralist and generative approaches that have been offered in the past and avoids analytical problems associated with their perspectives.

Chapter 5 illustrates an RNT approach to case through a description of the Polish genitive, one of six cases in this language. Eight different forms, related to numerous sememic roles with differing semantic functions, communicate this case when appended to a nominal or adjectival stem. An RNT model of genitive case assignment is elaborated to capture both frequent and infrequent possibilities.

Chapter 6 offers an RNT description of Spanish pronominal clitics and verb endings. While these units have been widely treated in the functional and cognitive linguistics literature, they have rarely been jointly modeled from a network-based perspective, despite their semantic, morphological, and morphotactic commonalities. The advantages of a relational treatment are highlighted in comparison to alternative accounts of the same phenomena.

Chapter 7 offers a relational network perspective on discourse-level phenomena, focusing on pronoun distribution in English narrative texts. Although countless nouns can be referred to by only a few (third-person) pronouns, the latter produce ambiguity in discourse relatively rarely, even when the actions of varied participants are described. Using RNT, we characterize relevant discourse and semantic constraints that can explain the establishment of clear reference ties in the absence of name/noun repetitions.

Chapter 8 shows how multiple types of speech errors (e.g., timing errors, tactic pattern errors, unintended blends, substitutions) provide evidence for subsystems in linguistic structure and the effects of processing. Because the linguistic system is biological in nature, asynchronies may occur if some of its parts take random rest periods. Moreover, imbalances may result when different potential realizations compete with one another. In either case, a speech error may result. Drawn from a large corpus collected in Polish and English, examples of the most common errors are presented and explained using relational networks.

The Afterword recapitulates our theoretical overview of RNT and the five studies presented thereon. In addition, we summarize the key ways in which RNT differs from mainstream formal linguistic theories. We conclude by describing directions for the further development of RNT and share our hopes for its prospects.

APPENDIX: AN INTERVIEW WITH SYDNEY LAMB

The Appendix offers a recent interview with Sydney Lamb, addressing historical, technical, and practical aspects of RNT. Profiting from Syd's decades-long involvement with the theory, this section offers a unique perspective on recent innovations and recurring queries, alongside valuable insights into the links between linguistics and cognitive neuroscience.

Introduction Endnotes

1. For example, Generative Semantics and Cognitive Grammar, tacitly or otherwise, include such Chomskyan assumptions as the centrality of syntax or focus on a single sentence.

2. Pulvermüller (2002, p. 129) considers that the brain cannot process some of the sentences through which Chomsky illustrates alleged complexities of natural languages. Loritz (1999) has attacked the notion of movement – a crucial element of all generative models – arguing that while it is posited as a metaphorical construct, nobody has ever ascertained what it is a metaphor of. Christiansen and Chater (2008), as well as Deacon (1997), provide evidence that Universal Grammar, the conceptual core of Chomskyan linguistics, is evolutionarily implausible. Furthermore, the very scientific nature of Generative Grammar has been called into question by Lakoff, who asserts that such a theory is built on 'a commitment to a program of speculative philosophy: to see what happens if you decide to study language given the metaphor that a grammar of a human language is a symbol-manipulation system in the technical sense' (1991, p. 62).

3. The use of the term whose physical existence has just been argued against does not entail a contradiction. In fact, there is a word *language* as well as a semological representation LANGUAGE (which can be related to different meanings). We can resort to both representations in much the same way as we can resort to the term

culture and the semological representation CULTURE, which would be subject to the same type of considerations. For descriptive and explanatory purposes, all sciences handle abstractions without a physical basis; yet, this is not equivalent to invoking the constructs proper as the objects of study. This last maneuver is what RNT seeks to avoid.

4.   Our sense organs do not capture every single aspect of the real world. For example, human hearing does not recognize sound frequencies beyond a certain level; hunters, for example, use whistles whose sounds are inaudible to humans. Human vision offers another good illustration: the retina contains three different types of photoreceptors, each endowed with specific wavelength sensitivities; together they derive a difference signal leading to color discriminations. However, since the colors of the real world must be filtered through the wavelength ranges of the photoreceptors, the signals we physically (not even cognitively) perceive do not capture the real-world color spectrum in its presumable totality.

Part I

Convergences

Linguistic, Operational, and Neurological Considerations

1 The Origins of Relational Network Theory

1.1 A Realistic Approach to Linguistics

As described in the Introduction, RNT was not originally devised to specify the cognitive mechanisms involved in language processing. Neither were relational networks first intended to represent neuronal circuits or cortical columns. Yet, nowadays the theory proves compatible with key neuroscientific facts. More than a mere coincidence, this correspondence is a natural consequence of its development. If RNT now seems broadly consistent with neurological findings, it is because it freed itself from analytical biases and unwarranted assumptions during what might be called its exclusively linguistic (pre-cognitive, pre-neurological) stage.

1.2 The Birth of Relational Network Theory

RNT sprang from the early work of Sydney Lamb. In the 1950s and 1960s, Lamb began shaping his views on linguistic structure by spotting theoretical shortcomings in what were then mainstream approaches – in particular, problems related to procedural orientation and the use of descriptive processes. At the same time, he found inspiration in the work of other linguists, including Jan Baudouin de Courtenay (1845–1929), Ferdinand de Saussure (1857–1913), Roman Jakobson (1896–1982), and, more directly, Louis Hjelmslev (1899–1965), Charles Hockett (1916–2000), and Michael Halliday (born in 1925). Here we briefly discuss the key antecedents of, and motivations for, the emergence of RNT.

1.2.1 Early Contributing Perspectives

As Halliday noted in the Foreword, Lamb's conception of language was reinforced by his studies of Saussure. In particular, we may recall Saussure's description of a defining shadow on the *parole* output.[1] Jakobson (Sullivan class notes, 1968) insisted that to Saussure, the meaning of a sign is not a thing but another sign (with another sign relation). This is compatible with a relational network approach, despite discrepancies in some respects.[2]

Additional antecedents to RNT can be found in the work of Baudouin de Courtenay, or *mon maître*, as Saussure referred to him. If we consider how the field has developed, reading Baudouin de Courtenay is like looking through a time warp. In several papers,[3] he builds up what is almost a twentieth-century picture of a phonological system, from alternating phones through something parallel to phonemes and, beyond that, something parallel to morphophonemes. In the process, he classifies six stages of alternations. He denies the existence of morphophonemes as such, stating that they result from 'paleophonetic alternations' between forms that are connected for 'psychological distinctions' (Baudouin de Courtenay, 1972, pp. 165-166). Though not explicitly a relational network description, his view is reminiscent of RNT postulates. A cognitivist mindset is evident in his thinking, as shown by statements such as: '[e]ach member of a speech community must accomplish for himself this process of associating concepts' (p. 165).

Jakobson (1962 [1929]) also describes phonological relations in a manner compatible with network approaches.[4] He begins with the fundamental notions of *oppositions de phonèmes corrélatifs* and *oppositions de phonèmes disjoints*. The former are syntagmatic relations and the latter are paradigmatic relations (p. 13 *et passim*), closely resembling RNT's distinction between ordered AND and OR relations. Expanded networks of relations were also immanent in Jakobson's conception of prosody, including notions such as synharmonism (p. 27) and open syllables. Later, in the 1930s, Jakobson and Trubetzkoy developed the concept of archiphonemic neutralization or suspension of phonemic oppositions (cf. Jakobson, Cherry, & Halle, 1962 [1953]). This is represented in RNT by an upward OR relation (Sullivan, 1974). However, as shown in the following pages, the upward OR is a more general formalization, as it applies to the logically identical relation at any level of the linguistic system, be it tactic or realizational.

In short, insightful and forward-thinking linguists were already operating in a manner compatible with RNT more than a century ago. Tacitly or otherwise, many of their contributions became the backbone of the connectionist conception adopted by the theory. However, as discussed below, RNT also emerged in response to other approaches used in linguistic analysis during the mid-twentieth century.

1.2.2 Linguistic Unrealities

Many linguistic theories are based on procedural description, assuming that a structural model must be based either on induction or deduction. According to Hjelmslev (1961 [1943], p. 12), induction can be defined as 'a progression from component to class' (e.g., from sounds to phonemes, from phonemes to syllables, and so forth), whereas deduction consists in 'a progression from class to component' (e.g., taking an unanalyzed text and progressively breaking it down into ever smaller units). For procedurally-oriented theories, no description of language is valid unless rooted in one of these approaches.

However, Lamb (2004c, pp. 86–87) argued that the aim of a linguistic theory should not be bound to any given procedure. He considered induction and deduction to be merely tactical approaches that could be adopted (or not) to describe a language. In fact, he regarded procedure as 'unnecessary and bothersome' (Lamb 2004c, p. 92), contending that a theory-construction approach is superior. That is, linguistic description must start off with a theory of the texts of the language, which means that:

> [w]e have to separate the practical procedure from the question of scientific validity [...] it doesn't matter how we arrive at our formulation. So we can use, for instance, intuition or guesswork to arrive at a hypothesis, provided we test our hypothesis. But with respect to practical procedure I would emphasize that we have to examine the linguistic data very closely. (Lamb, 2004d, p. 143)

So, in RNT terms, what determines the validity of a linguistic theory is not its emphasis on a pre-established methodology, but the appropriateness of the hypotheses to the available data. In this sense, Lamb (2004c, pp. 95–96) agrees with Hjelmslev that while a theory must at first circumscribe its object of study to make it manageable, it must then broaden its scope to correlate the postulated principles with as many linguistic phenomena as possible.

Lamb also objected to the so-called 'descriptive process' approach. Descriptive processes, or mutations, characterize static linguistic relationships (e.g., between phonemes and morphemes) in dynamic terms, as if certain forms existed solely as substitutes for others. Bloomfield (1988 [1933], p. 213), for example, referred to the phonological alternation found between *knife* and *knives* as a two-step process in which '"first" the [-f] is replaced by [-v], and "then" the appropriate alternant [-z] is added.' Descriptions of this kind interpolate a metaphorical temporal dimension into the characterization of synchronic units. Bloomfield himself acknowledged that '[t]he actual sequence of constituents, and their structural order [...] are a part of the language, but the descriptive order of grammatical features is a fiction and results simply from our method of describing the forms' (p. 213).

Such metaphorical descriptions provide an unrealistic conception of linguistic structure, for '[o]ne of the chief properties of the linguistic system is that it is a *non-process* type of system, there is *no motion* in the linguistic system itself' (Lamb, 2004d, pp. 156–157). Of course, this does not mean that linguistic systems are not engaged by processes. Speaking, understanding, and learning languages, for instance, involve continuous multi-level operations, which are ultimately implemented in the brain. The point is that while these involve use of the system, they must be distinguished from the system's organization as a set of options.

Descriptive processes are epitomized in the use of mutational rules. For example, in discussing examples of Russian phonology, Chomsky (1964) stated that his proposed rules must be ordered as given in his description. According to Lamb (2004e, 2004f), this implies that only one representation can be present at a time, and that only one rule can operate at a time. This leads to a number of problems: (a) the resulting order of rule application responds to artificial constraints, largely determined by the notation system; (b) mutation rules imply replacement of symbols, so that when an element y replaces an element x, the latter is no longer there and cannot serve as a conditioning environment for other rules; and (c) mutational accounts have built-in operations, in that linguistic information has no existence apart from the mutations.

Consequently, rules can be deemed artifacts of the descriptive technique, since they incarnate a particular type of description but are not part of linguistic structure itself. This conclusion is the backbone of Stratificational Grammar, the conception of language that served as a main stepping-stone towards RNT.

1.3   Stratificational Grammar

The origins of Stratificational Grammar date back to 1957, when Lamb was preparing his Ph.D. dissertation on Monachi. His project included a grammatical description of the language, a Monachi-English English-Monachi dictionary, and, more crucially, a new framework for linguistic description. As Lamb explains:

> [w]e linguistics students had been taught that there were two levels of structure: phonemic and morphemic [...] And the relationship between the two levels was supposed to be quite simple. Morphemes could have allomorphs, and allomorphs were phonemic forms, composed of phonemes [...] But I found for Monachi, as indeed also for English, it worked a whole lot better if we had two steps between morphemes and phonemic forms rather than one. (Lamb, 2004a, p. 27)

The intervening levels of structure, or strata, should then be identified as part of the language system. In *Outline of Stratificational Grammar* (Lamb, 1966a, p. 2), the notion of stratification was informed by the work of Hockett (1947, 1954) and, even more crucially, by Hjelmslev's Glossematics (1961 [1943]). Indeed, RNT can be seen as an extension of the latter approach.

In a critical review of Hjelmslev's *Prolegomena to a Theory of Language* (1961 [1943]), Lamb (2004c, pp. 111–112) subscribed to the distinction between expression and content planes, but deemed it insufficient, in that it subsumes sign-expressions and sign-meanings in just one level each. For instance, while the sign *undergo* can be broken down into the sign-components *under* and *go*, its meaning is not reducible to the sum of their respective meanings – *undergo* does not mean 'to go under' or anything of the sort. Since two-plane theories have no simple way to account for this fact, Lamb concluded that linguistic structure actually involves two sign-systems rather than one. Thus, there would be not two but three planes, so that '[t]he middle plane is "content" relative to the lower one and "expression" relative to the upper one' (Lamb, 2004c, p. 112).

To avoid terminological confusion, Lamb referred to these planes as 'strata'.[5] Four strata were initially identified, namely: phonemic (relating phonemic units of different complexity, such as /ʌ/ or /ʌn/), morphemic (describing the relations of morphemes, such as *under*), lexemic (relating lexemes of different complexity, such as *undergo* or the phrase *undergo a treatment*), and sememic (comprising meanings, such as the concept UNDERGO).[6] As illustrated in the preceding parenthetical examples, specific graphic conventions indicate which stratum a unit belongs to. Phonological units are placed within slanted bars; morphological and lexemic units are typed in italics; and semological units are identified with small capitals.

In agreement with Halliday, Lamb argued that all languages would be organized around three major components, or systems, namely: phonology, lexicogrammar, and semology.[7] Figure 1.1 depicts the basic organization of a stratificational grammar.

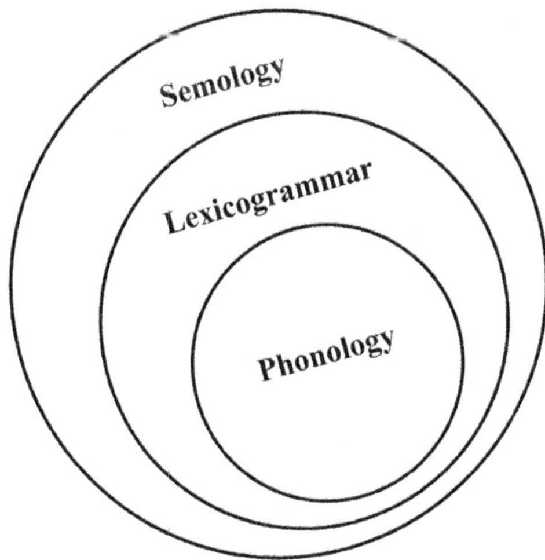

Figure 1.1: The three main systems in Stratificational Grammar.

With these three systems at its core, the structure behind a natural language is conceptualized as a hierarchy of strata. The number of strata posited will depend on idiosyncratic properties of each particular language. Lamb (1966a) claimed that all natural languages have at least four strata, while English and other languages may have as many as six. The terminology and subdivisions employed have undergone various changes over time and differ in various treatments, but the recognition of these three major systems, which may be considered as strata themselves, has remained a crucial axis of the theory. Figure 1.2 shows a five-strata model motivated for Polish, Russian, and English (see Chapters 4, 5, 7, and 8), where relations corresponding to Lamb's hypersememic stratum are considered part of cognition – note that to capture recent developments in cognitive science we now refer to this system as embodied/conceptual/executive cognition.[8] The phonemic system has: (a) a stratum for phonology, which deals with morphophonemics, contrast, and syllable structure; and (b) a stratum for hypophonology, which relates phonemic features to phonetic features and handles non-contrastive relations.

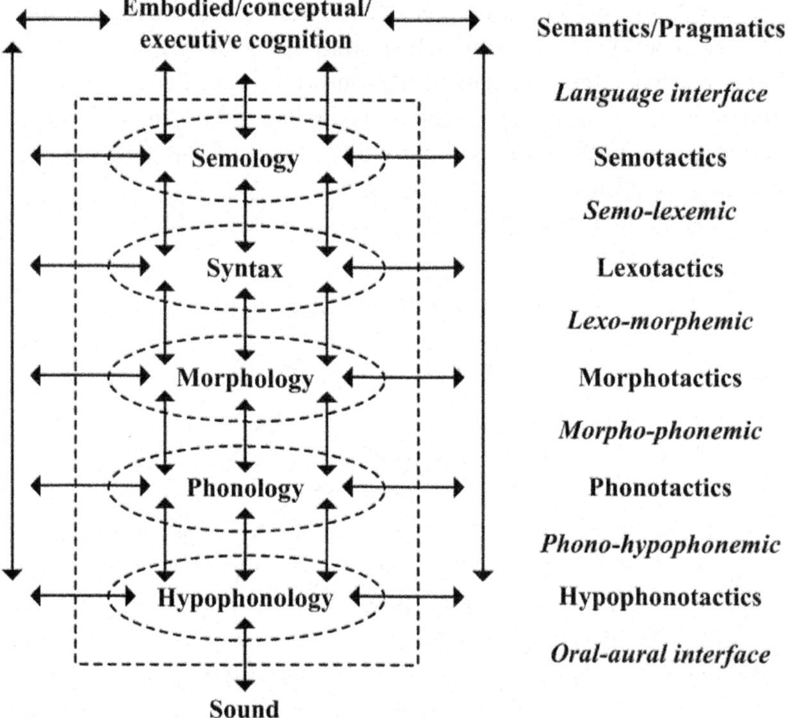

Figure 1.2: A five-strata model of the linguistic system, relative to embodied/conceptual/ executive cognition.

The above strata have internal levels of structure, each including its own patterns of arrangement. These patterns are termed 'tactics' or 'tactic patterns', so that the possible arrangements of phonemes are governed by 'phonotactics', those of morphemes (within the lexicogrammar) by 'morphotactics', those of lexemes (also within the lexicogrammar) by 'lexotactics' (more traditionally, 'syntax'), and those of sememes by 'semotactics'. Given these distinctions, Chomsky's famous *Colorless green ideas sleep furiously* (1957, p. 15) would be said to observe lexotactic constraints while diverging from typical or unmarked semotactic patterns.

The relationship between the units in a given system and those belonging to the immediately lower one is known as 'realization'. For instance, the sememic unit UNDERSTAND is realized in the lexicogrammar as *understand*, which in turn is realized in the phonemic stratum as /ʌndərstænd/. Through this notion of realization, the theory avoids the descriptive problems discussed in Section 1.2.2 and accounts for a number of linguistic complexities known as realizational discrepancies (Lamb, 1999, pp. 37–40).

The most typical kinds of realizational discrepancies include: (i) 'composite realization', (ii) 'zero realization', (iii) 'empty realization', (iv) 'portmanteau realization', (v) 'diversification', and (vi) 'neutralization'. Composite realization refers to the very frequent case in which a unit of a given stratum gets realized as more than one unit of the immediately lower stratum. For example, a single morpheme such as *dog* is realized phonologically as the sequence /d/ /ɑ/ /g/. Zero realization is present when a unit of a given stratum has no discernible manifestation at the lower level. The plural morpheme in the form *sheep* is a typical example of this discrepancy. Empty realization refers to units which appear at a given stratum representing nothing on the higher stratum. English presents a very frequent case in the lexeme *do*, when it serves exclusively grammatical purposes and points to nothing on the sememic stratum. Portmanteau realization occurs when a combination of, say, two morphemes leads to a phonemic representation which does not comprise two parts representing each of the morphemes. An example would be the form *went* as the realization of *go* and the past morpheme, usually realized as *-ed*. The term diversification denotes cases in which an element in a given stratum is represented by different units (e.g., suppletive allomorphs) on the immediately lower stratum. For instance, the element *good* is realized as *bet-* when in the comparative form *better.* Finally, neutralization is present when, for example, a unit in a lower stratum corresponds to two or more units in an upper stratum, as /bɛt/ corresponds to both *good* and *wager*.[9] Figure 1.3 depicts these types of realization.

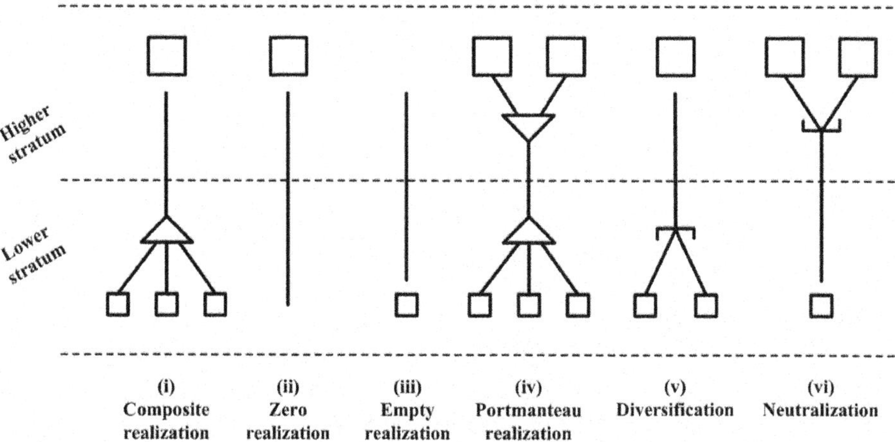

Figure 1.3: Six kinds of realizational discrepancies.

The notation used in Figure 1.3 is actually more complex than that originally proposed by Lamb. Stratificational Grammar first used a rule-like formulaic notation, which failed to exploit the notion of realization fully. The more explicit notational system illustrated here (Lamb, 2004a, p. 31) was consolidated in 1963, after Halliday shared with Lamb his own notation for systemic networks. This was a major milestone for the theory: '[w]ith two or three simple modifications to Halliday's network notation, I had the essentials of relational network notation' (Lamb, 2004a, p. 33).[10]

1.4   Relational Network Theory

In 1964, while relational network notation still included symbols in its formulations, Lamb began working on a review article for the second English edition (1961) of Hjelmslev's *Prolegomena to a theory of language*, originally published in Danish in 1943. As seen in the resulting article, titled 'Epilegomena to a theory of language,' Lamb (2004c) shared many, but not all, of Hjelmslev's ideas, and he discussed how his theory could be considered an extension of Glossematics.

First, Lamb conceived of language as the system underlying texts, rather than a collection of texts themselves. Therefore, to describe a language one would need to characterize that underlying system. Second, he agreed that, in order to be realistic, a theory must meet the requisites of completeness[11] (i.e., exhaustiveness in the potential to describe texts) and correctness (i.e., the description should not generate non-texts). Third, he supported the contention that, since theories must be rooted in reality, research had to begin from assessment of empirical data; only after such data have been meticulously gathered and analyzed would the linguist be in a position to formulate theoretical proposals.

Also during the preparation of this article, Lamb rediscovered a statement whose implications had not been hitherto fully appreciated. As a graduate student at UC Berkeley, Lamb had learned from Professor Mary Haas that '[t]he only way to understand a language is to understand it as a whole – everything in it as related to everything else' (Lamb, 2004g, p. 47). He would then find in Hjelmslev a critical insight regarding the wholeness of language:

> The recognition [...] that a totality does not consist of things but of relationships, and that not substance but only its internal and external relationships have scientific existence [...] may be new in linguistic science. The postulation of objects as something different from the terms of relationships is a superfluous axiom and consequently a metaphysical hypothesis from which linguistic science will have to be freed. (Hjelmslev, 1961, p. 61)

Accordingly, having rejected processes and rules, Lamb proposed that linguistic *structure* (as opposed to its manifestations) also lacks objects (i.e., items or symbols), since only *relationships* can be presumed to have real linguistic existence. By the mid-1960s, Lamb would dispense with symbols entirely in his theory. Again following Hjelmslev, he argued that while naive realism would have it that linguistic analysis consists in breaking down a given object into parts, neither the object nor its parts have any existence except by virtue of their mutual relationships. Analysis of linguistic data would then lead Lamb to establish that there are only two basic types of relationships in language, from which all specific relations can be derived: the BOTH-AND relationship (for co-occurring elements) and the EITHER-OR relationship (for mutually exclusive elements). The former is known as the AND relationship, whereas the latter is called the OR relationship.

The idea that the OR relationship is exclusive would eventually be refined. Henry Allan Gleason, Jr. (1917–2007) proposed that the OR relation was not itself exclusive, but inclusive: the exclusivity originally assumed to be part of OR nodes, he insisted, emerged from relations to the rest of the system. Further developments of this relation derived from the notion of threshold nodes (see Chapter 2).[12]

The AND relationship is present when two or more units occur sequentially (as in the case of phonemes) or simultaneously (e.g., the sememic representations UNMARRIED and MALE converge in the lexicogrammatical realization *bachelor*). The OR relationship, on the other hand, represents paradigmatic options within the system (e.g., the sememic unit ORDINAL could be realized either as *-st*, in *first*, OR as *-nd*, in *second*, OR as *-rd*, in *third*, OR as *-th*, in *fourth*, *fifth*, etc.

At this point, the new relational conception would prove crucial, for Lamb, in a very Whorfian vein, believed that 'any scientist's thinking is influenced by his notation system' (Lamb, 2004d, p. 169). A realistic approach should thus reflect nothing but relationships, which could be understood as points of convergence bringing together other points of convergence. The result would be a network of relationships, hence the name of the theory.

The first presentation of relational network notation, already freed from symbolic objects, took place in 1965, during a lecture at the University of Michigan. The notation first appeared in print in 'Prolegomena to a theory of phonology' (Lamb, 1966b), and it found its major manifesto in *Outline of Stratificational Grammar* (Lamb, 1966a). Since then, relationships have been represented with lines and nodes. Lines provide linkages between nodes by virtue of incoming and outgoing activation. For their own part, nodes can be classified according to three dimensions of contrast: (a) AND vs. OR; (b) downward vs. upward; and (c) ordered vs. unordered.

AND nodes are represented by a triangle, whereas OR nodes are depicted by a horizontal bracket. According to the vertical convention usually adopted in Stratificational Grammar, whereby meanings or functions are on the uppermost stratum and phonological expression is at the lowest one, each node can have an upward direction (leading from a given stratum to a higher one) or a downward direction (leading from a given stratum to a lower one).[13] Furthermore, all nodes have both a singular and a plural side, determined by how many other nodes they can be connected to on each end. Ordered nodes, whose lines lead to or stem from different points of the node, show sequential order in the emission or reception of their activation; unordered nodes, whose lines converge in or stem from a single point, show no particular sequencing of activation. Figure 1.4 shows some of the main nodes used in RNT and illustrates their functioning.

The first node in Figure 1.4 is an upward unordered AND, meaning that upward activation from 'a' goes to 'b' *and* 'c', while downward activation from 'b' *and* 'c' goes to 'a'. The second node is an upward unordered OR. In this case, upward activation from 'a' goes to 'b' *and* 'c', and downward activation from 'b' *or* 'c' goes to 'a'. In the third node, a downward ordered AND, downward activation from 'a' goes to 'b' *and later* to 'c', whereas upward activation from 'b' *and later* from 'c' goes to 'a'. Finally, the rightmost node is a downward ordered OR, which means that downward activation from 'a' goes to 'b' if possible, and otherwise to 'c'; on the other hand, upward activation from 'b' *or* 'c' goes to 'a'.

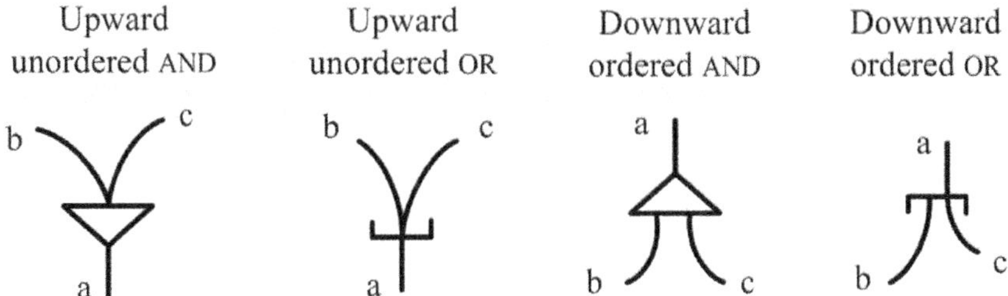

Figure 1.4: Some of the main nodes in RNT.

Since linguistic structure consists of nothing but relationships, a single node cannot be the basic unit of the model, for it fails to show where activation is coming from – i.e., which specific relationships the node is subsuming. The most basic unit in RNT, then, is a linkage between two nodes or, in technical terms, a *nection*. Nections come in different varieties, some of which are shown in Figure 1.5.

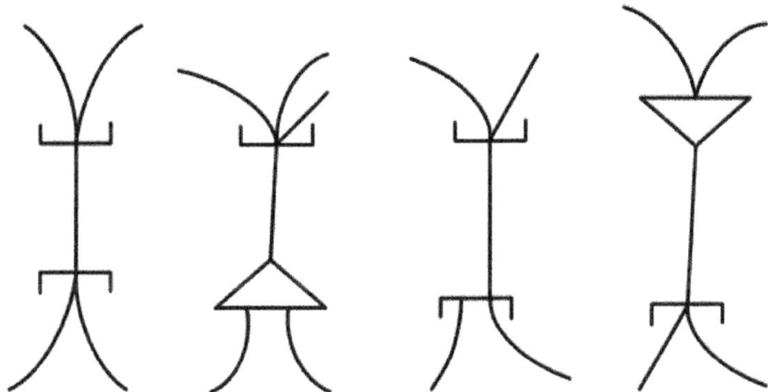

Figure 1.5: Some examples of nections.

At this point, it may appear that either the nodes or the nections are tantamount to the symbols postulated in other theories. That is not the case. Nections represent points of convergence within the system, so that they only exist insofar as the relationships exist. One could of course attach a symbol or label to a node, but such a symbol would not be part of the structure itself. The linguist can rely on peripheral symbols as a signaling convention, much as street signs function in a city. A given corner constitutes a distinguishable, unique point in the city's network of streets. For the benefit of drivers and pedestrians, street signs are placed at that point, but that point, which is part of the street structure, does not require any sign to be unique and distinguishable and to fulfill its specific function in the overall system. In fact, the sign can be removed without altering the structure in any way – the corner labeled 'Leeland and Louisiana' in Houston will continue to be what it is, even if a hurricane sweeps the sign away.

If a linguist's task is to describe the structural system underlying language, then non-structural elements, such as symbols, should not be interpolated in the description. It would be a mistake to conceive of nections in the ways depicted in Figure 1.6; for relational networks do not represent symbols, either within nodes (Figure 1.6a) or within lines (Figure 1.6b).

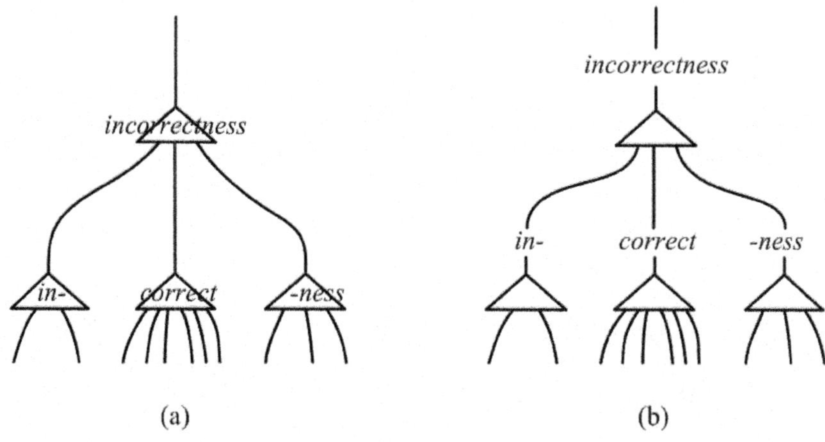

Figure 1.6: Two wrong conceptions of relational networks.

Instead, the appropriate conception of nections as units of linguistic structure could be represented as in Figure 1.7, with labels located outside the network for the benefit of the reader. Linguistic structure itself is thus represented as what it is, a network of relationships.

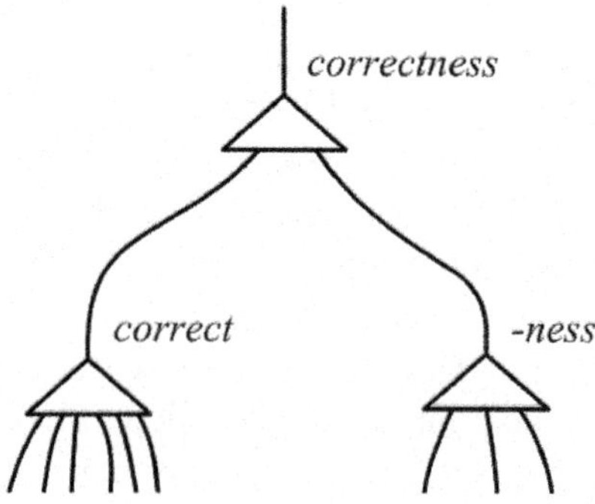

Figure 1.7: The appropriate conception of relational networks.

This notation enables efficient handling of verbal phenomena involving multi-relational mappings of meanings and form that traditional accounts treat with limited success (see Chapters 6 and 8). Another advantage of relational network notation is that it reflects the real ordering of linguistic units (cf. Lamb, 2004e), unlike rule-governed systems which force artificial ordering on linguistic structure. Furthermore, relational networks ultimately touch on substance at the phonetic and perceptual ends, linking language with low-level sensorimotor systems.

To illustrate the comprehensiveness, ease, and utility of the notation for a slightly more complicated case, Figure 1.8 offers a representation of *under*, *go*, and *undergo*. Let us analyze it from the perspective of reception (from bottom to top). Hearing the word 'under' activates the nections subserving the phonemes /ʌ/, /n/, /d/, /ə/, and /r/, in that order. The ordered AND, which captures the linear nature of phonemic units, gets activated only if it receives activation from those five nodes. As such is the case, activation proceeds upwards from the AND node to the ordered OR. At this point activation branches out following the two ascending lines. Activation going through the left-most line (the so-called precedence line) dies out upon reaching the node representing *undergo*, as it has not received activation from the node processing *go*. The other line ascending from the ordered OR for *under* reaches a sememic nection providing a link to the meaning UNDER.

However, if the perceived word is *undergo*, activation proceeds sequentially along nections for the phonemes /ʌ/, /n/, /d/, /ə/, /r/, /g/, and /o/, first engaging the node for *under* and then the node for *go*. Activation moves upwards along the lines ascending from these upward OR nodes; since both precedence lines are sending activation, the ordered AND for *undergo* gets activated, at which point the activation ascending through the other line in each of the OR nodes vanishes. Ultimately, this ignites the sememic nection for UNDERGO, representing a meaning that is distinct from those of UNDER and GO, even if the lexeme *undergo*, at the lexicogrammatical stratum, receives activation from the individual nodes for *under* and *go*.

The question has sometimes been posed whether relational networks are not metaphorical, that is to say, artificial. To this, Lamb (e.g., 2004d, 1999) responds that relational networks result from analyzing language exclusively in terms of its own structure. Note that the connectivity principles outlined so far have been formulated without imposed external categories, methods, or procedures. On this point, RNT differs from several linguistic theories, in particular generative models. The reasoning traced throughout this chapter indicates that linguistic structure (as Hjelmslev insisted) is a network of relationships, composed by reciprocal links between nodes, in the absence of any other types of element. In RNT terms, this approach yields plausible accounts of language architecture.

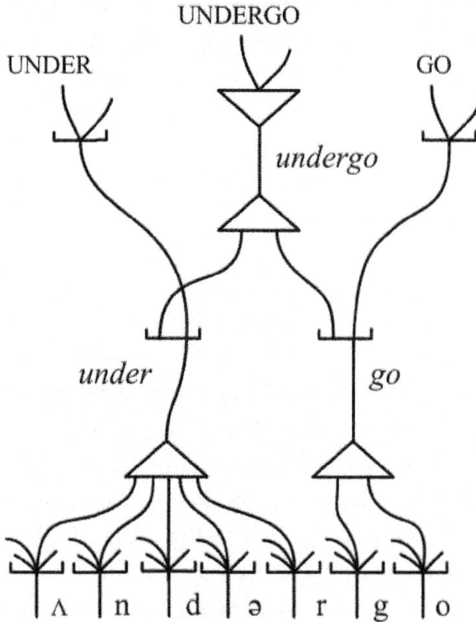

Figure 1.8: The lexeme *undergo* as a network of relationships.

In the early formulations described above, networks sought to capture linguistic structure as a static mesh of connections. With the passing of time, when the networks were put into action to account for language processing, more sophisticated types of notation had to be introduced (see Chapter 2). Still, this initial phase in the development of RNT provided enough ground to define language as a stratified complex of multiple subsystems whose units have no existence except by virtue of the relationships they represent.

The next step in the exploration was to check the theory for operational and developmental plausibility – in other words, to determine whether RNT, in addition to being structurally realistic, was also cognitively realistic. Results from this search are described in Chapters 2 and 3.

Notes

1.   Sullivan, encountering this characterization for the first time, got the impression of a seine, or net.

2.   For example, in the essay 'Saussure's error: Objects of study in linguistics and other sciences', Lamb (2004h) discusses some infelicities in Saussure's epistemological conception of linguistic constructs and their relation to real-world phenomena.

3.   In particular, 'An attempt at a theory of phonetic alternation', 'Phonetic laws', and 'The difference between phonetics and psychophonetics', which have been

reproduced in Baudouin de Courtenay's (1972) collected works as chapters VII, XIV, and XV, respectively.

4. This monograph was composed in Russian and completed in 1926. It was translated into French for publication in the *Travaux du Cercle linguistique de Prague*. The Russian original was lost or accidentally destroyed. Trubetzkoy was not happy with the French text and he corresponded about it with Jakobson. Still, the relational network nature of Jakobson's thinking, though at a preliminary stage, is easily recognizable.

5. Incidentally, Hockett (1961) proposed the same term. While Hockett's publication preceded Lamb's, neither scholar claimed precedence, as Lamb seemed to follow Hjelmslev in this notational variant required by the elaboration of the system.

6. Later, he renamed the same strata that in 1958–1959 he had referred to as *phonemic* (remained phonemic), *hyperphonemic* (renamed morphemic), *morphemic* (renamed *lexemic*), and *hypermorphemic* (renamed *sememic*) (Lamb, personal communication).

7. The phonological system also includes other units such as the syllable, the phonological word, and the phonological phrase, which realize certain lexemes and phrases at the lexicogrammatical stratum. Some current treatments (see Chapters 4, 5, 7, 8) use the term 'hypophonology' to refer to part of the phonological system. Phonetics has conventionally been considered part of phonology, though the units in each system are essentially different. Elements of instrumental phonetics (articulation, acoustics, audition) may be separated from systemic phonetic or hypophonological properties and referred to collectively as phonetics (proper).

8. We use the term embodied/conceptual/executive cognition to refer to neurocognitive systems which participate in verbal communication but are neither exclusively nor distinctively linguistic. First, embodied cognitive systems encompass all sensorimotor networks which ground high-order mechanisms, such as verbal semantics (Barsalou, 1999; Gallese & Lakoff, 2005). For example, hearing the word *kick* yields distinctive activation patterns in leg-specific areas of the motor cortex (Pulvermüller, 2005), while verbs denoting manual actions are critically grounded in networks specialized for programming and controlling hand movements (García & Ibáñez, 2016a, 2016b). However, such embodiment effects are not exclusive to language. For instance, cortical and subcortical motor-related regions are engaged by both execution and imagery of visually guided movements (Binkofski *et al.*, 2000), including manual and mental rotation (Parsons *et al.*, 1995). Second, linguistic systems also interact profusely with amodal conceptual processing systems, which integrate signals from lower-level unimodal sensory modalities, giving rise to more abstract, disembodied representations. Critical neural regions for these networks include Wernicke's area, the superior temporal sulcus, and, crucially, the anterior temporal lobe (Patterson, Nestor, & Rogers, 2007; Visser, Jefferies, & Lambon Ralph, 2010), which are engaged in both linguistic and non-linguistic tasks. Finally, executive functions encompass complex mechanisms which regulate activity in other cognitive systems. These include working memory, attentional allocation, inhibitory control, and cognitive flexibility, and rely critically on prefrontal networks and subcortical networks (Zillmer & Spiers, 2001). All of these functions are essential to language processing across strata.

9. Of course 'neutralization' is a familiar term from the phonological analyses of Jakobson and Trubetzkoy. In RNT, this notion is implicit in the usage of upward OR nodes, as illustrated in detail at the phonemic level in Sullivan (1974).

10. A full account of Halliday's notation for systemic networks, recognizing several types of relationships between 'systems', 'entry conditions', and 'features', can be

found in Halliday (1967/1968, pp. 37–38). A more extended discussion of Halliday's influence on Lamb's network notation can be found in Halliday, Lamb, & Regan (1988, pp. 7–8).

11.   Here Lamb points out that no complete account can be given of a linguistic system, so that 'partial completeness' is the best a linguist can achieve.

12.   Successive adjustments were inevitable, given the swirling dynamic of thinkers contributing to the theory's takeoff. The afternoon classes run by Lamb during the late 1960s were regularly visited by Gleason and his students from the Hartford Seminary Foundation, and joined by Halliday during his residence at Yale. Gleason provided important insights into the nature of OR relationships. Additional contributions were made by David Bennett (1937–2013), David Lockwood (1939–2007), and Peter Reich. The latter, in particular, was at that time developing the idea of spreading activation as an alternative method of implementing encoding/decoding processes through a linguistic network. Note that spreading activation and threshold nodes are compatible logically and neurologically, and it is not necessary to exclude one or the other. The important point is that these were the initial efforts at moving from a logical to a more neurological network. Neurocognitively plausible tenets (e.g., emergent knowledge) grew from this and from the implicit knowledge inherent in the logical network, as developed then and later by Sullivan.

13.   The system can also be conceived of as three-dimensional, i.e., vertical, horizontal, and deep. And it can be rotated conceptually, so that a part horizontal at a given moment can differ from what was horizontal a moment before. What remains constant is the relationships.

2　From Language Structure to Language Processing

2.1　Introduction

RNT strives to provide a realistic model of how we process language, from cognition to articulation and from perception to cognition. Details of its architecture and operation are motivated in response to linguistic evidence, which critically reflects the system's structural constraints. With that architecture in place, RNT has advanced specific hypotheses on how information flows across systems and strata, thus addressing the requisite of operational plausibility. This chapter introduces the key constructs devised to such an end.

We begin with an overview of language processing as a dynamic activity related to other cognitive processes. We consider how the assumption of spreading activation and quantum firing can model actual language processes. Our focus is on the distinctions between different types of nodes, their interconnections (via nections), and the means by which they can exchange information. Two types of notation are introduced: abstract notation, which represents information flow bidirectionally; and narrow notation, which represents information flow unidirectionally.

Next, we consider tactic patterns as a representation of how elements combine to form the structures related to each stratum (e.g., phonemes, morphemes, lexemes, clauses, predications). The tactics should be understood as the generalized structural relations between the emes of a given stratum, such that the phonotactics constitute the syntax of phonemes, for example. We also consider how realizational relations link the tactic patterns of adjacent strata, eventually describing a complete linguistic system. AND and OR nodes, or, alternatively, diamond nodes where realizational relations meet tactic patterns, are described with respect to their coordination of information flow throughout the system.

In the final sections, we consider the linguistic system in relation to cognition, perception, and learning, and show how RNT can account for complex processing phenomena that strictly serial, algorithmic theories may have difficulty explaining.

2.2　A Dynamic View of Language Processes

Already in the 1960s, initial efforts were being made to specify how relational networks must behave to produce and understand speech. The term 'cognitive linguistics' was soon introduced to refer to any theory incorporating a viable performance model (Lamb, 2004a). From this perspective, and against the generativist ethos of the era, the real-time workings of cognition at large were seen as undetachable from language mechanisms.

The reasoning was that if a linguistic system can be appropriately described in terms of nodes and connections, these must be capable of acting dynamically, for actual verbal processes put linguistic systems into operation. More generally, since language draws upon and informs other cognitive systems, RNT must account not just for how language works, but also for how cognition functions in general. In an interview given in 1973, Lamb (2004d) expressed his desire to explore the overall cognitive applicability of the model; and in 1988, during a conversation with Halliday at Claremont Graduate University, he asserted that a number of cognitive systems other than language can be accounted for in terms of hierarchically arranged nections (cf. Lamb, 2004i).

Still, the primary aim of the theory was to account for the linguistic system of the individual. Specifically, to meet the requisite of operational plausibility, the model must be able to function in real time, observing the possibilities and constraints of actual linguistic performance. Thus, at the most basic level, the model must be able to handle information processing – and note, once again, that processing is not part of linguistic structure per se, but the result of putting the system into operation.

2.3   Linguistic Processing as Spreading Activation

In RNT, information processing is conceived as the spreading of activation along the lines – or pathways – linking different nodes. That is to say, activation flows through the lines connecting one node to another. It follows that relational networks are inherently dynamic: a node is activated by receiving enough activation from other nodes, and it then sends further activation along its output lines, in a context of co-constraining activation patterns.

Spreading activation combines with quantum firing as a means of communication within the network. By way of illustration, consider the difference between an incandescent bulb and a capacitor. In electrical systems there are two ways a current moves through a circuit. Spreading activation is exemplified by what happens in an incandescent bulb. When the supply is connected, the current begins to flow through the wires. When it reaches the bulb, the wire in the bulb begins to heat and glow, starting with deep red and moving up through yellow to white. If another bulb is attached in series to the first and the circuit is open, even while the current was heating up the wire in the first bulb, the current would be spreading to the next bulb, always lagging behind but still moving. In short, the progress of the current through the circuit is gradual and spreads continuously.

A more straightforward account of spreading activation in a relational network has been proposed by Peter Reich (personal communication). When activation reaches the singular side of a node, that node sends out via its plural side a lesser degree of activation to the nodes it is related to. Each node reached in turn sends out a lesser activation to all the nodes it is related to. And so on. For the system to keep working, spreading activation must be inputted from other parts of the upper system. If it is not, the existing activation fades.

Quantum firing is more like what happens with a capacitor. A capacitor accepts and stores electrical energy until its capacity is reached. When the capacity is breached by another bit of electrical energy, the capacitor discharges its stored energy, giving a boost to the system. In a relational network, quantum firing is what we envision for nodes with a particular activation level. Until that level is reached, they just store input. When the activation level is reached, they fire.

Spreading activation and quantum firing are not mutually exclusive; both could be happening in different parts of a network at the same time, on different activated lines. They would also be compatible with harmonic vibration in the system.

However, several specifications need to be introduced for these mechanisms to explain actual linguistic phenomena. A very basic (yet non-trivial) observation is that people are able to both produce and understand language. This means that the linguistic system is bidirectional. Following the stratificational metaphor that meaning is at the top and expression is at the bottom, linguistic production goes from top to bottom, whereas understanding goes from bottom to top.

Also, actual individuals (as opposed to idealized speakers/hearers in the generative tradition) do not process information serially, in a linear fashion; rather, our minds are constantly doing many things at once. For example, while we articulate part of an utterance we are typically planning what to say next. To account for such phenomena, relational networks are proposed to operate in loose parallel – i.e., different flows of information may be processed at the same time, regardless of their upward or downward processing orientation.

Moreover, a nection (a relational structure linking two nodes via a single connecting line) is assumed to operate by virtue of its connections to other nections located at different (oftentimes distant) points in the network. Consequently, information in relational networks is widely distributed. The activation of a node at one point in the system depends on the concerted input from nections located throughout the system.

The three preceding paragraphs summarize some of the key processing features in a linguistic system. In short, for RNT the linguistic system relies on bidirectional parallel distributed processing: it processes information both downwards and upwards, in parallel, so that nections can be appropriately linked irrespective of their reciprocal distance.

Note that nections constitute a connectional abstraction of the linguistic relationships established within and across strata. In keeping with RNT tenets, they do not contain symbols or representational objects of any kind. This leads to a modified understanding of traditional linguistic units, as RNT conceptions are based on relationships, formalized as the nections within each stratum. Nections at the phonemic stratum are called 'phononections'; those at the morphemic stratum are 'morphonections'; those at the lexemic stratum are 'logonections'; those at the sememic stratum are 'semonections'; and those belonging to embodied/conceptual/executive cognition are 'ideonections'. Thus, for example, what object-based theories call a 'phoneme' would, in RNT, find its cognitive basis in a specific 'phononection', a purely relational entity. This is, of course, a simplification, since phononections can actually represent units larger than the single analytical phoneme, and they need not correspond to alphabetical units.[1]

2.4   Abstract Notation *vis-à-vis* Narrow Notation

Relational network descriptions can be presented in algebraic form, as seen, for instance, in the interlocking Boolean statements set forth by Coleman (2009). This notation can be seen in Chapter 4 as an illustrative alternative to graphic networks – the two types describe the same connective structure, and are true examples of mere notational variants. Some find the linear algebraic formulations easier to follow, though they may be subject to misinterpretation. Those familiar with Chomskyan linguistics see the labels and slash marks of algebraic notation and read them as generative rewrite rules with arrows and real objects. So an algebraically expressed network written 'Syl / Onset Rhyme' would be mistakenly read as 'Syl => Onset Rhyme', or as 'syllable is replaced by an onset followed by a rhyme', instead of a tiny part of a network. Yet, while syllable, onset, and rhyme in a generative framework are real items of the system, an RNT approach makes no such assumptions about the cognitive existence of linguistic entities.

To reduce the chances of implying such reifications, we prefer graphic descriptions, which are more representative of relational network thinking. In RNT, only the network is in any sense real, though not a tangible thing as such, and the labels just refer to specific points in the network. Not to put too fine a point on it, but hallmark RNT graphic networks tend to frighten students and even mature scholars. (The secret of success in relational network thinking is in the ability to read a map and relate it to the territory, as Korzybski said.) That being said, note that the graphic notation used in most relational network descriptions, and adopted here, is a formalism (that is, a formalized description) and should not be mistaken for the theory itself. Formalized descriptions can be written in words without accompanying graphics, as in the accompanying text.

There are other reasons for our insistence on using graphic notation. There are many reasons. First, we are conditioned to think in terms of things that are arranged in relation to each other. This is fine for distributing furniture around a room, but it is backwards with regard to the analysis of a linguistic system that must be abstracted from its real-world manifestations. Hence, we favor graphic networks, where units of linguistic information can be referenced to points on a diagram. Second, this notational convention has long facilitated our ability to think of the linguistic system as a network of relations in which emes and their constructs are defined by the relations they contract. Finally, graphic networks provide a natural, non-arbitrary means of differentiating between different linguistic strata inductively. All levels of the linguistic system are described by the same basic set of logical relators: AND, OR, ordered, and unordered, with either upward (toward meaning / toward tactic superiority) or downward (toward sound / toward tactic subordinacy) orientation. The strata are then identified by the differences in local networks as well as by the strata they are related to.

Formalisms can be presented in a graphic network of different degrees of delicacy. In RNT, networks are presented in two notation systems: abstract and narrow. The former is more basic and proves simpler to draw and read. Critically, abstract notation assumes that nections are bidirectional – i.e., any given nection can process activation both upwards and downwards – and bidirectionality is represented by a single node with both upward and downward lines indicating direction of flow. In narrow notation, however, such a structure is decomposed into a pair of nodes leading upwards and downwards, respectively. Figure 2.1 presents two examples of abstract notation nodes translated into narrow notation.

In narrow notation, the nodes specifying the number of necessary input lines are called *junction nodes*, and the digit inside them is the *threshold*. When the threshold is satisfied, the node sends activation along its output line. On the other hand, the nodes represented by a tiny solid circle are called *branching nodes*; in these, incoming activation spreads out along both lines. As seen in Figure 2.1, the difference between AND and OR nodes in narrow notation is shown by their thresholds: AND nodes have a threshold of 2 or higher, whereas OR nodes always have a threshold of 1.

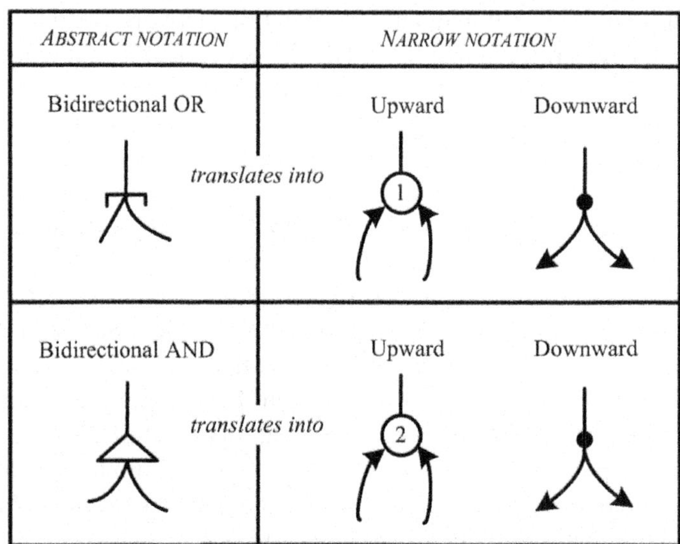

Figure 2.1: Two abstract notation nodes translated into narrow notation.

Furthermore, connections (i.e., lines) can be either *excitatory* or *inhibitory*. Excitatory connections are those which convey positive strengths, as they add to the amount of activation entering a node. On the contrary, inhibitory connections convey negative strengths, so that they reduce the amount of activation the node receives, as described further below. Excitatory connections can be either local or distant. They can lead to nodes located either within the same subsystem as those from which they stem, or to nodes located in other subsystems – e.g., they can connect two nections within the phonemic stratum, or a nection in the morphemic stratum to one in the phonemic stratum. On the other hand, inhibitory connections are only local, which means that they can only connect nodes located within the same subsystem – e.g., two nodes within the morphemic stratum.

Inhibitory connections are especially important for characterizing the operation of OR nodes. An OR node receiving activation from its singular side will send activation along both of its output lines, since it has no way of 'knowing' in advance which of the two lines will carry activation leading to satisfaction downstream.[2] However, at some point one of the two output lines will typically get blocked.[3] The blockage will usually be provided by an inhibitory connection – although, technically, a line reaching an AND node which does not get its threshold satisfied will also get blocked.

Inhibitory connections come in two types: either a blocking element may act directly on the node, or the blockage may operate on the connecting line. These connections are particularly important, for instance, in handling ordered OR nodes. Figure 2.2 exemplifies the operation of blocking elements acting on connecting lines in a case of portmanteau realization (*went* as past of *go*) involving ordered OR nodes in narrow notation. Blocking elements are represented by the two fork-like terminals.

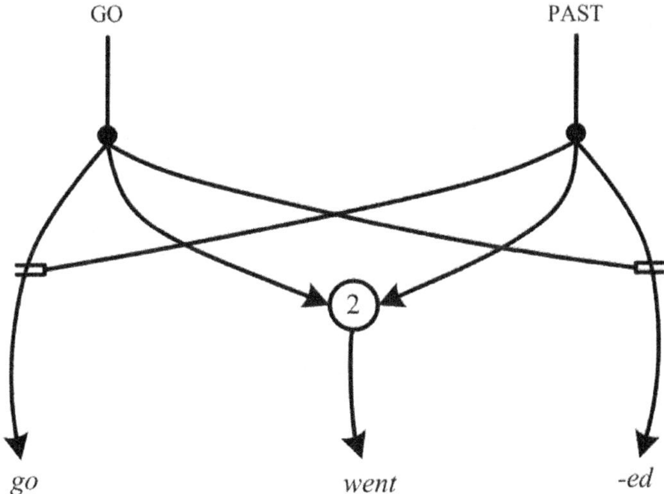

Figure 2.2: Inhibitory connections acting on output lines of an ordered OR node: The case of a portmanteau realization.

Activation builds up rather than reaching its full charge suddenly. Thus, even if some activation flows along the non-desired output line of an OR node, it does not mean that its target node will ignite. The blocking element will hinder the passage of activation before all of it has traversed the pathway. In addition, inhibitory connections may connect directly to a node, as opposed to a line. These connections reduce the total amount of activation entering the node. As will be seen below, the threshold of a node performs a running summation of the activation of its incoming lines by adding excitatory (positive) connections and subtracting inhibitory (negative) connections. Figure 2.3 shows an inhibitory connection (represented by a tiny hollow circle) acting directly on a node. In this example, since the node's threshold is 3 and one of its four input lines is inhibitory, the node does not get activated unless the inhibitory line is inactive.

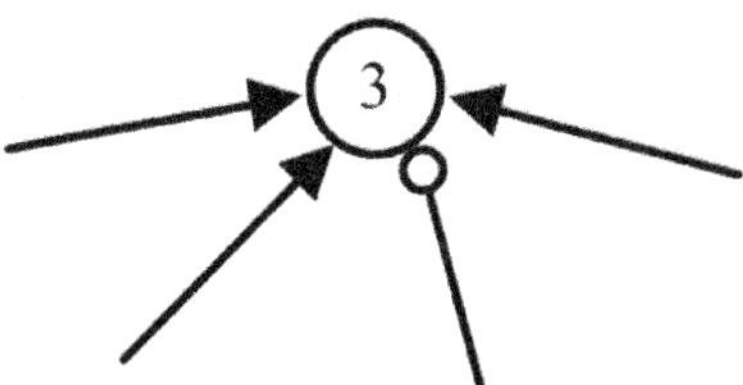

Figure 2.3: An inhibitory connection acting directly on a node.

Inhibitory connections are crucial to explain finely tuned temporal dynamics during language processing. The same is true of the ordered AND node. In this case, activation sent along the second line (and third, and fourth, if applicable) must be put on hold while the activation flow along the first, leftmost line is in progress. Furthermore, the activation sent through the second line must 'know' how long to wait. Otherwise, the ordering specified by the node may not function properly. In this case, there is another possibility. Activation fades over time, and it may be that the rate of fade determines how long the activation should wait. Further neurological research is needed before the choice between these possibilities can be clarified.

The required timing constraints could be implemented by several (neurally plausible) mechanisms, each of which may operate in a different portion of the network. Let us discuss one of them, called *feedback timing*. This mechanism is illustrated in Figure 2.4. Outgoing activation travels along both output lines at once. Yet, to prevent *go* from being processed before *under*, the second line has a loop which keeps the activation flowing in circles until *under* is fully processed. Note that the threshold for the loop is 1, so that the activation of that line alone is enough to maintain an iterative flow. On the other hand, the node leading to *go* has a threshold of 2, so that no single line is enough to activate it. Once the morphonection for *under* is satisfied, it sends activation upwards to a branching node. One of the lines of this branching node blocks the loop, whereas the other sends activation to the junction node with a threshold of 2. The activation that traveled in circles around the loop now has only one pathway to follow, and the junction node becomes satisfied.

While narrow notation is suitable for formulating neurologically oriented hypotheses in RNT (see Chapter 3), abstract notation can be safely adopted as a more convenient resource for basic description of linguistic phenomena. This is so because: (a) the diagrams are less cluttered and hence easier to read; (b) narrow notation nodes require explicit indication of threshold values, which can only be speculatively postulated; and (c) full operational details of threshold adjustments, connection strengths, and excitation-inhibition tradeoffs are not yet well understood (either in RNT or in cognitive neuroscience). Thus, while the degree of detail captured by narrow notation is important for constraining the theory, formulating more stringent hypotheses, and taking a step toward characterizing the biological basis of language, introductory RNT characterizations of linguistic phenomena can be more efficiently achieved via abstract notation. Indeed, since the present book focuses on descriptive applications, this has been our approach in the following sections and throughout the case studies of Part II.

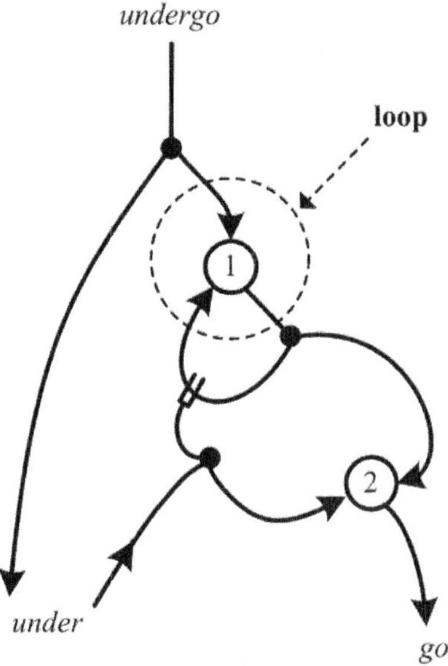

Figure 2.4: Handling timing in the ordered AND node via feedback timing.

2.5   Tactics

As seen in Chapter 1, RNT dismisses grammar rules as introjective artifacts, so they are not a cognitively plausible option for construing an operational model. The alternative is to have nodes which receive acceptable input and whose outgoing lines specify ordering information. This means that syntactic ordering should also be handled by combinations of different node types.

Building on Stratificational Grammar, RNT recognizes various tactic patterns, that is, network configurations that indicate the structural relations between elements (emes) on a particular stratum. With any eme (sememe, lexeme, morpheme, phoneme, hypophoneme), the relationships may include combinations of functional relations (up, to the next higher stratum and ultimately toward meaning), formal relations (down, toward phonetic form), and tactic relations (relations to other emes on the same stratum). The tactic relations may be upward, toward larger constructs, or downward, toward smaller ones. The upward tactic relations define the element's range, while the lower tactic relations define its domain. A unique combination of such relations suffices to define any particular linguistic element at any level of the linguistic system.

RNT scholars have explored various proposals to handle tactics. We shall here introduce two by way of illustration and to lay the foundation for their use in the descriptive applications (Part II). Although not all strata will be discussed, the basic properties of the tactics presented below are, in principle, applicable to all linguistic levels. Once again, for descriptive convenience, the following figures will be drawn using abstract notation.

2.5.1 Handling Tactics with AND and OR Nodes

In RNT, AND and OR relationships, respectively, capture conjunctive and disjunctive relationships among linguistic entities. The distinction between 'ordered' and 'unordered' nodes also responds to basic observations about linguistic structure. For example, co-occurring entities may either merge to give rise to a new entity (unordered AND, as in the portmanteau realization *went*), or be organized in succession (ordered AND, as in the realizations of *undergo* as *under* and *go*).

Thus, the ordered AND can be seen as the basic unit of tactic relationships, for it necessarily specifies sequential ordering of activation. As such, any tactic pattern in RNT will contain at least one ordered AND node. Figure 2.5 shows a very basic syntax – or lexotactics – for a simplified

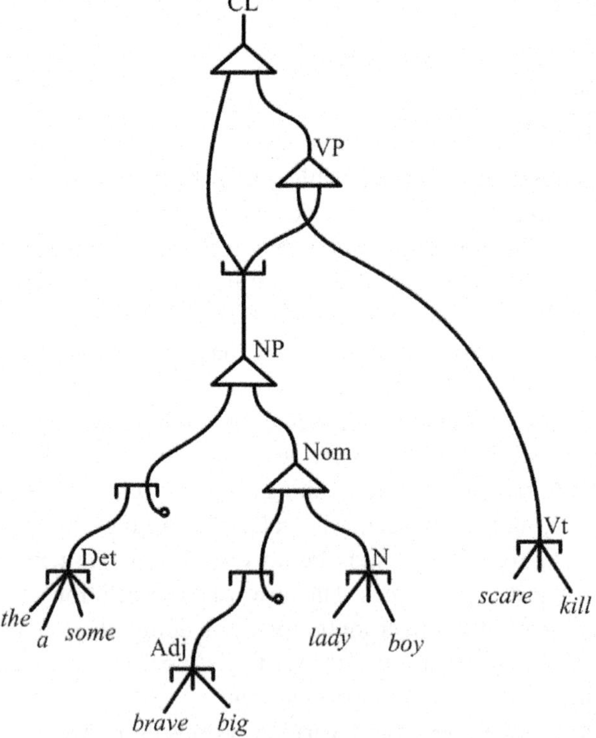

Figure 2.5: A simplified portion of English lexotactics for unmarked, affirmative, active clauses.

conception of the unmarked, affirmative, active English clause (CL), as in *the big boy scared a lady.*

The network in Figure 2.5 indicates that unmarked, affirmative active clauses in English are related to a Noun Phrase (NP) and a Verb Phrase (VP), in that order. The NP node specifies that Determiners, if present, occur before the Nominal (a unit intermediate between the NP and the Noun), while the Nom node determines that an Adjective, if present, occurs before the Noun. The possibility of an NP having no Det or Adj is represented by the tiny hollow circle in the downward ordered ORs. For its own part, the VP node shows that a Transitive Verb always occurs before its object NP, whose structure is conditioned by the same constraints described for the first NP. Thus, this extremely simplified network provides the tactic ordering for a myriad of English clauses, while establishing that English is an SVO language.

As a further example of how lexotactics can be treated using relational networks, consider Figure 2.6, taken from Lamb (1999, p. 98), which represents a simplified syntax for yes/no questions in English.[4]

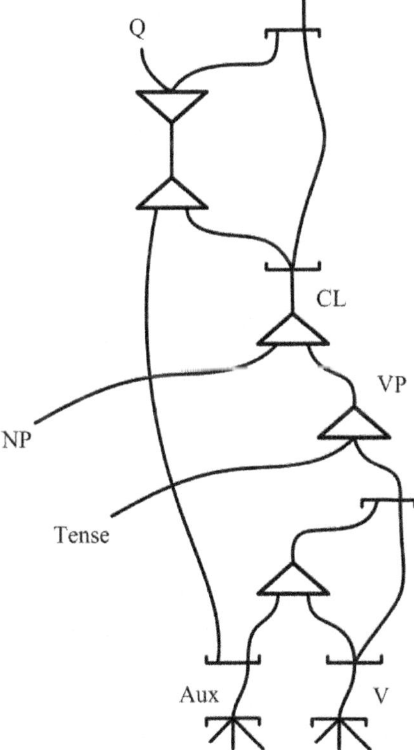

Figure 2.6: A simplified lexotactic network for English yes/no questions. Authorized reproduction of Figure 6.13 from: Lamb, S. M. (1999). *Pathways of the brain: The neurocognitive basis of language.* Amsterdam: John Benjamins. Used by permission of John Benjamins Publishing and Sydney Lamb.

By virtue of the first downward ordered AND node, Figure 2.6 posits that in the production of an English yes/no question, activation first flows down to the Aux node and then to a CL node, which will in turn activate first an NP node and then a VP node. The unordered downward VP node, once satisfied, will send further activation downwards to simultaneously realize a specific Tense and either a single verb or a combination of an auxiliary and a single verb (this possibility is accounted for by the ordered OR node right below the VP node).

All in all, in this type of account, tactic patterns are implemented as networks whose nodes connect with other nodes of a given stratum to specify their relative order of processing. While these examples have been treated with what might be called a 'vertical' approach to tactics, there are other approaches which may be just as valid – or perhaps even more valid (cf. Lamb, 1966a, 1980, 1999; Lockwood, 1972). Be that as it may, the bottom line is that RNT offers an operationally plausible characterization of tactics which not only does without rules, but is also capable of providing ordering at all linguistic levels without relinquishing the notion of realization (see Chapter 1), now reconceptualized as bidirectional spreading activation.

2.5.2 An Alternative Account: Incorporating Diamond Nodes

Another approach to tactics within the RNT framework relies on a notational device called a 'diamond node'. Diamond nodes were introduced in the late 1960s as a means of intersecting the tactic patterns and realizational portions of each stratum. It was thought that the knots linking such portions had a special kind of timing function which could account for anataxis, or what is typically called (synchronic) metathesis. Tactic patterns were defocused in RNT research in the 1980s and 1990s, as Lamb ventured into the neurocognitive domain. However, other scholars kept working on the issue.

From that time period, Sullivan recalls a conference organized for linguists of different theoretical persuasions to face a set of challenging syntactic phenomena and explain them in terms of their respective theories. For example, participants were asked to specify whether the explanation required Subject-Object or Agent-Patient or Topic-Comment structure, whether it could all be done with NP, VP, command structure, and transformations, etc. One proposal offered depended on a (long) series of movement transformations, which could be traced to a mistaken original (i.e., underlying) form, from which other sentences (with differing surface forms) had to be derived by reordering. Sullivan (1980) approached the problem by taking a relational approach, with a semotactics whose predications grouped sememes hierarchically but not linearly, and which was realized by lexemes that were linearized in two or more different ways in the lexotactics, depending on the functions the lexemes expounded. Soon thereafter Sullivan reasoned that the same methods would account for all anataxis. The consequence was that this required somewhat generalized tactic patterns, which Lamb no longer saw the need for. However, such patterns have remarkable overall utility; in fact, a generalized tactic pattern solution that worked for specific examples of anataxis could be extended to account for all anataxis (see Sullivan, 2000) and an even wider variety of speech errors.

Since speech errors are productive, they suggest that Lamb turned away from generalized (not necessarily optimized) tactic patterns too soon. His method of elaborating realizational patterns and reducing tactic patterns requires that the potential for speech errors be added to the system deliberately. This could be done, but the patterning of the errors would directly reflect the construction bias of the builders. The treatment of a variety of errors in two languages in Chapter 8 suggests that the argument for generalized tactic patterns is empirically sound. The model adopted in that chapter predicts the possibility of these errors without construction bias and provides a general approach to tactics, based on diamond nodes.

Diamond nodes come in seven varieties, at least. Each one can be described using combinations constructed of AND nodes as nections, a point to which we return below. In Figure 2.7, we see AND nodes expressing the same information as the diamond node version, which is notationally more efficient and offers the same possibilities of timing function. The first diamond we consider has a four-way connection (Figure 2.7a).

In Figure 2.7a, the path defined by 1–2 leads from the next higher tactic pattern to the next lower one. The path defined by 3–4 relates a superior tactic pattern structure to an inferior tactic pattern structure. This diamond node is useful, for example, to characterize a morpheme marked for accent. In this case, Line 1 relates to the morphology, specifically to all morphemes marked for accent. Line 2 relates to the hypophonology and the phonetic signals of accent (increased loudness, length, general articulatory energy, change in pitch). Line 3 leads to the range of word accent – e.g., once in a phonological word (Pword). Line 4 leads to the domain of accent, which is the syllable. So, the diamond notation could neatly integrate both the tactic pattern and realizational properties of the accent phoneme in Russian, for example. Similarly, a four-way diamond is used in the description of the genitive case in Polish (cf. Chapter 5, Figure 5.4).

As shown in the following panels within Figure 2.7, there are several possible three-way diamonds. The diamond in Figure 2.7b represents a typical eme (e.g., a phoneme) at the bottom of a tactic pattern. Line 1 relates

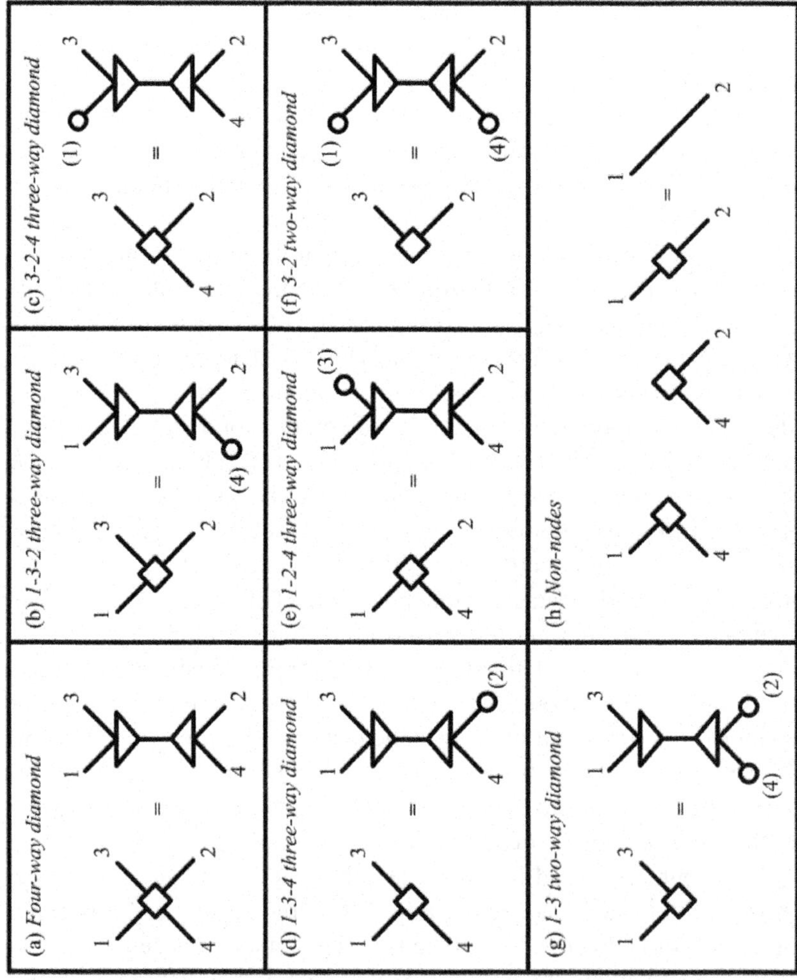

Figure 2.7: The seven varieties of diamond nodes and four types of non-nodes.

to all morphemes distinguished by that phoneme. Line 2 relates to the relevant phonemic feature or features of that phoneme. Line 3 relates to the OR node that defines the set of phonemes that share that feature. Line 4, which appears only in abstract notation, has a zero relation – i.e., it is related to nothing. This is why it does not appear at all in the diamond diagram. For examples of phonemes described by this type of diamond, see Chapter 4, Figure 4.11.

The function of the diamond in Figure 2.7c is to supply a determined tactic feature to the encoding process. Determined features relate to the next lower tactic pattern and to domain and range in their own tactic pattern, but they have no direct relation to the next higher stratum. For example, if line 4 is related to a conjoined pair of singular nouns in subject position, line 2 could provide plural subject–verb agreement, even though neither noun is semantically plural. Another example can be found in Chapter 7, Figure 7.2, with the line leading to New (¶).

The type of diamond in Figure 2.7d is usually found in marked-unmarked oppositions. Line 1 relates to the marked (left-hand) line of an ordered OR node, which is line 3 to the diamond in the figure. Line 4 realizes the marked form. This type is useful, for example, to describe the many possibilities of case-endings in some languages. We use such diamond nodes to describe the Polish genitive in Chapter 5, Figure 5.5 (note the realization of pl 'plural', which evokes the set of plural endings at node 1). See also the realization of ¶ in Chapter 7, Figure 7.3.

While the preceding three-way diamonds have been useful in descriptions of Slavic languages as well as English, there is a fourth possibility, given in Figure 2.7e, as posited by Sullivan on the basis of speculation. In particular, he surmises that the diamond illustrated should be present at the top of each tactic pattern. The reasoning behind this choice is as follows, cast in terms of the semotactics. Line 1 comes from embodied/conceptual/executive cognition and can be labeled 'intent to communicate'. It provides the starter signal for semotactic processing of the input from ideonections to semonections. Line 4 relates to the semotactics, and a signal down this line is the start of semotactic processing, which groups sememes into predications and provides sememic roles (semantic role relations, in Halliday's terminology). At the same time, line 2 connects to line 1 at the top of the lexotactics, and a subsequent signal down line 4 at the top of the lexotactics sets processing activation to work there, and so on in sequence.

There are also two two-way diamonds. The diamond in Figure 2.7f is located at the bottom of a tactic pattern and is related only to a superior tactic structure. It also has relations to the next lower stratum but no direct relations to the next higher stratum. So it is an eme with relation to form but with no direct functional relation. Line 3 is the culmination of a series of unmarked choices, like the nominative singular in Polish morphology (see Chapter 5, Figure 5.5, at node 5).

The other two-way diamond is given in Figure 2.7g. This is the relation for an eme with zero realization. It has relation to function, whether to meaning or to the next higher stratum. It is also related to superior structures in the tactics of its own stratum. The genitive plural ending in Polish feminine nouns has exactly this kind of diamond (see Chapter 5, Figure 5.5, below node 2).

No reason has been advanced to posit the 1–4 and 2–4 two-way nodes using diamond notation, as illustrated in Figure 2.7h. A diamond relating lines 1 and 2, or lines 3 and 4, is not a diamond. As indicated, such a relation reduces to a simple line.

In short, diamonds are simply a shorthand for a back-to-back nection of two unordered AND nodes rather than a new node. Their notational efficiency makes them convenient in graphic description.

2.6   The Linguistic System in Relation to Cognition and Perception

All considerations to inform the formulation of RNT so far pertain to the linguistic system alone. However, the linguistic system interfaces with several other cognitive and perceptual domains. Language enables us to make reference, for example, to visual, auditory, and somatosensory phenomena, and it also allows us to speak about constructs with no direct physical basis, such as *justice*, *honor*, and *confusion*. To be cognitively realistic, the theory must be able to account for these facts.

This requires broadening the scope of inquiry. Consider the model's abstract stratified architecture, as illustrated in Chapter 1 (Figure 1.2). At the bottom, the linguistic system connects with the sensorimotor interfaces (the articulatory organs, the ears, and even the digitomanual system, for writing); the highest linguistic stratum relates to thoughts and meanings, which, in turn, receive inputs from the perceptual and motor systems, whose lowest strata are also next to the interfaces (the eyes, the ears, the hands, etc.). Therefore, from a broader cognitive standpoint, what began as a vertical stratified system now becomes a stratified arch (Figure 2.8).

This arch brings together linguistic, perceptual, and otherwise cognitive systems in general. Beyond the interfaces lies the real world, which we can only apprehend indirectly on the basis of our cognitive constraints. The schematic divisions of the arch allow for the distinction between three major systems: (a) the *human information system*, which includes all cognitive systems as well as the interfaces; (b) the *human cognitive system*,

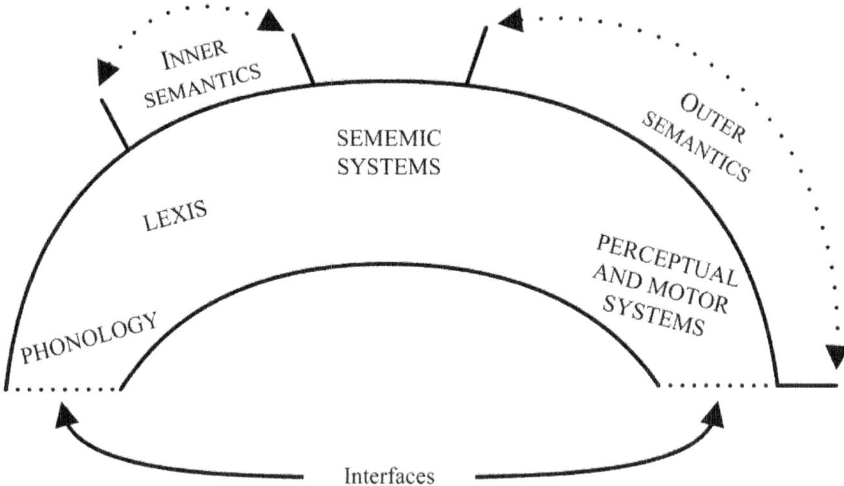

Figure 2.8: The locus of the linguistic system in the stratified cognitive arch. Authorized reproduction of Figure 9.3 from: Lamb, S. M. (1999). *Pathways of the brain: The neurocognitive basis of language.* Amsterdam: John Benjamins. Used by permission of John Benjamins Publishing and Sydney Lamb.

which could be defined as the network connecting all the interfaces; and (c) the *human linguistic system,* which is a subnetwork within the latter.

At the bottom of the arch lie the perceptual and motor systems. Each constitutes an independent subsystem processing unimodal representations – the visual system, for example, is specialized for visual information. Besides, RNT distinguishes between *percepts* (unimodal perceptual representations) and *perfuncts* (individual motor representations). Like language, each of these unimodal systems is hierarchically organized.

The realm extending from lexis to the perceptual and motor systems constitutes sememic structure. The sememic systems provide integration for the different unimodal meanings that belong within the perceptual and motor systems. The nections integrating information from different perceptual modalities are called *concepts* (e.g., an integration of visual, auditory, and tactile information pertaining to a dog), while those integrating information from different perfunctual domains are known as *confuncts* (e.g., a coordinated representation of the various individual movements involved in the process of tying one's shoes). Figure 2.9 shows various percepts (unimodal perceptual nodes) integrated by the conceptual category DOG, where conceptual (C), tactile (T), lexical (L), auditory (A), and visual (V) hubs are indicated. Once again, this is a very simplified depiction, since any concept is bound to integrate numerous percepts from each modality.

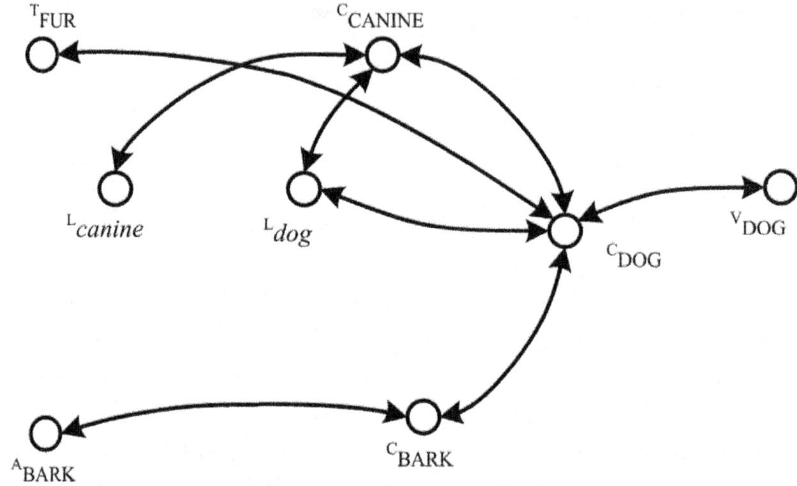

Figure 2.9: A simplified diagram of the connections involved in the conceptual category DOG.

Within sememic structure, a distinction is made between inner semantics and outer semantics. Inner semantics is the dimension of exclusively linguistic meanings, as realized by lexis. Outer semantics refers to the relationships between sememic systems and perceptual and motor systems, which support a composite model of experience.

The linguistic end of the cognitive arch leads to phonology, which is necessarily involved in both speech production and perception. In other words, phonology has a production facet and a reception facet. As Lamb (1999) explains, the structures needed for phonological production are quite different from those needed for reception. They also follow different developmental trajectories. For instance, a child learning a language is able to understand his parents' speech long before he is able to produce any speech of his own. Also, most adults are capable of understanding many more words than they are able to produce spontaneously.

Thus, the one phonological system is closely related to the speech organs (motor systems), while the other has abundant connections with the hearing system (perceptual systems). Yet, both must be connected, since human beings are able to 'hear' their inner speech and to reproduce new words upon first hearing them even without knowing their meaning – i.e., even if no connections have been established between the phonemic, morphemic, lexemic, and sememic strata. Moreover, people actually hear their own overt production. This oftentimes overlooked fact is crucial for monitoring purposes. The decision of what to produce next is partly determined by the input we receive from ourselves.

Note that these two phonological systems are distinct from the motor and perceptual interfaces on which they depend. A monolingual English speaker with a perfectly functional hearing mechanism may listen to a Japanese speaker and, although he will hear the sound waves produced by the latter, he will likely fail to recognize the ensuing phonemic contrasts. Hence, he will not be able to establish connections with lexis or semology. Therefore, while phonological production and phonological perception are inextricably bound to the systems for articulatory production and auditory perception, they are distinct. Also, they are further removed from the interfaces than these systems. Figure 2.10, based on Lamb (1999, p. 127), illustrates the relationship between both phonological systems.

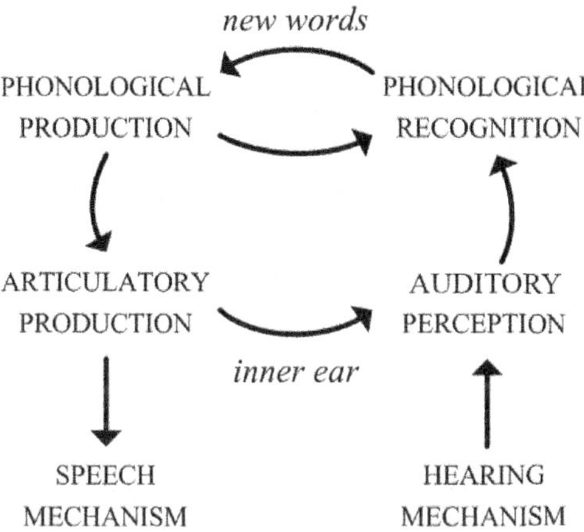

Figure 2.10: Interacting phonological subsystems (based on Lamb, 1999, p. 127).

As regards the lexico-grammatical stratum, a distinction between grammar and lexis must be recognized. Similar considerations to the ones applied to phonology led Lamb (1999) – *mutatis mutandis* – to hypothesize that there may be a difference between grammatical production and grammatical recognition.

Grammar would thus be a broad term for a series of independent, though related, tactic production networks and tactic reception networks. For its own part, lexis, acting as an intermediate layer between linguistic content and expression, must be related to everything that a person can think of and manifest linguistically. However, not everything that a person can think of is of the same status. For example, in discussing process categories (or confuncts), Lamb (1999, pp. 139–140) recognizes a difference between 'object categories' (those constructed through direct experience, like WALKING and EATING), and 'abstract categories' (those constructed through observation only, such as FLYING and RAINING). The subsystem for abstract categories might be seen as comprising the ideonections for immaterial referents, such as *justice* and *honor*.

However, not all possible features of a concept need to be activated for it to be evoked. To capture this aspect of semantic processing, we need to introduce a new notational element known as the *threshold node* (distinct from the threshold of a node, discussed in section 2.4 above). This construct is vital for understanding the process of conceptualization introduced above as well as some of the learning and processing phenomena which will be discussed below. Indeed, AND and OR nodes are not enough to account for the many 'fuzzy' aspects of language.

An AND node is satisfied only when all of its input lines get activated; as such, it is an all-or-nothing node. It would thus appear that a nection gets activated only when necessary and sufficient conditions are present. However, everyday linguistic experience contradicts such a postulation, for people are able to identify entities (i.e., to activate nodes) by having access to just about any combination of their relevant properties. Consider, for example, the conceptual category DOG, as in Figure 2.9. Not all percepts connected to it need to send activation for it to be satisfied. Moreover, no set of properties proves either necessary or sufficient to account for what a dog is. One could propose, perhaps, that a dog is defined by having four legs, a tail, being furry, barking, being small, etc. Yet, there are tailless dogs (corgi), hairless dogs (Chinese crested), dogs that yodel (basenji), and dogs of various sizes (Great Dane to teacup chihuahua). And they are all dogs to some degree.

So, even if some percepts that typically get activated upon seeing a dog – e.g., TAIL, BARK – do not get activated when we encounter a tailless, barkless dog, the concept DOG will still get activated. Neither AND nor OR nodes can handle this situation. The solution is provided by the threshold node, a type of node whose threshold does not necessarily coincide with the number of incoming lines. Thus, the threshold may have a value of 2 while being connected to five input lines. In such cases, it does not matter which of those five lines are active at any one time; it takes only two of them for the threshold to be satisfied.

The introduction of the threshold node leads to a redefinition of the AND and OR nodes, which can now be seen as special types of threshold nodes. An AND node is a threshold node whose threshold is equivalent to the number of incoming lines it has, while an OR node is any threshold node with a threshold of 1. Consequently, all nodes may be seen as threshold nodes. Figure 2.11 illustrates some simple types. Note that the first node in that figure coincides with an OR node (since the number of input lines from below exceeds the threshold value), whereas the second one is equivalent to an AND node (the number of input lines is equal to the node's threshold value).

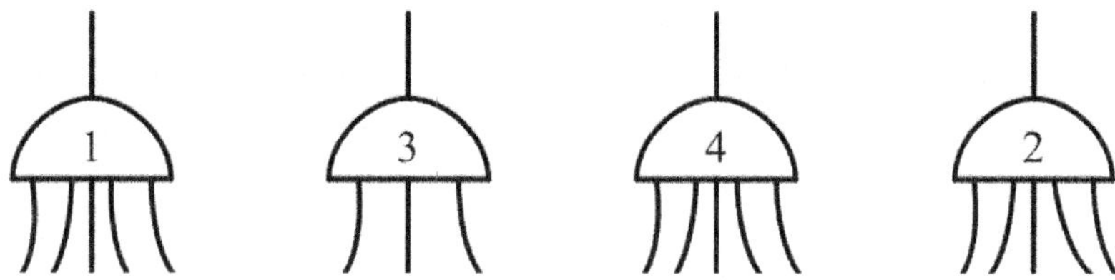

Figure 2.11: Examples of threshold nodes.

Admittedly, specifying the threshold for any node is, practically speaking, impossible. How many properties associated with DOG are enough to activate the node? And for whom? Realistically, we never process only four or five percepts when apprehending a real-world entity; the chances are that the number of perceptual representations we process at any given time ranges in the hundreds, or even thousands. Yet, the notion of threshold nodes is useful to illustrate the non-trivial theoretical considerations discussed above.

2.7   The Process of Learning

In addressing the requisite of developmental plausibility, RNT conceives of language learning as a process that starts in very early life (even prenatally) and continues until death. In this sense, it differs considerably from the generative framework, which aims to account for native language acquisition mainly with reference to children, counterfactually idealizing the process as if it were instantaneous or consisting of discontinuous, instantaneous steps.

RNT acknowledges the contribution of both endowment and experience to learning, but it emphasizes the latter. Lamb (1999) proposes that all nections and their possible connections are built-in features of our neurocognitive systems. However, in their initial stage, all connections are latent, possessing zero or near-zero strength. This means that, from birth, any given nection is connected to most (though not all) of the nections with which it can establish direct connections, but no nection is predetermined to process a particular type of high-level information. What information a specific nection ends up processing will depend on a number of factors, largely guided by experience.

Once a nection receives activation for the first time, it goes from *latent* to *established*. In other words, the connection will no longer be dormant, but it will serve a specific function within the system. With time, and through iteration of activation, the nection will go from *established* to *dedicated* (see Figure 2.12). As such, the nection will process only the information it has come to subserve within the overall network. More importantly, any cognitive activity calling upon the information processed by a given nection will necessarily activate that nection – except for specific cases of redundancy, in which case more than one nection may become the key hub of a given representation.

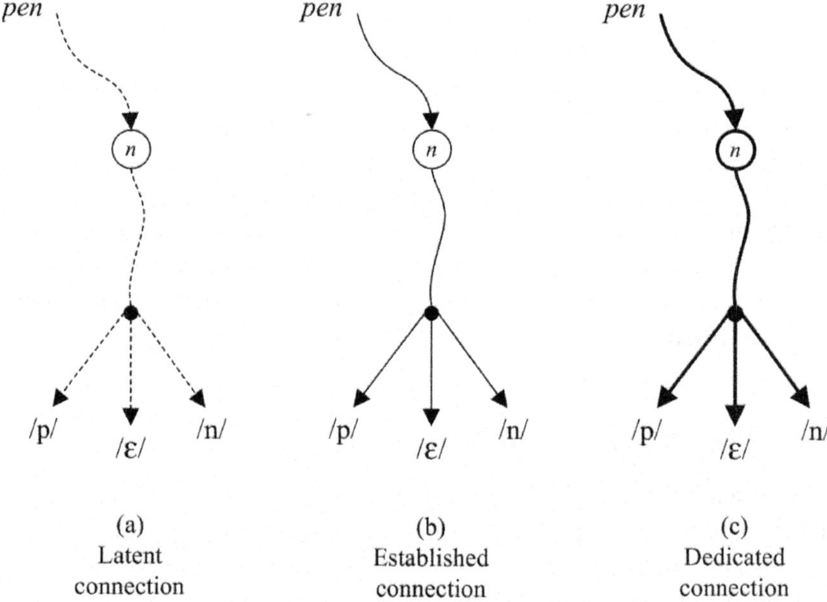

Figure 2.12: Three states in the strengthening of connections.

In relational network terms, learning occurs as connections strengthen and thresholds are adjusted. These processes are driven by bottom-up mechanisms triggered in the lower levels of the cognitive arch. Such information flows upward towards higher levels of integration and is constrained by top-down expectations and previous knowledge. Thus, concept formation involves a series of steps. First, low-level percepts are activated by means of pre-established connections with the interfaces. Within each modality, these low-level percepts get integrated by higher-level nections capturing recurrent partial similarities among the representations processed by the lower-level nections. The process is repeated throughout all the hierarchical layers of each perceptual modality. Finally, the highest perceptual nections processing related information within each modality send activation to a central coordinating node constituting a concept – i.e., a multimodal association nection.

For instance, upon seeing a dog, one activates nections at the lowest visual level. This level, being in closer contact with the interfaces to the outer world, offers a great degree of detail and specificity; its nections process fine-grained visual information about the dog at hand – e.g., the length and distribution of the hairs in its fur, the amount of separation of its eyes, etc. At the next higher level, individual nections will integrate activation coming from two or more nections processing similar information at the immediately lower level; for instance, the different individual percepts of the dog's hairs will get integrated to yield a more abstract representation of a dog with relatively uneven fur – details of the actual length and distribution of those hairs will not be present at this level. Then, at an even higher level of integration, different mid-level nections processing information of different dogs' fur will have converging connections to a high-level visual nection processing a very abstract representation of, simply, dog fur. The same process takes place within each perceptual modality, so that concepts, integrating information coming from the highest levels of each perceptual subsystem, bring together very abstract information – that is, they process representations which are several steps removed from phenomena in the outside world. As a result, concepts are categorical – rather than exemplar-specific – in nature.

Connections come in different strengths; some are weak, some are strong. What determines the strength of any given connection is, in brief, repetition. The more a connection is used, the stronger, or more entrenched, it becomes. Thus, the more often we activate, say, the nection for the lexeme *daddy*, the stronger its connections will become.

Yet, each node has a threshold function specifying the minimum amount of activation it needs to receive to reach full activation. A node can receive both excitatory (positive) and inhibitory (negative) connections. The internal structure of a node performs a summation of its incoming activation, adding the strengths of excitatory connections and subtracting the strengths of inhibitory ones. If the result is enough to satisfy the threshold, the node gets activated and it sends activation along its output lines. (Of course, it may also be the case that the result does not reach the threshold, in which case the node will be only weakly satisfied; over a short period, this weak activation fades.)

When a node has its threshold satisfied, its connections become strengthened and its threshold is raised a little. The reason for the latter effect is to prevent the threshold from being too easily satisfied in the future (see below). As regards the strengthening of connections, Lamb maintains the following:

> [...] a connection is strengthened when it is active while the node to which it is connected has its threshold satisfied by virtue of also receiving activation from other connections. In other words, success is rewarded: a connection is successful when it contributes to

the satisfaction of a threshold of a node, and its reward is that it gets strengthened. (Lamb, 1999, pp. 177–178)

One additional element of this learning hypothesis concerns numerical considerations. RNT requires that extremely large numbers of nections be disseminated throughout the network. That is precisely what Lamb (1999) upholds in establishing the *abundance hypothesis*: latent nections must be available for recruitment in all areas of the network where new information might need to be integrated, and those nections need to possess abundant latent connections.

Lamb (1999, p. 47) estimates that the linguistic system of the typical monolingual contains nections representing analytical elements in the following ranges: '(1) ten to fifteen phonons (phonemic features), (2) fifteen to sixty-five phonemes, (3) five to ten thousand morphemes, (4) tens of thousands of lexemes.' The number of necessary nections becomes remarkably larger if one includes conceptual areas. As Lamb (1999, p. 216) states, '[a] model to represent an actual human being would have to start with hundreds of thousands of latent lexical nections and millions of latent conceptual nections.' In fact, it is not even necessary to consider conceptual nections for the quantitative requirements of the model to dramatically increase, as the theory acknowledges the existence of phononections representing syllables and other phonological complexes (e.g., phonological words, phonological phrases, etc.). Lamb actually suggests that the Phonological Recognition system of a monolingual might include as many as 50,000 nections.[5]

Moreover, the figures increase even more in the case of a bilingual or polyglot, as his system will include many more nections for lexemes, morphemes, and tactic patterns (and probably also for sememic units), although phonemes and especially phonons do not necessarily need to be more numerous – many polyglots in fact speak their foreign languages using their native phonological systems. Of course the plausibility of this hypothesis, like that of all other hypotheses considered so far, will need to be checked for neurological plausibility.

Note that the system does not need to 'know' where to establish the specific connections required for linguistic performance during the learning process. What the system does is engage in a Darwinian process by which it proliferates possibilities beforehand, so that learning becomes a process of selection rather than construction. Of the multiple connections that each node has in its initial stage, only some of them will get selected, or recruited, as learning progresses. Those which do not get selected may either remain latent for future recruitment or wither away and become unusable.

The selection or recruitment of nections will always start at the lower levels, so that nections located at higher levels will only be candidates for recruitment if other nections at the immediately lower level have already been recruited to serve a specific function. As Lamb (1999, p. 178) maintains, 'higher-level nodes cannot emit activation until they get recruited by virtue of having a few of their incoming connections converted from latent to established by this learning process.' This means, among other things, that an information system that has never been exposed to at least one dog (or, alternatively, to at least one picture or recording of a dog) will not be able to recruit a nection for the concept DOG.

It follows that the human cognitive system is a vast network of interconnected nections. Since the present learning hypothesis is based on properties of nections and their connections, RNT would fall within the category of domain-general theories. Language learning would not be a distinct process occurring by virtue of specialized mechanisms which differ from those involved in other types of learning. On the contrary, the basic mechanisms of learning would be similar across cognitive subsystems.

Consequently, all the above considerations about learning in general apply to language acquisition. At the perceptual level, a child hears his parents' speech as a collection of sound waves. With time and repetition, similar low-level auditory percepts get integrated by higher-level auditory recognition systems. As a result, specificities of the percepts get abstracted to form phononections – i.e., relational representations of phonemes. Little by little, certain nections within the child's Phonological Recognition system become dedicated to, say, the phonemes /d/, /ɑ/, and /g/; and perhaps a nection may become dedicated to the unified phonological sequence /dɑg/.

Of course, words do not occur in a contextual vacuum. As the child establishes those phonological connections, other perceptual systems provide high-level integration for the features of the dog being perceived. At one point in the learning process, the child will have both high-level integration nections for the phonological representation /dɑg/ and for the concept DOG, each located at different points in the network. Because all cognitive events that repeatedly occur together tend to become associated, the phononection /dɑg/ and the ideonection DOG will get connected, the result of their connection being the logonection *dog*.

Following the proximity principle, the logonection *dog* will be in an intermediate location between the corresponding phonemic and sememic nections that it connects. Finally, as the child abstracts the grammatical constraints applying to the logonection *dog*, he will begin (tacitly or otherwise) to recognize the pattern of distribution of that logonection and to establish and strengthen the connections linking it to the nection for Noun.

Importantly, the basic unit of learning at the lexicogrammatical level is not the word, but the lexeme. Lexemes can be of different sizes. Some, like *dog*, are coterminous with morphemes; others, like *undergo*, correspond to two morphemes of analytical linguistics; still others, like *in the nick of time*, constitute an analytical phrase; and there are also clausal lexemes (e.g., *If I were you*), sentential lexemes (e.g., *You know what I mean*), and even longer ones (e.g., the lyrics to a national anthem). Thus, the number of constituents that can be analytically identified in a given unit is not a critical point from a lexemic perspective. What matters is that a unit, regardless of its length, can have specific connections to other nections which are not shared by its analytically derived constituents.

Still, when a logonection for a given lexeme is activated, it will probably send activation downwards to the relevant morphonections. For example, from a production perspective, when the ideonection UNDERGO is activated it sends activation downwards to the logonection *undergo*, and not directly to the morphonections *under* and *go*, respectively. However, the nection for *undergo* is then bound to send activation to those two morphonections, which will in turn send activation to the corresponding phononections (see Figure 1.8). This is a source of redundancy in the system.

In sum, learning is conceived as a continuous bottom-up and top-down process in which connection strengths and threshold levels become adjusted by experience. But how does the theory explain long-lasting memories of learned information in the absence of symbols? If there are no symbols, representations cannot be retrieved, and that is precisely the point. In relational network terms, the entire cognitive network is memory itself. Once a nection becomes dedicated to a certain function, all it takes to process that function again is to reactivate the corresponding nection. No separate memory needs to be postulated because each nection is its own processor. Remembering, then, would be the result of sending activation along connecting lines that have already been established and dedicated to a given function. The more one experiences something, the stronger the connections that process its representation, hence the easier it will be to remember it by reactivating the corresponding nection.

2.8   Handling Complex Processing Phenomena

Despite major simplifications, the framework laid out in this chapter allows us to describe numerous features of language use. In fact, a relational account offers elegant treatments of several common phenomena that pose major challenges for non-relational theories (Lamb 2004j, pp. 331–334) because of their complexity:

(1) Coexistent alternative catalyses (cf. Lamb 1999).
(2) Multiple parallel interpretations of complex lexemes (cf. Müller 2000, Lamb 1999).

(3) Disambiguation of ambiguous words using linguistic and extra-linguis-
     tic context (Lamb 1999).
(4) Context-driven lexeme selection (Lamb 1999, Reich 1985).
(5) The interpretation of puns (Reich 1985, Lamb 2004j).
(6) Complex associations in slang lexeme formation (Eble 2000).
(7) Phenomena involving association, such as literary allusions (Lamb
     1999).
(8) Degree of entrenchment of idioms and other complex lexemes (Lamb
     1999).
(9) Gradualness of learning (Lamb 2004k).
(10) Slips of the tongue (cf. Dell & Reich 1980a, 1980b [cf. also Chapter
     8]).
(11) Prototypicality phenomena (cf. Lamb 1999).
(12) Realistic means of accounting for speaking and understanding (Lamb
     1999).
(13) On-line cognitive processing in conversation (cf. Meyer 1991, 1992,
     2000; Lamb 1999).

To the above list we could add (14) inner speech, (15) misinterpreta-
tions, (16) overgeneralizations, and (17) mutable lexemes. All these phenomena indicate that relational networks are inherently dynamic: they
undergo changes as they are put to use, as connections strengthen and
weaken, as threshold levels are raised and lowered, and as certain connections get blocked. Let us briefly exemplify how RNT would handle some
of the phenomena listed above.

Consider Eble's (2000) treatment of complex associations in slang
lexeme formation (item 6 in the list above). She describes the process
whereby a lexeme, by virtue of sharing certain phonological connections
with other lexemes, may come to establish connections with the ideonections connected with the latter. Eble illustrates the process with the particular case of *ho/hoe*, which may be seen as a dialect pronunciation of *whore*
or as a standard name of a garden tool. Lamb (2004j, p. 333) presents
Eble's example in network notation, as shown in Figure 2.13.

In this case, the lexemic nection *ho* acts as the anchoring point for the
new slang term to appear. The nection for *ho* has (relatively) direct connections to the concepts WHORE and HOE, which have very strong connections to the concepts PROMISCUOUS WOMAN and GARDEN TOOL, respectively.
The nection for GARDEN TOOL is strongly connected to the lexemic nection
garden tool, and the resulting concentration of activation in the network
favors the establishment of a connection from the lexemic nection *garden
tool* to the concept PROMISCUOUS WOMAN, the whole process having been put
in motion by a case of homophony.

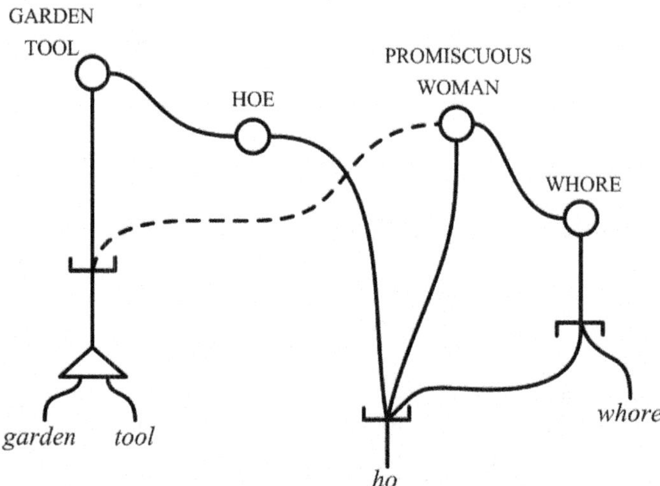

Figure 2.13: Complex associations in slang lexeme formation (from Lamb 2004j). Used by permission of Bloomsbury Publishing Plc.

Let us consider one more example. In certain complex lexemes – e.g., phrases, clauses, or sentences learned as a unit – one constituent may be deliberately replaced to evoke the lexeme's key meanings in combination with new semantic effects. This is what Lamb (1999) calls a mutable lexeme (added item 17 above). Typical examples of mutable lexemes are excerpts from literary pieces or speeches which undergo an internal modification so as to link the sememic representations that the excerpt conjures up with a present situation. Lamb (1999, pp. 264–265) gives some examples: the lexeme *the mother of all battles* has become mutable as the constituent *battle* became variable. For instance, a pilot has been recorded saying *the mother of all meteors* – and most of us have encountered similar examples. The pattern involved could be formulaically expressed as *the mother of all <Thing>s*. Likewise, Shakespeare's *Something is rotten in the state of Denmark* can give rise to *Something is rotten in the state of California*, on the basis of the formula *Something is rotten in the state of <State/Country>*.

Let us consider another case of a mutable lexeme based on a Shakespearean quote. In October 2003, Switzerland hosted the IV Palliative Care Meeting for cancer patients. One of the panels of the meeting was entitled 'To eat or not to eat. That is the question.' Now, was the expression *to eat or not to eat* formed following syntactic rules, or does it instantiate a mutable lexeme? The first option would not capture the overt intention to bring a famous literary piece to mind. On the contrary, the mutable lexeme hypothesis is sensitive to this deliberate meaning effect, as illustrated in Figure 2.14.

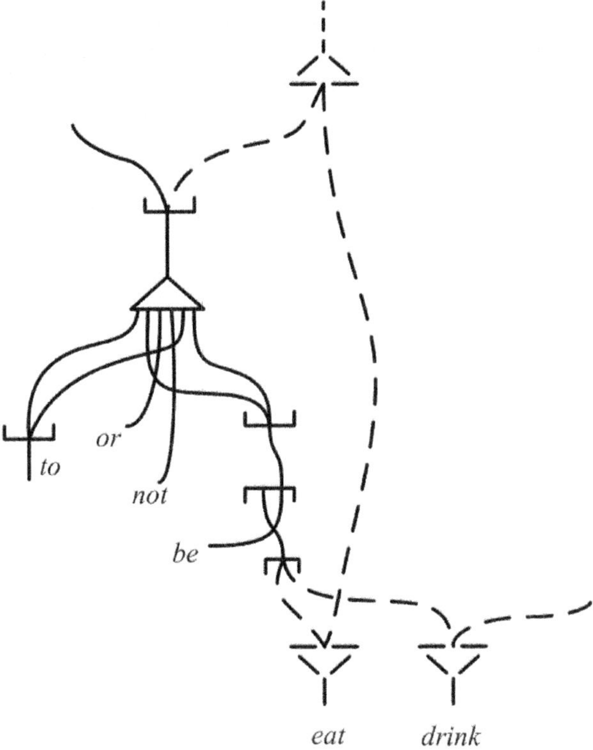

Figure 2.14: Network representation of a mutable lexeme.

In Figure 2.14, the solid ordered downward AND processes the original lexeme. The variable constituent is presented as a downward ordered OR. The default line leads to *be*, as it is probably more entrenched than any variation that may be introduced in the lexeme. The precedence line of the ordered OR leads to an unordered OR which offers connections to the constituents that may be used to replace *be*. In this case, an upward unordered AND for *eat* is shown as having connections to both the lexeme itself, in the structural positions where it occurs, and to the uppermost downward ordered AND, which represents the sememic unit(s) that the original lexeme, and now the variable constituent, can evoke by virtue of its/their connections.

2.9   Conclusion

As seen in this chapter, the theoretical apparatus of RNT provides useful tools to characterize the dynamic nature of the human linguistic system and its relation to the human information system as a whole. Crucially, it provides a workable model for describing processes involved in ordinary language use – which is fundamental to pass the test of operational plausibility – and language learning – which is fundamental to pass the test of developmental plausibility. In Chapter 3, the theory's main theoretical proposals will be tested against neuroscientific evidence to determine how successfully RNT meets the requisite of neurological plausibility. Finally, the studies compiled in Part II show how relational network constructs and hypotheses can be applied to describe varied phonological, lexicogrammatical, and semantic phenomena across languages.

Notes

1.   In fact, the notion of the phoneme as a circumscribed entity (for example, as traditional accounts would have it, the size of a letter of the alphabet) is an arbitrary and unnecessary assumption (see Sullivan, 2005).
2.   The outcome may not be satisfied at the next node, and it is possible that both output lines will lead to ultimate satisfaction in the case of the upward OR.
3.   But not in the case of puns, for instance. See Reich (1985).
4.   The network is simplified, among other things, in that it does not make explicit the nodes and connections needed to process a yes/no question beginning with the verb *be* (e.g., *Are you cold?*), which represents a special case in English syntax, as *be* is not (just) an auxiliary. We can also consider *do* questions (e.g., *Do you have a dog?*). *Be* and *do* questions are critical in showing that 'AUX' is not a thing but rather a label on a node – and its locus is a matter of choice regarding the network, not whether *be/do* is or is not an AUX.
5.   It is also possible that serious generalization could occur during the acquisition process, leading to more efficient storage, which would then allow nections that are no longer used to decay and become available for recruitment to other purposes, e.g., learning of a second language.

3 From Neurological Structures to Language Processing

3.1 Introduction

As stated in the Introduction, RNT seeks operational, developmental, and, finally, neurological plausibility. Chapter 2 described how a model of linguistic relations gave rise to specific accounts of real-time verbal processes – that is, issues related to operational and, to a lesser extent, developmental plausibility. Yet, in pursuit of neurological plausibility, RNT must consider how neuroanatomical and neurofunctional findings constrain the constructs proposed so far. In other words, the ensuing model must convergently incorporate relational restrictions present in language structure and in the neurological system.

Linguistic descriptions in RNT terms have not yet been directly tested in neurolinguistic experiments. However, systematic synergies can be noted between the constructs introduced in Chapters 1 and 2 and well established findings from neuroscience. In the quest for structural and functional compatibilities between aspects of language and aspects of the brain, this chapter introduces basic neuroanatomy and explains how neurons work to exchange information, with an emphasis on macroanatomical and microanatomical structures involved in language processing.

First, we introduce key distinctions at the macroanatomical level, considering successive levels of detail: from hemispheres to lobes to gyri and Brodmann areas. At the microscopic level, we describe neurons, synapses, and basic neural networks, with emphasis on critical aspects of interneuronal communication, including activation and inhibition as well as strengthening and weakening. Finally, we refer to the organizational roles of cortical columns and functional webs, discussing how neurons could coordinate their activity to subserve specific cognitive processes, such as those triggered by a word.

Next we return to RNT constructs and consider the evidence and rationale through which they can be interpreted in neurological terms. In particular, the diagrammatic conventions, notational devices, and associated terminology of RNT are considered against the backdrop of relevant neuroscientific findings. For example, several correspondences can be noted between nections in a relational network and cortical columns in the brain, whereas changes in connection strength may be seen as structural or functional synaptic adjustments. While RNT does not relate to several intricacies of neural architecture and physiology, its notation system and cognitive assumptions are broadly compatible with neurological facts. The biology of the brain, in this sense, constitutes an additional source of empirical constraints for RNT.

3.2   Basic Notions of Neuroanatomy

The brain is part of the central nervous system. It is located in the skull, weighs roughly three pounds, and contains over 100 billion neurons. Many of these neurons extend through the spinal cord and connect to other cells in the body, with which they exchange electrochemical signals. All of our experiences are associated with activity patterns in specific neural networks.

The brain comprises various structures. A traditional division distinguishes between the myelencephalon (medulla oblongata), the metencephalon (pons and cerebellum), the mesencephalon (midbrain), the diencephalon (thalamus and hypothalamus), and the telencephalon (neocortex and cerebral hemispheres). These structures can be seen in a midsagittal section of the brain, as shown in Figure 3.1.

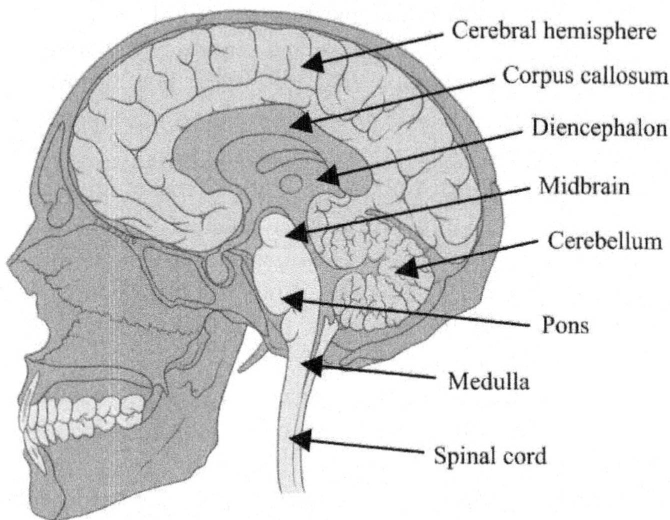

Figure 3.1: Midsagittal section of the brain.

The outer surface of the cerebral hemispheres is known as the neocortex. The regions included in the diencephalon and midbrain are called subcortical structures. In general terms, neocortical structures are specialized for cognitive processing (e.g., language, visuospatial information), whereas subcortical structures play a crucial role in the regulation of physiological

and emotional processes. However, such functions are not exclusively subserved by either of these broad divisions.

3.2.1 Some Language-Related Subcortical Structures

Subcortical structures are varied and complex. Language processing critically involves at least three of them, namely: the basal ganglia, the hippocampus, and the cerebellum. These are shown in Figure 3.2.

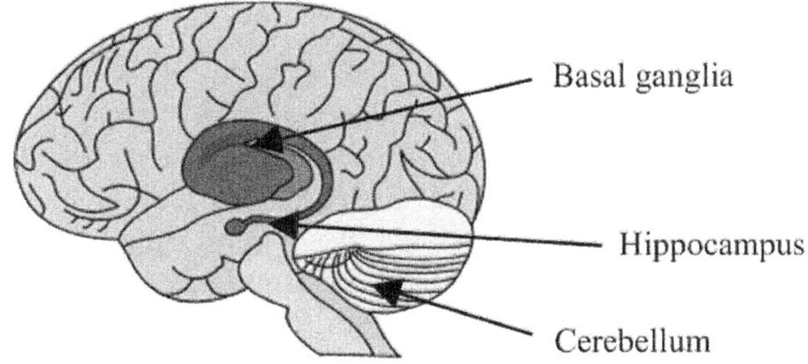

Figure 3.2: Some subcortical structures involved in language processing.

The basal ganglia are composed of various parts, such as the neostriatum (caudate nucleus and putamen), the globus pallidus, and the substan-
tia nigra. While each of these structures subserves different functions, the
basal ganglia, as a whole, are implicated in body posture, planning, motor
coordination, and learning of sequential and hierarchical information patterns. As regards language, they are critically involved in syntax (Bocanegra *et al.*, 2015; Hochstadt *et al.*, 2006; Lieberman *et al.*, 1992), pragmatics
(Holtgraves & McNamara, 2010; Monetta & Pell, 2007), verbal fluency
(Raskin, Sliwinski, & Borod, 1992), and action-verb semantics (Bak,
2013; Bocanegra *et al.*, 2015; Cardona *et al.*, 2013; A. García & Ibáñez,
2014; A. García *et al.*, 2016).

The hippocampus is included in the vast medial temporal lobe network.
It is profusely connected to varied locations within the neocortex. One of
its main functions is to regulate the exchange of signals between cognitive and emotional mechanisms distributed throughout the neocortex and
subcortical regions. Crucially, the hippocampus is involved in long-term
memory, as it seems indispensable for the construction of new memories.
In the language domain, the hippocampus and its connections with the
temporal lobe are crucial for lexico-semantic processing (Ullman, 2004).

Posterior to the pons lies the cerebellum. This very complex structure
represents just 10% of the brain's overall volume, but it contains more
than half of its neurons. Its main function is to integrate sensory and motor

signals to control perceptual input and coordinate bodily action. Thus, the cerebellum is critical for controlling and sequencing fine motor movements, such as those needed to play the piano or shuffle cards. More generally, the cerebellum has been implicated in searching for and retrieving conceptual information for subsequent processing in other brain areas. With respect to language, it appears to contribute to the mapping of lexico-semantic information onto syntactic structures (Ullman, 2004), as well as verbal fluency and sequencing skills (Ardila, Bernal, & Rosselli, 2015).

3.2.2 The Neocortex

The neocortex contains the most important areas for language processing. It is divided into two roughly symmetrical halves, namely, the cerebral hemispheres. Separated by the longitudinal fissure, the hemispheres are bidirectionally connected through the corpus callosum, a bundle of long-distance fibers. Although both hemispheres work in a coordinate fashion during most human activities, each of them subserves different functions. Language processes, in particular, are lateralized to the left hemisphere in approximately 97% of the population (Springer *et al.*, 1999). Also, as shown in Figure 3.3, each hemisphere can be divided into anatomically defined lobes, which can in turn be subdivided into smaller portions called gyri.

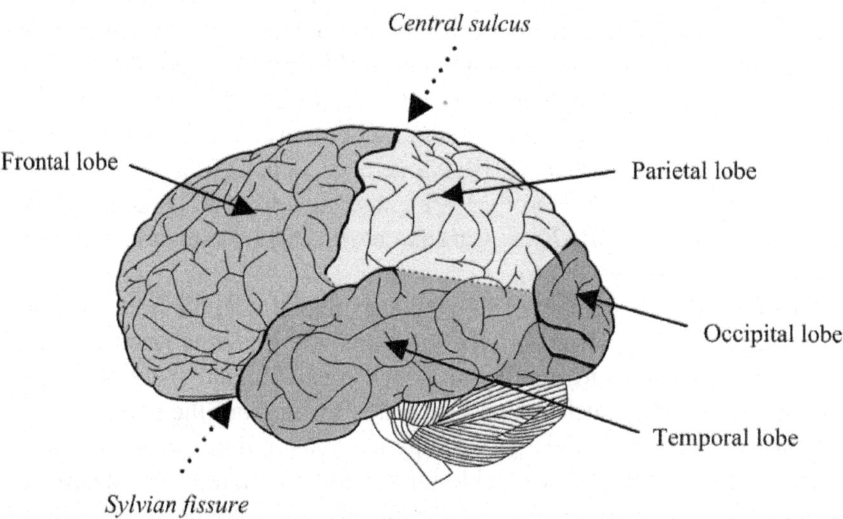

Figure 3.3: Lateral section of the left hemisphere.

Figure 3.3 shows two main grooves: the Sylvian fissure and the central sulcus. Both constitute anatomical landmarks to delimit broad areas within each hemisphere. The Sylvian fissure separates the temporal lobe from the frontal and the parietal lobes, while the central sulcus separates the latter two. The frontal lobe lies anterior to the central sulcus and superior to the Sylvian fissure. It is mainly concerned with motor action and functions such as planning behavior and coordinating information coming from the rest of the brain. The temporal lobe lies posterior and inferior to the Sylvian fissure and is specialized for auditory processing, in addition to more specific functions. The frontal and temporal lobes include the most critical regions for language processes, including key functions such as phonological recognition, lexico-semantic access, morphosyntactic processing, and phonological production, among many others (Ardila, Bernal, & Rosselli, 2015). As these regions surround the Sylvian fissure, they are known as perisylvian areas. Superior to the temporal lobe and posterior to the central sulcus is the parietal lobe, which processes somatosensory information coming from all over the body. The hindmost part of each hemisphere comprises the occipital lobes, which are critical to the representation and processing of visual information.

Each lobe has its own internal divisions. In particular, the frontal and temporal lobes consist of three gyri (inferior, middle, and superior). For example, the superior temporal gyrus is the part of the temporal lobe lying immediately below the Sylvian fissure. The middle and inferior temporal gyri can be found in succession. Each gyrus subserves specific functions within each lobe.

All brain regions are widely connected with one another. No region is self-sufficient for processing high-order functions, such as thought, visuospatial orientation, memory, or language. These require the concerted action of multiple neural structures, which may be quite distant from one another. However, certain areas are critical to or indispensable for the proper functioning of specific cognitive domains.

The brain's astounding connectivity is enabled by neurons. In the neocortex, the cell bodies of neurons make up the outer surface of the hemispheres – more precisely, a layer ranging from 3 mm to 6 mm in thickness called gray matter. Neurons may be interconnected either locally (to other neighboring neurons) or remotely (to other distant neurons). Long-distance connections depend on white matter, that is, long myelinated axons beneath the gray matter which connect cells within or across lobes, or even across the hemispheres. White matter also affords connections between nearby cells.

All neurons possess similar features (e.g., they all consist of a cell body, an axon branching into output terminals, and multiple dendrites with input spines). However, there are different types of neurons, which can be classified according to their form and function. A detailed account of the physiological and molecular aspects of neurons falls outside the scope of this chapter, but it is worth mentioning that there are subtle differences in the distributions of cell types from one cortical area to another. The first scientist to draw a map of such differential distributions was Brodmann (1909), who identified 52 cytoarchitectonic areas within each hemisphere. Such areas have become known as Brodmann areas (BAs). The main BAs are shown in Figure 3.4.

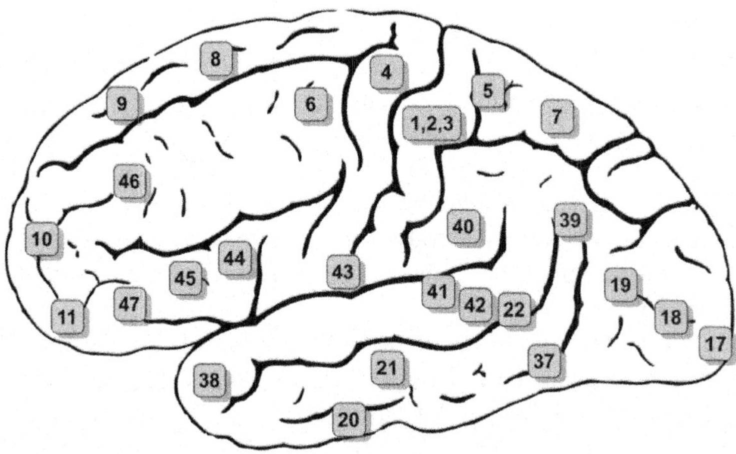

Figure 3.4: A depiction of some Brodmann areas.

As seen in Figure 3.4, BAs can be mapped throughout neocortical (and also subcortical) regions. They enable us to conceive of anatomical structures in terms of groupings of cell types. As they are usually more fine-grained in their reference than gross anatomical landmarks, they allow us to identify more precisely which regions are crucial for a specific cognitive system or the processing of a specific function. (Note, however, that there is no one-to-one relation between BAs and cognitive domains.) Table 3.1 lists some BAs which prove important for different linguistic functions.

Table 3.1: Brodmann areas and neuroanatomical loci implicated in key linguistic functions

Brodmann area	Approximate neuroanatomical location	Associated linguistic function
BA 44 BA 45	Inferior frontal gyrus (Broca's area)	Phonological production, grammatical processing
BA 4	Frontal lobe: precentral gyrus (primary motor cortex)	Muscle control needed for articulation and writing

Brodmann area	Approximate neuroanatomical location	Associated linguistic function
BA 41	Superior temporal gyrus (primary auditory cortex)	General auditory processing, sound discrimination
BA 42 BA 22	Posterior portion of the superior temporal gyrus	Phonological recognition, lexico-semantic representation and processing
BA 1 BA 3	Parietal lobe: postcentral gyrus (primary somatosensory cortex)	Representation of somatosensory and semantic/conceptual information
BA 17	Posterior occipital lobe	Visual processing, reading, graphemic representation

3.3   Neurophysiology: Neurons and Synapses

Neurocognitive activity results from complex processes occurring both within and between neurons. Each neuron is composed of three main parts: a soma (or cell body), multiple dendrites, and a single axon typically possessing many branches (Figure 3.5).

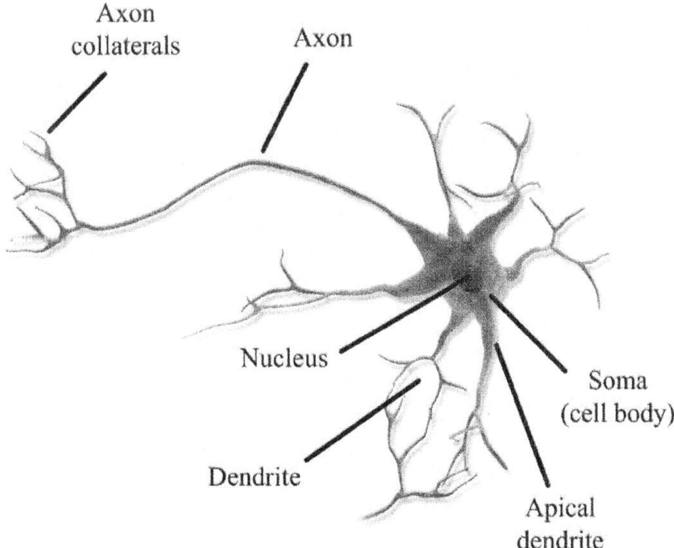

Figure 3.5: Structural components of a neuron.

The soma, which contains the neuron's nucleus, stores genetic material and produces proteins and other molecules needed for the cell's survival.

The dendrites and the axon are nerve fibers enabling interneuronal communication. Dendrites are afferent (input) pathways, meaning that they receive signals from other neurons. The axon is an efferent (output) pathway, as it sends signals to other neurons via its multiple collaterals. Axons can reach both neighboring and distant cells; some of them, in fact, are several centimeters long.

Due to their structure, neurons possess two key properties: convergence (each neuron may receive input from multiple efferent neurons) and divergence (each neuron may send output to multiple afferent neurons). The point of contact between any two neurons is called a synapse. Each neuron in the brain establishes synapses with thousands of neurons in various brain locations. According to DeFelipe & Farinas (1992), a typical pyramidal neuron has roughly 50,000 efferent synapses and 50,000 afferent synapses. This profusion of connections is largely responsible for the complexity of human cognition.

3.3.1 Interneuronal Connections: Basic Principles and Types

In general terms, communication between neurons occurs when the axon of an efferent neuron releases specific molecules of a neurotransmitter (at the presynaptic membrane), which flow across the synaptic cleft (typically about 20 nm) and through the postsynaptic membrane on a dendrite or cell body of the afferent neuron. This process is illustrated by the synapse in Figure 3.6.

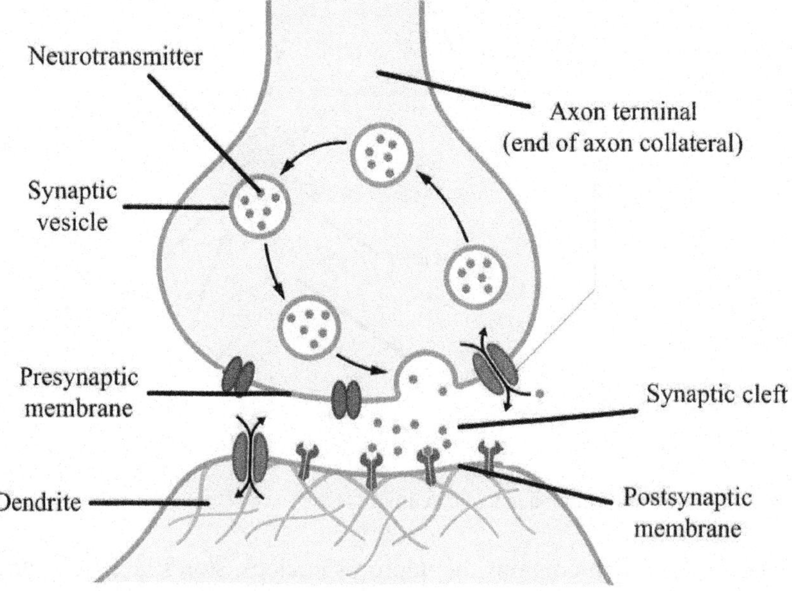

Figure 3.6: A rough illustration of a synapse.

Receiving neurotransmitters from a single presynaptic terminal is not enough stimulation for the input neuron to respond. However, when neurotransmitters arrive from a sufficient number of efferent connections at the same time (or within the lapse of a few milliseconds), the input neuron generates an action potential, that is, an electric signal which propagates along the axon in order to promote activity in other receiving neurons. Thus, the input neuron now acts as an output neuron. In sum, interneuronal communication follows an electric-chemical-electric sequence: electric signals running along axons result in the release of neurotransmitters (chemical substances), which, if certain conditions apply, will enter the afferent neuron and trigger a new electric signal in it.

Connections between neurons can be either excitatory or inhibitory, with each connection type involving different neurotransmitters. The former contribute to the activation of the receiving neuron and can be established between neighboring or distant cells. Conversely, inhibitory connections tend to mitigate activity within the receiving neuron. The latter are typically established between neighboring cells.

The main neuron types featuring excitatory connections are pyramidal and spiny stellate cells. Neurons with inhibitory properties come in various forms. In the neocortex, some of the most typical ones are large basket cells, double bouquet cells, chandelier cells, and smooth stellate cells. There are two types of inhibitory connections. Axoaxonic inhibitory connections are established on the initial segment of a neighboring axon, whereas axosomatic inhibitory connections are established on the soma of a neighboring cell.

At the point where the soma meets the axon, every neuron features a structure known as the axon hillock. Signals entering the receiving neuron are here summated and if their aggregated intensity increases rapidly or if they exceed the neuron's activation threshold, an action potential is triggered (that is, the neuron fires). Conversely, if the overall voltage falls below the threshold, the neuron remains inactive. These processes reflect the main difference between excitatory and inhibitory connections: while the former increase the voltage of the receiving neuron, thus favoring its activation, the latter reduce the voltage and tend to deactivate it.

Action potentials are all-or-none responses, that is, either they are generated or they are not. There is no such thing as a partial action potential. Also, the action potential does not attenuate as it propagates from the axon to the multiple synapses located next to each of the axon's collaterals. On the contrary, postsynaptic potentials (generated in the receiving neuron's postsynaptic membrane and capable of increasing or reducing overall voltage) are analog signals which gradually attenuate as a function of the time elapsed since their release and the distance covered throughout the corresponding dendrite.

The strength of a synaptic connection may change through time. Specifically, synaptic connections are strengthened if the synapse is frequently used. This follows from the so-called Hebbian principle, which states that 'any two cells or systems of cells that are repeatedly active at the same time will tend to become "associated", so that activity in one facilitates activity in the other' (Hebb, 1949, p. 70). At the same time, neuronal connectivity depends on the opposite process: independent (antiphasic) activation of any pair of cells or cell systems will weaken their reciprocal connections (Tsumoto, 1992). Such modifications in connectivity strength result from varied biochemical and even structural changes in the neurons involved (Kandel, 1991), such as the growth of dendritic spines (Braitenberg & Schüz, 1998). In sum, any connection between two neurons is strengthened by their joint activity and weakened by their independent firing.

Another important property of interneuronal connection in the neocortex is that connections between areas tend to be reciprocal. If there is a group of neurons sending signals from region A to region B, more often than not there will be another group of neurons sending signals from region B to region A. However, note that the groups of neurons involved in signal transmission in each direction are not the same, so that they are subject to different processes of activation, inhibition, strengthening, and weakening over time (Pandya & Yeterian, 1985; Young, Scannell, & Burns, 1995).

3.3.2 Cortical Minicolumns and Functional Webs: Cognitive Processing as Neuronal Teamwork

No neuron can support a cognitive representation on its own. A single cell is insufficiently efficient to process information by itself, as its inner processes may be rendered noisy by other signals around it (Pulvermüller, 2002). Moreover, cellular deterioration and death may occur at such rapid rates that if each representation depended on a single neuron, it would be practically impossible to retain information for long periods of time.

It has been proposed that the minimal processing module in the neocortex is the cortical minicolumn (Mountcastle, 1998). A minicolumn is a group of roughly 100 neurons aligned vertically throughout the six layers of gray matter and operating together as a functional unit (Mountcastle, 1998; Burnod, 1990; Arbib, Érdi, & Szentágothai, 1998). Each minicolumn is approximately 4 mm in length and 35 µm (microns) in diameter. Some 70% of neurons in a typical minicolumn are pyramidal, meaning that they possess excitatory connections. In comparison, a substantial portion of the remaining neurons possess inhibitory connections. Hence, a minicolumn is capable of sending both excitatory and inhibitory signals to other minicolumns.

The evidence about the structure and function of minicolumns comes mainly from studies with cats, monkeys, and rats. Hubel & Wiesel (1962, 1977) showed that visual cortex nodes in these species are implemented as hierarchically organized cortical columns: each successive level integrates features processed by the immediately lower level so as to then send activation to higher layers. Therefore, higher hierarchical levels in a cortical structure subserve more abstract cognitive relationships. For his own part, Mountcastle (1998) reached similar conclusions by examining the primary somatosensory and auditory cortices of cats and monkeys: such brain areas, and presumably other areas, too, are organized in terms of columns.

Since the cortices of cats and monkeys are similar to those in our own skulls, neuroscientists sometimes extrapolate findings from the former and apply them to their models of the human brain. The topological and cellular similarities between the cortices of these species and our own are such that it is not unusual for neuroscientists to work on the assumption that people's linguistic, perceptual, and conceptual systems are also organized in hierarchical networks of cortical minicolumns.

It requires an additional extrapolation, and one that may seem extreme, to derive hypotheses about human language processing from research on the brains of cats or monkeys. Indeed, the specific complexities and functional properties of language are simply absent in other species. However, just as cats and monkeys possess cortical columns specialized for representations so specific that they fire upon stimulation of a single digit, so does the human cortex possess minicolumns and even individual neurons which fire only in the presence of certain visual stimuli. This has been demonstrated by Quian Quiroga *et al.* (2005), whose experiments with epileptic patients showed that a single neuron may selectively respond to stimuli as precise as pictures of American actress Jennifer Aniston, NBA legend Michael Jordan, or the Leaning Tower of Pisa.

There are other types of neuronal systems which also work as integrated processing units but are more widely distributed throughout the brain. Functional webs are a case in point. These structures support complex cognitive representations involving sub-representations belonging to remote systems – for example, the concept DOG, which subsumes unimodal representations such as FOUR-LEGGED (visual percept, mainly subserved by occipital networks), BARK (auditory percept, mainly subserved by temporal networks), and SOFT FUR (somatosensory percept, mainly subserved by parietal networks).

According to Pulvermüller (2002), a functional web is a widely distributed functional microsystem of nerve cells which features a well defined topography and whose dynamics can be characterized in terms of four activity states: rest, ignition, priming, and reverberation. Rest refers to the lack of (significant) electrochemical activity in a web; ignition is the state attained by a web receiving sufficient activation to make it fire; priming is the effect whereby a web receives a small amount of activation as a result of its connections to other fully active webs; and reverberation refers to the state in which a web retains its internal activity for a few seconds.

That cognitive representations are supported by cortical minicolumns and functional webs implies that not every neuron participates in every cognitive process. This fact has an important consequence: since the number of neurons in the brain at any point in life is finite, each cognitive representation necessarily depends on a finite number of neurons, which need not always be the same. At the same time, a neuron or a column may participate in different neural networks and, consequently, in different cognitive processes. Nevertheless, the particular population of neurons subserving a given representation is unique, despite possible partial overlap among different neurocognitive networks.

Note also that while minicolumns and functional webs are composed of several nerve cells, they share some overall features with individual neurons. For example, these complex structures have properties such as input and output, convergence and divergence, susceptibility to and capacity for excitation and inhibition, strengthening and weakening.

3.4   Correspondences between Relational Networks and Neurological Structures

We have considered aspects of neuroanatomy at the macro- and microstructural levels, focusing on the role of neurons and neuronal networks in processing information. Below we discuss how these properties of the brain correlate with RNT constructs. While relational networks simplify the complexity of neurological structures, they are a useful source of preliminary insights into the neurobiological basis of linguistic representations.

3.4.1 Nections *vis-à-vis* Cortical Minicolumns

In trying to interpret relational networks in neurocognitive terms, correlations can be posited between nections and cortical minicolumns. In this sense, Lamb (1999) has proposed that a nection in narrow notation could be implemented as a cortical column. Irrespective of the precise location and distribution of the neural substrate represented by a nection, the latter will necessarily capture two key aspects of its putative basis: the properties of afference (input) and efference (output), and the attributes of convergence and divergence. Indeed, just like minicolumns (and functional webs), nections usually require activation from multiple incoming connections to become active and, once activated, they can send signals to several other nodes.

If we interpret neurological connections in RNT terms, all lines reaching a node would represent sets of synapses between various axon terminals and dendrites or cell bodies. The same applies to all lines stemming from a node. Communication between nodes depends on spreading activation along connections, following the orientation of the corresponding arrows. Activation, thus, would be neurally implemented as the release and reception of neurotransmitters among neurons, plus electrical activity traveling along nerve fibers (axons and dendrites).

Note that for RNT all nections (irrespective of the stratum they are located on and the complexity of the information they process) would be implemented as cortical minicolumns. That is, a nection may process information patterns corresponding to varied levels, modalities, and analytical lengths (e.g., percepts, concepts, or syntactic, lexemic, morphemic, syllabic, and phonemic representations). More extended functional webs would further support multiple links among hubs in each of these levels and modalities.

3.4.2 Bidirectionality and Reciprocal Connections between Areas

Bidirectionality is the property by which neighboring and remote areas connect through reciprocal flows of activation. Such reciprocity in inter-regional connectivity actually constitutes 'one of the universal neuro-anatomical and neurophysiological properties of the cortex' (Pulvermüller, 2002, p. 21). Also, at a larger scale, bidirectionality is a functional attribute of neurocognitive systems whereby partially autonomous subsystems are specialized for receptive and behavioral processes. Both forms of bidirectionality must be contemplated in a model that seeks to account for production and comprehension processes. At a cortico-cortical level, this is achieved by virtue of long-distance connections linking remote areas of the cortex (Aravena *et al.*, 2010; Friederici, 2009). Indeed, processing a given function involves joint transmission of activation in both directions (Friston, 2002).

Reciprocal connections between areas are functionally independent. In other words, they rely on different sets of interneuronal connections. A neural fiber which sends activation from area A to area B cannot itself send activation in the opposite direction. This principle is captured in Figure 3.7.

While abstract notation nodes are bidirectional, they are proposed to correspond to two unidirectional narrow notation nodes running in opposite directions. Thus, connections between any pair of linguistic representations in abstract notation can be straightforwardly related to this principle of neural connectivity if framed in narrow notation terms. (On notational contrasts, see Chapter 2.)

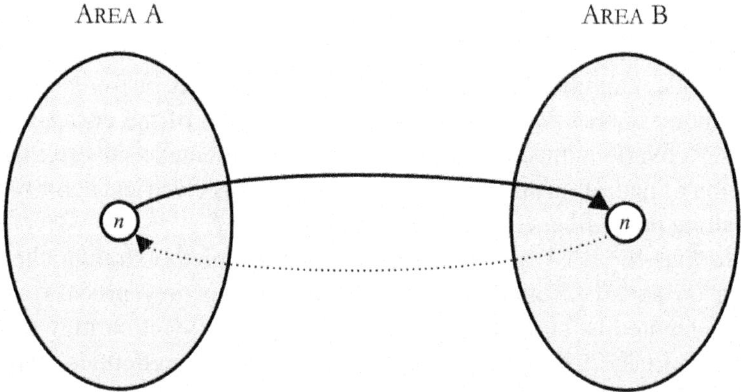

Figure 3.7: Reciprocal connections between areas depend on separate neural circuits.

3.4.3 Connection Length

Not every notational aspect of RNT can be interpreted isomorphically. Such is the case with the length of the lines connecting nodes and nections in a diagram. These lines do not reflect the extension of the dendrites and/or axons which would physically implement them in the brain. In fact, what determines the length of lines in relational networks is simply graphical convenience.

Nonetheless, it must be recognized that certain pairs of nections will actually be further apart than others. This is no trivial observation, given that the correct operation of certain relational networks requires specific flows of activation coming from diverse portions of the system to reach the receiving node simultaneously or with a minimal time-gap. In this sense, RNT notation is not inconsistent with neural functioning. In fact, different types of neurons are capable of transmitting their signals at varying speed ranges, so that an afferent minicolumn can receive simultaneous input from both neighboring and distant cells. The axons of pyramidal neurons are wrapped in myelin, an insulator which increases signal transmission speed between distant neurons; the thicker the axon, the faster its conduction rate. Still, the main factor underlying speed differences between cells is the presence or absence of myelin. Whereas an unmyelinated axon can send signals at an average of 1 mm per millisecond, myelinated axons do so at an average of 100 mm per millisecond. Therefore, one and the same neuron or minicolumn can receive impulses coming from distant regions at roughly the same time as those coming from nearby regions.

3.4.4 Changes in Connection Strength and Node Thresholds

As seen in section 3.3.1, interneuronal connections have varying strengths. In RNT notation, connection strength is indicated by the thickness of the lines: the thicker the line, the greater the strength. Figure 3.8 represents different percepts involved in the activation of the concept BIRD. The small hollow circle on the line for SWIMMING represents an inhibitory connection (see section 3.3.1). This network shows that the percepts FEATHERS and FLYING are more strongly associated to the concept BIRD than the percept SMALL. Moreover, it is assumed that the percept SWIMMING tends to deactivate the concept BIRD – that is, when faced with a bird that can swim but cannot fly through the air, such as a penguin, a person will find it harder to accept it as an exemplar of the category BIRD.

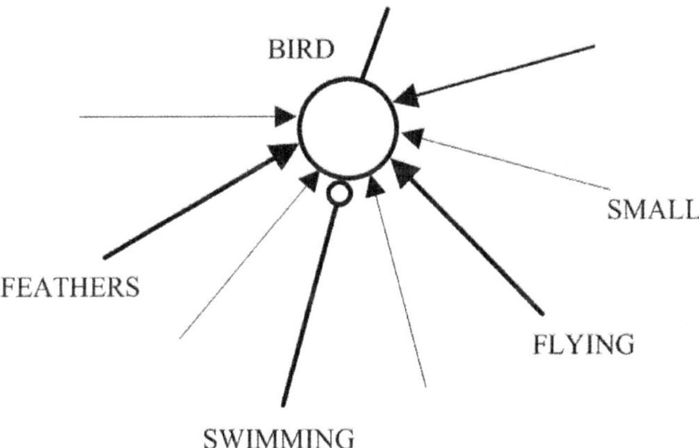

Figure 3.8: Connections with different strengths linked to the concept BIRD.

Connection strengthening goes hand in hand with the Hebbian principle (see section 3.3.1): the more two neural systems become coactivated, the stronger their connections become. As described in Chapter 2, RNT posits that connections can go through three main states. In their initial state, they are latent, meaning that they are structurally present in the system but they have not yet been recruited to process any particular representation. Once a nection is recruited to process specific information, its connections become established, that is, active within the system. With time, and as activation flows travel repeatedly along them, connections are dedicated, so that they will not be able to process any other type of information. The more a nection is activated, the easier it will be to activate it in the future. These three states were illustrated in Chapter 2 for the construction of the main connections linking *pen* to /p/ /ɛ/ /n/ (Figure 2.12).

Another important property related to neuronal connections is that nodes possess varying thresholds. The total intensity of the sum of postsynaptic potentials needed to trigger an action potential in a neuron changes over time. Repeated activation of a neuron or a neuron circuit lowers its activation threshold, so that, with the passing of time, such a neural substrate will require ever less intense signals to fire.

Following the same principle, when a neuron remains inactive for too long, its activation threshold rises (Braitenberg, 1978a). Notationally, in RNT, the thresholds of junction nodes (represented by a number within the node) are not static; rather, they vary through time. As a person acquires more information related to a certain category, relevant nodes will require lesser amounts of incoming activation for their thresholds to be satisfied. It is the same process through which repeated processing of a representation eases its activation in the future.

3.4.5 Connection Types: Long and Short Distance, Excitation and Inhibition

Braitenberg (1978b) observed that the dendritic tree of pyramidal neurons possesses lateral ramifications called basal dendrites, usually accompanied by a vast ascending branch called an apical dendrite. Neurons which are close to one another are mainly linked through synapses on their basal dendrites. On the other hand, distant cells are connected by way of synapses involving their apical dendrites. The system composed of basal connections (the B-system) and the one integrated by apical connections (the A-system) have different functional attributes for cognitive processing (Braitenberg & Schüz, 1998).

Compatibly, relational networks involve different types of connections. First, a distinction is drawn between local and long-distance connections. The former are established within a given subsystem (e.g., within the phonological production subsystem) and the latter connect representations belonging to different systems (e.g., the semological and syntactic systems).

The neurological distinction between excitatory and inhibitory connections is captured explicitly in RNT notation. Excitatory connections send positive signals (so they contribute to the activation of the receiving node) and may be either local or long-distance. Conversely, inhibitory connections send negative signals (so that they tend to shut off the receiving node) and can only be local. In Figure 3.8, for instance, the signals sent from the nodes for FLYING, FEATHERS, and SMALL are excitatory, whereas the signal sent by the concept SWIMMING is inhibitory.

As explained in section 3.3.1, inhibitory connections can be axoaxonic or axosomatic. This distinction is explicitly captured in RNT notation. Axoaxonic inhibitory connections are represented with fork-like terminals blocking the flow of activation along the line on which they land, as illustrated in Figure 2.2 from Chapter 2 (here reproduced as Figure 3.9).

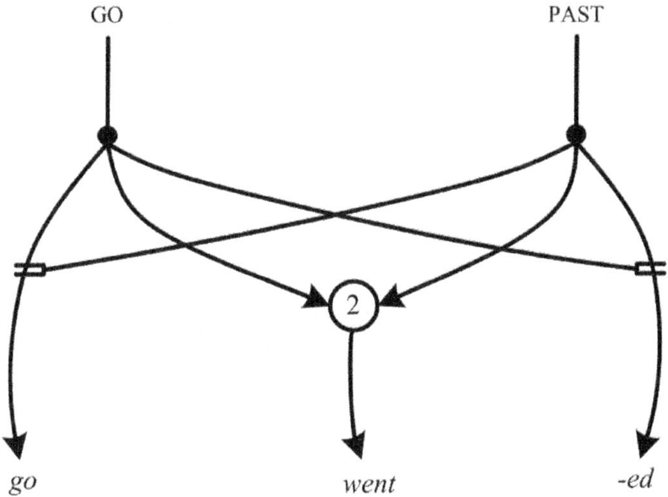

Figure 3.9: A type of inhibitory connection in RNT corresponding to an axoaxonic inhibitory connection.

Upon firing, a branching node will send activation through all of its output lines. In producing the word *went*, for example, a speaker must simultaneously activate the semantic representations GO and PAST. When GO is active (in a downward direction, for production), activation is simultaneously transmitted to the lexical representations *go* and *went* (and to all other representations linked to the node for GO). However, one or more of these lines will be blocked to prevent the concurrent activation of two incongruent representations, which would result in the production of anomalous forms such as *goed* or *go-went-ed*. A similar process occurs in processing PAST, as this node sends activation to both *went* and -*ed*; but the line leading to -*ed* is also blocked by inhibitory connections. Note that this also implies similar inhibitory connections blocking every other possible strong verb representation, although these are not included in the figure to avoid cluttering. In sum, this network can successfully handle the processing of *went* by virtue of the interplay between excitatory and inhibitory connections.

On the other hand, axosomatic inhibitory connections are represented by an empty circle which lands on a junction node and subtracts activation from the summation performed by its threshold. This second form of inhibitory connection is exemplified in Figure 2.3, here reproduced for convenience as Figure 3.10.

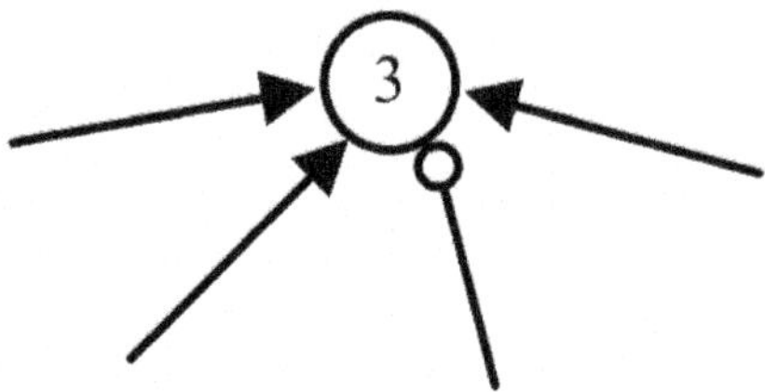

Figure 3.10: A type of inhibitory connection in RNT corresponding to an axosomatic inhibitory connection.

Figure 3.10 depicts a node with a threshold of 3 which receives three excitatory connections and one inhibitory connection (represented by the tiny hollow circle). If the inhibitory connection is active, the summation with three incoming signals yields a total of 2. Thus, the threshold is not satisfied, the node does not fire, and activation does not proceed along the output line.

Lamb (1999) maintains that relational networks are implemented at the neocortical level. While it is true that most inhibitory neurons can be found within cortical columns in the neocortex, inhibitory mechanisms also rely on subcortical structures. Wickens (1993) describes one such mechanism as a loop formed by projections leading from the cortex to the neostriatum (caudate nucleus and putamen), then to the paleostriatum, then to the thalamus, and then back to the neocortex. The connections linking the neostriatum with the paleostriatum and the latter with the thalamus are mostly inhibitory. In particular, neostriatal neurons can inhibit other cells within the neostriatum, so that competition between rival circuits would take place subcortically, before the thalamus synchronizes the resulting signal with other incoming signals and sends it to the neocortex. Even though relational network notation fails to capture such neurophysiological details directly, it does explicitly show how excitatory and inhibitory processes operate jointly during neurocognitive processing, while recognizing the existence of different types of inhibitory connections.

3.5   Conclusion

Fueled entirely by linguistic observations, Chapter 2 showed how abstract (bidirectional) notation, which is particularly useful for descriptive applications, supported an operationally plausible view of online language processing. This chapter has further suggested that such an account is also compatible with basic macroanatomical and microanatomical aspects of the brain. Non-trivial convergences become evident from a comparison between the model's narrow notation system and the way neurons connect and transmit electro-chemical signals. While we claim no direct isomorphisms, the parallels are extensive and suggest that the constraints RNT assumes for language are at the least broadly consistent with neurological constraints.

One way to foster informative dialogue between linguistics and neuroscience and other disciplines is to provide testable (therefore, falsifiable) characterizations of specific linguistic networks assumed to underlie particular linguistic facts. To this end, in Part II we present five chapters describing varied linguistic phenomena in different languages (Russian, Polish, Spanish, and English). For the sake of simplicity and notational convenience, we formalize those descriptions using abstract notation (although they could be translated into narrow notation to derive more specific neurologically oriented hypotheses). These aim to shed light on the links between phonology, morphology, syntax, and semology, and relations between the linguistic system and cognition. Chapters 4–7 focus on the description of grammatical phenomena. Chapter 8, which offers an account of speech errors in English and Polish, incorporates processing hypotheses. These descriptive applications are intended to illustrate comprehensive examples of relational network description and demonstrate the utility, efficiency, and potential of RNT. Let us turn to them now.

Part II

Descriptive Applications

4 An RNT Approach to Russian Obstruent Onsets

4.1 Introduction

Much confusing discussion surrounds the concept of the syllable, ranging from definitional to methodological and even ontological debates. Here, as a working principle, we will assume that the syllable, as a construct, is both analytically informative and cognitively plausible, even if it lacks clear-cut boundaries in the speech chain. But what is the relation of something like a syllable to phonemes, especially if the exact nature of the two concepts, syllable and phoneme, is moot? In the RNT framework, such questions are not primary for two reasons. First, the key organizational elements of the theory are lines and relations (AND and OR, ordered and unordered), as opposed to predefined emes. Second, phonemes and other linguistic elements, whether basic emes or constructs like syllables, are defined by, and in, the network of relations. In cognitive terms, they are emergent knowledge. To put it briefly, in RNT we analyze phonological phenomena as a network of relations without a prior definition of phonemes. The phonemes, the syllable, and other phonotactic constructs (or, more precisely, the underlying relational patterns) emerge from the description.

The present chapter brings together analytical and descriptive work on Russian phonology and considers it from an RNT perspective. Russian has a very complex syllable structure, with the syllable onset being the most complex part. Maximal word-initial clusters may have four phonemes, of which the final one is always a sonant (e.g., /r/). This resolves to word-initial obstruent onsets of up to three phonemes. Together they constitute the majority of onsets in both type and token. Here we focus precisely on obstruent onsets.

In earlier work, other scholars sought to define the phonemes of Russian in accord with one formalism or another (cf. Trager, 1934; Jakobson, Cherry, & Halle, 1962 [1953] – hereafter JCH, 1953). We have no scruples about borrowing or even expropriating the best of their work. Our study of Russian obstruents begins with a short summary of research performed using various methodologies, starting with the inventory of Trager (1934) and modifications introduced in JCH (1953), and outlining certain modifications to JCH (1953) adopted in Halle (1959).

4.2   Previous Descriptions of Russian Obstruents

4.2.1 Three Early Descriptions

Trager (1934) provides a classical description of Russian obstruents from the viewpoint of neo-Bloomfieldian phonemics. His inventory of obstruent phonemes (stops, fricatives, and affricates) is given in Table 4.1, modified and simplified for present purposes. For the sake of brevity, we leave out nasals, liquids, glides, and vowels, which can ultimately be handled in the same way as the obstruents.

Note the modifications made in Trager's inventory. First, the bilabials and labiodentals are combined in a single column. Only the fricatives are labiodental; all other labial phonemes are bilabial or involve both lips in rounding. Second, long, soft š and ž (i.e., [š:] and [ž:]) are left out. JCH (1953) correctly pointed out that these phones appear where we expect to see šč (cf. *čišču* 'I clean' [čiš':u]) and zž (cf. *jezžu* 'I ride' [jež':u]).

Table 4.1: Segmental obstruent phonemes of Russian per Trager (1934)

		labial		dental		palatal		Velar	
		hard	soft	hard	soft	hard	soft	hard	soft
Stops	voiced	b	b'	d	d'			g	g'
	unvoiced	p	p'	t	t'			k	k'
Affricates	voiced								
	unvoiced			c			č'		
Fricatives	voiced	v	v'	z	z'	ž		ɣ	ɣ'
	unvoiced	f	f'	s	s'	š		x	x'

Conversely, we retain two marginal or even controversial entries. The hard and soft voiced velar fricatives, /ɣ/ and /ɣ'/, were archaic even before Trager's work. But they had persisted because of their appearance in words like *Bog* 'God' [boɣ] and the influence of Ukrainian pronunciation on Orthodox liturgical language.

Next came the seminal work of JCH (1953), which we will only briefly discuss here. Although that study does not directly address our present topic, it made relevant conceptual contributions. First, the distinctive features provide the contrasts, not the alphabet-sized emes, as in Table 4.1 (cf. Sullivan, 2005). Second, these features may be marked or unmarked in a particular context. Third, the features in a particular phonological slot should be treated like the answers to questions involving contrast. Finally, the order of questions should be determined by position in the chain and the answers given to previous questions. With these premises, JCH hoped to minimize the number of phonemic features per segment. They went some distance but were ultimately unsuccessful.[1] Yet these are laudable goals, and they can be achieved in a relational network approach. We return to this question in section 4.5.2.

The next step was taken in Halle (1959), which was formulated specifically to provide a phonological component to the transformational-generative syntax in Chomsky (1957). Halle abandoned some of the characteristics of JCH (1953), among them contrast and the idea of changing the order of feature-determining questions. What he brought to the table was a detailed examination of some clusters. This had been a feature of previous descriptions, but the clusters were inventoried in word-initial, word-medial, and word-final positions. Halle limited the clusters to morpheme-initial, morpheme-medial, and morpheme-final positions. This resulted in a set of morpheme structure constraints and permitted him to make certain simplifying generalizations in the rest of his description.

Sullivan studied Halle (1959) carefully before beginning the phonological part of his work (cf. Sullivan, 1969), and noted that a description based on the syllable could improve on the morpheme structure constraints and account for the fact that native speakers of Russian had no difficulty in pronouncing certain clusters found originally only in borrowings. However, he limited word-initial onsets to those found in monomorphemic lexemes, thus avoiding controversies about prefix boundaries and word boundaries. Still, native speakers normally produce a string of syllables that ignore syllable or word boundaries, if indeed such boundaries exist. Moreover, ignoring morpheme boundaries gives a larger set of examples to incorporate in an overarching description of onsets, in general, and obstruent onsets, in particular, though Jakobson's comments on the size of an obstruent cluster still hold.[2] The next full study of Russian phonology appeared in Sullivan (1969), and the description provided in this chapter is to a great extent based on that one.

4.2.2 More Recent Descriptions

In recent years, a number of studies on Russian have appealed to the syllable or to syllable parts. In general, these works assume the existence of the syllable and look at its effects on other questions. For example, Gouskova (2001) refers to onsets and syllable contact but focuses on Russian loanwords in languages with CV[C] syllables. Gribanova (2009) looks at differences between Russian prepositions and verbal prefixes, with a focus on the fleeting vowels or jers. This involves syllabification, but it is a very restricted data set with only simple syllables. Also, the author's focus on L2 acquisition proves peripheral to our purpose of describing onsets. The same holds true of Kulikov's (2011) work on L2 acquisition of palatalization, and Ostapenko's (2005) study, which does deal with onsets but as related to errors during L2 acquisition. Finally, working from a purely phonetic stance, Howie (2014) presumes fully-formed syllables but does not identify their structure.

More relevant to this chapter are the studies by Kornai (1993) and Chew (2003). Kornai (1993) claims that feature geometry is demonstrably necessary and sufficient for describing the structure of natural classes. In essence, he tries to establish a phonological base (cf. Sampson, 1975), beginning with Chomsky's consistent demand that linguistics must search for substantive universals. Yet, Kornai notes that '[c]urrently there is no single generally accepted feature geometry' (1993, p. 44), partly (or mainly) because there is no metatheory constraining the number of features or the geometry of the tree. The metatheory therefore overgenerates, providing more than one answer. Thus, the current situation is unacceptable, though he holds out hope for productive research. We discuss feature geometry further in relation to RNT and the current study in section 4.5.2.

Like Kornai (1993), Chew (2003) attempts to provide a phonological base for a generative description of Russian phonology. He provides a set of context-free phrase structure rules to identify the permissible segment orders and qualifies them with probabilistic constraints. His work also includes insights into morphophonemic alternations and the realization of stress. However, whereas Chew deviates from Halle (1959) by couching rules in terms of distinctive features, he follows that author in treating each column of distinctive features as segments. He combines the phrase structure rules to a certain extent, but there is no overall generalization. There are other problems with the study, most of which can be traced to the assumptions of Chomskyan phonology. For example, it goes from the level of syllable structure to that of feature directly, limiting the possibilities for intermediate generalizations (cf. Figure 4.11). Another weakness is the assumption of a universal set of binary ($\pm$) distinctive features, essentially the same set introduced in Chomsky & Halle (1991 [1968]). Neurocognitively, however, the biggest shortcoming of Chew's work is the use of 'probabilistic constraints in the syllable structure grammar to explain why constraints on word-marginal onsets and codas are weaker than on word-internal onsets and codas' (Chew, 2003, p. 3). Our brains do not operate in terms of strict mathematical probability. As described in Chapter 2, there are at least two possible modes of neurological activation (spreading activation and quantum firing), and the two may be combined with each other or with the effects of harmonic vibration in the system. Moreover, it remains to be discovered whether there is some completely different mode of neurological activation. Until that question is resolved, we might assume some neurocognitively plausible mode of operation or not, but there is no need to assume a mathematically elegant but neurocognitively implausible mode. While serious and thought-provoking, Chew's (2003) study is limited by the theoretical assumptions under which it was carried out.

4.3   An RNT Approximation of Russian Obstruent Onsets

Our present RNT treatment of Russian obstruent onsets finds an antecedent in Sullivan (1969), who rejected Chomskyan assumptions and deviated from Halle (1959) – and, incidentally, from Chew (2003) – in two key respects. First, it abandoned binary ($\pm$) features in favor of singulary features. Second, it posited that singulary features relate to the articulators (cf. Lamb, 1966b; Hockett, 1975), since place of articulation is never phonemic in Russian obstruents. The result was a pure relational network description that incorporates contrast and full specification of the entire set of obstruents, as in Table 4.2.

However, Sullivan (1969) retained Halle's (1959) restriction of the data set to monomorphemic clusters.[3] This is another unnecessary assumption incorporated into the early stage of Chomskyan phonology, and it arbitrarily restricts the data set. Most important, however, it is an assumption that has nothing to do with phonology, as it involves single morphemes and position in a word and has never been justified. We therefore abandon it in the present study. It does, however, require us to account for a larger set of exemplars, but this turns out to be no problem.

As a beginning to our description of Russian obstruent onsets, we retreat to the traditional (and, we maintain, incorrect) notion that the phonemes of Russian are alphabet-sized segments, grouped into a table according to the features that identify the articulators (as in Tables 4.2–4.4). The next step is an inventory of onset clusters in word-initial syllables, supplemented by the obstruent portions of word-medial and word-final clusters (Tables 4.5 and 4.6) under the preliminary assumption that all may fit into onset position.[4] Combination and generalization follows, with a description in terms of algebraic formulae. We repeat the step-by-step process and develop a diagrammatic relational network description in abstract notation. As described in Chapter 2, the two notation systems express the same information; here, the algebraic rules are useful in describing the development of the analysis sequentially, but overall, we find abstract notation less clumsy, less likely to be confused with generative rule formalisms, and more commensurate with an RNT perspective.

4.3.1 A First Approximation

The preliminary set of obstruents is given in Table 4.2. We use the symbol Y to indicate phonemic voice. Following traditional notation, the apostrophe after a consonant (C') indicates a phonemically soft consonant with a fronto-palatal coarticulation. In connected speech, a soft consonant results in a fronted preceding vowel and a fronto-palatal offglide into a following vowel. Unvoiced hard consonants are not marked [- voice] or [- soft]; they are merely not marked for voice or softness.

Table 4.2: Preliminary inventory of Russian obstruent phonemes

		Lb		Ap		Fr		Do	
		-	'	-	'	-	'	-	'
Cl	Y	b	b'	d	d'			g	g'
Cl	-	p	p'	t	t'			k	k'
Gr	-			c			č'		
Sp	Y	v	v'	z	z'	ž		ɣ	ɣ'
Sp	-	f	f'	s	s'	š		x	x'

Key: Cl = oral closure; Gr = groove release; Sp = spirant friction; Lb = labial; Ap = apical; Fr = frontal; Do = dorsal; ' = phonemic softness; Y = phonemic voice.

Of the 28 obstruent phonemes in Table 4.2, some (e.g., f', ɣ) are marginal, with a low informational load – i.e., they do not help to realize many morphemes and there are few or no minimal pairs to be found. Still, they can be heard in the speech of native Russians.[5] This refers specifically to the voiced, soft counterpart of č. Neither do native Russians have any difficulty pronouncing a voiced apicodental grooved affricate, which is not phonemic in Russian but occurs phonetically in a context like *otec doma* 'father's at home', where the *c* is non-contrastively voiced. These and other phones do not violate any phonotactic patterns, so it can do no harm if we construct the phonotactics in such a way that it permits the possibility of processing (encoding or decoding) them. To see how the hypophonotactics handles this situation, see Sullivan (2002).

Now, however, it is necessary to introduce a pair of refinements.

4.3.2 Further Approximations

Russian obstruent clusters are either entirely voiced or entirely unvoiced, and the voice character of the cluster is determined by the voice character of the final obstruent (Halle, 1959; Sullivan, 1977), even across word boundaries. Thus *vaš dom* ('your home') is pronounced [važdom].

In neo-Bloomfieldian linguistics this was accounted for by a phoneme replacement rule, something like 'before a voiced obstruent (here d), an unvoiced obstruent (here š) is replaced by its voiced counterpart (ž).' This works well enough descriptively, so long as the obstruent in question has unvoiced-voiced counterparts.

But we cannot call on a phoneme replacement rule to account for the above-mentioned *otec doma* 'father's at home', which is pronounced [at'edzdoma]. That is, /c/ has no voiced phonemic counterpart. Instead, any description or explanation of what is happening here must be couched in terms of the actual element of contrast: the feature voice, rendered here by Y. The effect of this in RNT terms is that, at the AND nodes that relate morphemes to phonemes, Y must be extracted from the rest of the obstruent. We return to the relational network details below. Consider now the effect this has, as in Table 4.3.

Table 4.3: Russian obstruents: Factoring out voice

		Lb	Ap	Fr	Do	
Cl	hard	P	T		K	
	soft	P'	T'		K'	
Gr	hard		c			(Y, Ø)
	soft			č'		
Sp	hard	F	S	Š	X	
	soft	F'	S'		X'	

Table 4.3 allows each consonant, hard or soft, to occur with or without voice. Of course, c and č never occur with phonemic voice, but this is taken care of in the realizational portion, where morphemes are related to phonemes (as illustrated in Figure 4.7). At that point, for example, c is simply a one-to-one line from morpheme to phoneme, with no relation to phonemic voice. An examination of the network in Figure 4.7 shows that Y is a phoneme, but it is a dependent phoneme. That is, its phonotactic relations are always dependent on the presence of other phonemes (actually archiphonemes of neutralization, cf. section 4.4.2) and it never occurs alone. We return to this question in section 4.5.1.

Softness, like voice, generally occurs only once in a cluster. The situation with softness is more complex than it is for voice and it involves sonants as well as obstruents, but for present purposes we can ignore the complexities. The traditional treatment that we have been following shows the softness as part of the consonantal phoneme. In a relational network description, this analysis becomes unnecessary and untenable. Like voice, softness is a dependent phoneme occurring with other phonemes and never alone. So we can factor out softness, giving a third approximation of the Russian obstruent inventory, as seen in Table 4.4.

Table 4.4: Russian obstruents: Factoring out voice and softness

	Lb	Ap	Fr	Do	Voice	Softness
Cl	P	T		K		
Gr		c^{a,b}	č^{a,b}		(Y, Ø)	(', Ø)
Sp	F	S	Š^b	X^c		

Key: a = not contrastive for voice; b = not contrastive for softness; c = marginally contrastive for voice and softness.

Table 4.4 provides the full set of Russian obstruent (archi)phonemes that appear in the onset clusters described in the remainder of the chapter. The initial description is focused on the phonotactics of obstruent clusters as denoted with these symbols, but rendered in our description first as algebraic formulae representing relational networks and second in abstract notation.

4.4   Describing Russian Obstruent Onsets in RNT

As mentioned above, obstruent onsets in Russian can be one, two, or three phonemes in size. They may appear alone or with a sonant (most often r) following. A non-exhaustive set of typical three-place clusters is given in Table 4.5. Some of these also occur voiced or soft – e.g., [vzd], which is voiced, or [pšč'], which is soft. Added combinations appear in interword context.

Table 4.5: Some three-place onset clusters

tšč	pšč	kšč	fšč		
tsk	psk	ksk	fsk		xsk
tst	pst	kst	fst	šst	xst
			fsp		
			fsx		

Similarly, a non-exhaustive set of two-place obstruent clusters is given in Table 4.6. Again, many of these occur voiced or soft.

Finally, note that any obstruent can occur alone, plain, soft, voiced, or both, with exceptions as noted in Table 4.3. We are now in position for phonotactic generalization, beginning with three-place onsets. We provide the descriptions first in algebraic, then abstract notation, followed by a summary diagram and a general discussion of how RNT accounts for the onset possibilities.

Table 4.6: Typical two-place onset clusters[6]

pt	pč	pš	ft	sc	sf
tp	?tč	tf	fp	fč	sx
kt	kč	ks	fs	sš	sk
		kx		šč	

4.4.1 Method 1: An Algebraic Generalization

Note that in algebraic terms, an OR relation is symbolized with a comma, as in (Y, Ø) 'voice OR nothing' and (', Ø) 'softness OR nothing'. Henceforth, we adopt a slightly simpler formalism for optional phonons, like voice and softness. (Y, Ø) will be written [Y] and (', Ø) will be written [']. Linear order is represented by an ordered AND relation and is symbolized by a simple string, as in SVO vs. SOV in syntax. The generalized set of potential onset clusters begins with the ordered AND relation given in (1), where each branch must be realized with a single (archi)phoneme. Yet, not every phoneme can occur in every position.

(1)   3ObOnset / A B C

Each branch on the plural (right-hand side) of (1) has a number of possibilities. This means that A, B, and C are related to OR relations connecting each of them to a number of (archi)phonemes. These three branches, elaborated from Table 4.5, are given in (2)–(4).

(2)   A / P, T, K, F, Š, X

(3)   B / Š, S

(4)   C / P, T, K, X, č

Note that the subset of stops, (p, t, k), is related to both A and C. This suggests an intermediate level, call it A_1, that is related to the set of stops. A and C are modified to reflect this in (5) and (6), with the intermediate level elaborated in (7).

(5)   A / A_1, F, Š, X

(6)   C / A_1, X, č

(7) A_1 / p, t, k

If we look at (3) and (5)–(7), it seems as if a pattern might be developing: the full set of stops can occur in positions A and C. Only fricatives can occur in all three positions. And we only see an affricate in position C. The distribution of obstruents is not fully symmetric, so we make no more of it here; but there are two sets of obstruent onsets to go. We return to the possible patterns when the other sets are merged with the three-place onsets.

We can split the two-place onsets into two subgroups, those that begin with a stop (9) and those that begin with a fricative (10).

(8)   2ObOnset / D, E

(9)   D / (P, T, K) (F, S, Š, X)

(10) E / (F, S, Š) (P, T, K, F, S, Š, X, c, č)

D and E are both related to two-place combinations. Note that A_1, (P, T, K), is present in first position of D and second position of E. We provide that generalization in (11) and (12).

(11) D / A_1 (F, S, Š, X)

(12) E / (F, S, Š) (A_1, F, S, Š, X, c, č)

Now note that the set of fricatives is related to the second position of D in (11) and E in (12). Let the fricatives occupy an intermediate position, like the stops, and we have (13), which is merged with (11) and (12) in (14) and (15), respectively.

(13) A_2 / F, S, Š, X

(14) D / A_1, A_2

(15) E / (F, S, Š) (A_1, A_2, c, č)

Now consider (5) and (3), repeated here for convenience.

(5)   A / A_1, F, Š, X

(3)   B / S, Š

Remember that (5) shows the relations of the first position in a three-place onset to archiphonemes and (3) shows the relations of the second position in a three-place onset to archiphonemes. In addition to A_1, (5) has all the fricatives but S. The question arises as to whether this is an accidental gap or a structural gap. If it is an accidental gap, it can safely be ignored. Consider that three-obstruent onsets are relatively much rarer than two-place onsets, so a particular gap may well be only accidental. Yet, it might also result from a hypophonotactic timing factor of the sort that predicts what happens in the contrast between *prelest'* ('charm') and *prelestnyj* ('charming'), whose corresponding cluster is generally pronounced [sn], with the apparent disappearance of the *t*. With three apical consonants in a row, two unvoiced and two with complete oral closure, pronouncing *stn* would require articulating the oral closure before the nasal passage is opened and voice is turned on. Such complex timing procedures can be simplified or subject to error.[7]

Alternatively, as a first approximation, one may assume that the lack of S in (5) is an accidental result of other factors. In fact, there are lexemes where we would predict the onset sš, as in the perfective infinitive *sšit'* ('sew'), cf. *sošju* 'I'll sew'. What we get is [š:š]. Then (5) should have the potential for the full set of fricatives, (F, S, Š, X). This lets us rewrite (5) as (16).

(16) $A / A_1, A_2$

At the same time, (3), which shows relations to the second position in a three-place onset, has only two of the fricatives. In fact, when Sullivan (1969) originally described the Russian syllable, it was almost possible to restrict the inventory of position two to S, using morphophonemics to account for any discrepancies. Yet, when the restriction to monomorphemic onsets was lifted, it became no longer possible. Still, position two is missing F and x, but this is of minor significance: F and x are the rarest in the Russian fricative inventory. The [f] originally appeared only in foreign borrowings, though when the jers dropped, an archiphonemic F (v without voice) appeared – compare [fx] in *vxodit'* ('enter, impf.') with [v] in *vojti* ('enter, prf.'). Moreover, native x originally appeared in Slavic only after IE *r, *u, *k, *i, and thus had a restricted range. The morphological sequence for an X to have arisen in this position is lacking. Finally, in lexemes where the X is expected, it is realized as Š. That leaves us lacking only f in position two. Given the rarity of the phoneme, we again ignore the gap and posit the full set of fricatives.

Now we can see that a third intermediate level appears in the most general description. It comes about like this:

(17) a. ObOnset / D B E
    b. $D / A_1, A_2$
    c. B / A_2
    d. $E / A_1, A_2$, c, č

But let $(A_1, A_2) = A_3$, so, expanding to (archi)phonemes:

(18) a. ObOnset / F B G
    b. F / A_3
    c. B / A_2
    d. G / A_3, c, č
    e. $A_3 / A_1, A_2$
    f. $A_1 / P, T, K$
    g. $A_2 / F, S, Š, X$

Two things remain. We must include the realization of phonemic voice in (18) and allow two- and one-place onsets. All two-place onsets are accounted for if line B does not occur – i.e., if it is structurally optional. Putting brackets for optional occurrence around B suffices here. And the one-place onsets could not be simpler. By itself, line G relates to all obstruents. B is already optional, so if we make F optional, too, that will allow G to occur alone. This modifies (18a), producing (19a).

(19) a. ObOnset / [F] [B] G

All that remains now is to account for phonemic voice. Recall that an obstruent cluster in Russian is either entirely voiced or entirely unvoiced. The choice is determined by the phonemic character of the last obstruent in the chain. Thus, accounting for voice is easy: we simply attach it to G; it is structurally optional and is thus written in brackets. This further modification of (18a) is provided in (20), where Y = phonemic voice. Providing voicing for F and B is easily taken care of in the hypophonotactics (cf. Sullivan, 2002, p. 129).

(20) ObOnset / [F] [B] (G[Y])

This completes the algebraic description of Russian obstruent onsets. An equivalent abstract description follows, with correspondences noted for reference.

4.4.2 Method 2: An Abstract Description

The algebraic statements given in (20) + (19a) + (18b–g) certainly look like a set of context-free phrase structure rules. They are not. They constitute a clumsy attempt at representing a relational network without a diagram. If they look like phrase structure rules, that is an artifact of the formalism. Yet, they can be used to construct an abstract description of Russian obstruent onsets as a pure relational network. The graphic description that corresponds to (20) + (19a) + (18b–g) is given in Figure 4.11. However, proceeding immediately to Figure 4.11 may be too much of a leap, so we will construct the diagram from (18b–g) + (19a) + (20), working from the bottom up, in a fashion parallel to the way we built up (18b–g), beginning with (18f) and (18g).

The labels on the diagrams are of two sorts: archiphonemes (capitals) or phonemes (lower case), which are across the bottom; and labels that simply refer to the formulae cited.

At the tactic level just above Figure 4.1 is (18e) or A_3. A_3 is given graphically in Figure 4.2.

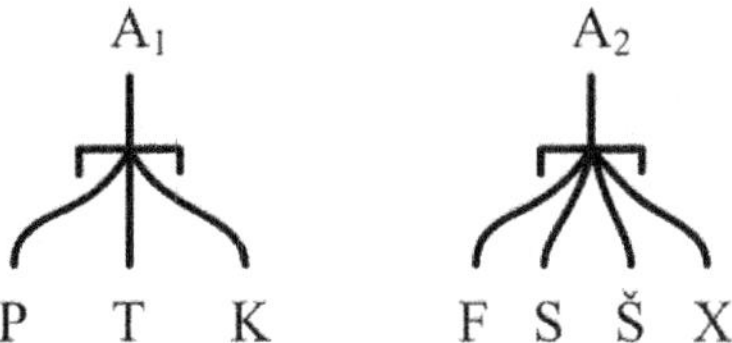

Figure 4.1: A_1 / P, T, K and A_2 / F, S, Š, X.

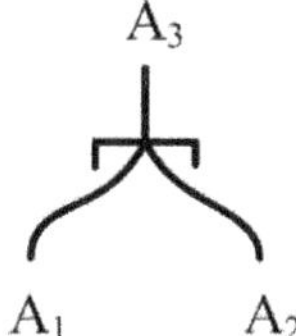

Figure 4.2: A_3 / A_1, A_2.

Above Figure 4.2 we reach a subnetwork with relations to the obstruent onset (ObOnset) cluster. Before we complete this subnetwork, we jump to the top of the cluster, (18a), in Figure 4.3, to provide grounding for the connections that are shown in subsequent figures.

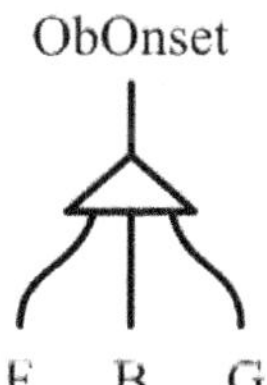

Figure 4.3: ObOnset / F, B, G.

We are now in a position to look at the network between Figure 4.2 and Figure 4.3. In subsequent figures (e.g., Figure 4.11), the network in Figure 4.3 will be seen above Figure 4.2. The first step is provided in Figure 4.4, which combines algebraic (18b) and (18d). Note that we add the affricates c and č to the set available for G.

In Figure 4.5 we bring B into the picture presented in Figure 4.4. Both these figures require the use of upward OR nodes, turning what has heretofore looked like a tree into a reticulum – a fully three-dimensional network. Lines B and the left-hand line from the OR node below G cross on the two-dimensional diagram, but they do not meet. They are skew.

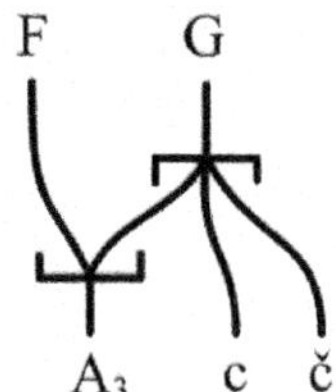

Figure 4.4: F / A₃ and G / A₃, c, č.

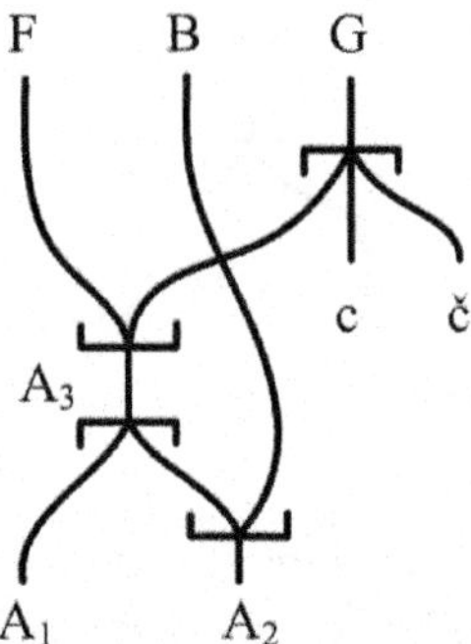

Figure 4.5: F / A₃ and B / A₂ and G / A₃, c, č.

Before connecting Figures 4.5 and 4.3, it is necessary to modify the latter according to (20), repeated here for convenience:

(20) ObOnset / [F] [B] (G[Y])

The first two relations in (20), F and B, are optional. This allows for two- and one-obstruent onsets. The third relation, G, leads to onsets that are unvoiced (simply G) or voiced (G & Y). Modifying Figure 4.3 to allow these choices is, as discussed above, very simple. The result is seen in Figure 4.6.

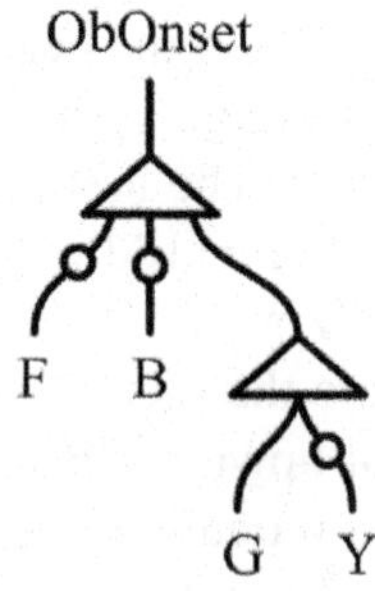

Figure 4.6: ObOnset / [F] [B] (G[Y]).

One step remains before the summary integrated diagram can be constructed. That is, we must explain the relation of voice to the rest of the cluster. Picture it this way. The input from the morphology to the phonology comes from morphemes distinguished by relation to a voiced obstruent (e.g., b), and from other morphemes distinguished by relation to an unvoiced obstruent (e.g., p). The phonemic occurrence of voice is with the last obstruent in a cluster. All other potential appearances of voice are excluded or realized as zero: *oves* ('oat(s)') with [v], but genitive *ovsa* with [fs]. In that position, no voice contrast can be established, so the [f] cannot be said to be phonemic /f/. Trubetzkoy called it an *archi*phoneme. This is as good a name as any, for it correctly identifies the sound's phonological (here phonemic + phonetic) character. In practice, what happens is that when a potentially voiced-voiceless pair is part of the input to phonology in Russian, the voiced member is related to the unvoiced member AND potential voice – i.e., to voice (Y) or zero. The Y line is then related to the voice (final) position of the onset. This is presented in Figure 4.7.

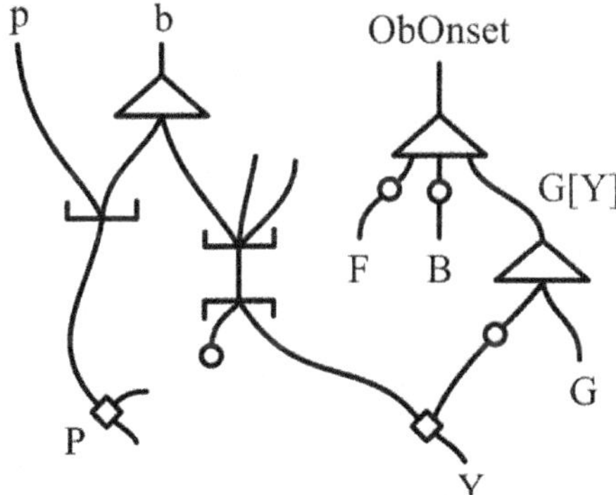

Figure 4.7: The realization of the p,b archiphoneme P and its relation to voice.

Every voiced-voiceless pair has a realizational network like the one given for (p, b). Two obstruents, c and č, which do not occur in voiced-voiceless pairs, do not have such a network. Each of them is related to a set of morphemes, just as p and b are. Yet, below these morphemes there is a one-to-one relation to c and č at the bottom. So, although P and T and K and the rest are *archi*phonemes of neutralization (the upward OR node near the upper left), c and č are simply phonemes.

4.4.3 A Summary Diagram

Presented as an integrated summary diagram, Figure 4.8 is not yet a complete description of the Russian onsets. Modifications are needed to account for word-final or syllable-coda details, and a good deal of structure must be added to describe the interrelations of sonorants and phonemic palatalization to onset position. Other modifications are needed to account for productive morphophonemic alternation.

Still, Figure 4.8 has a good deal to offer. For example, recall that c and č are phonemic but without voiced counterparts. This is guaranteed by the lack of any relations to voice (Y) at the input from the morphology (upper left). However, the tactic relations of G[Y] predict correctly that native speakers of Russian can still produce and perceive [dz] and [dž']. More importantly, Figure 4.8 does this without any added mechanisms. This prediction is what can be called emergent knowledge or implicit competence.

Yet, Figure 4.8 is not our stopping point with Russian phonology. Each line at the bottom of Figure 4.8 should have a set of relations to a diamond, just as P does. The lines leading down from these diamonds relate the (archi)phonemes to phonemic features or hypophonemes. The next step is to add these networks and perform some mechanical simplifications on them. This will lead us to the solution to a number of questions raised by attempts at underspecification, as in JCH (1953) and Archangeli (1984), and in the analyses of more recent proponents of feature geometry.

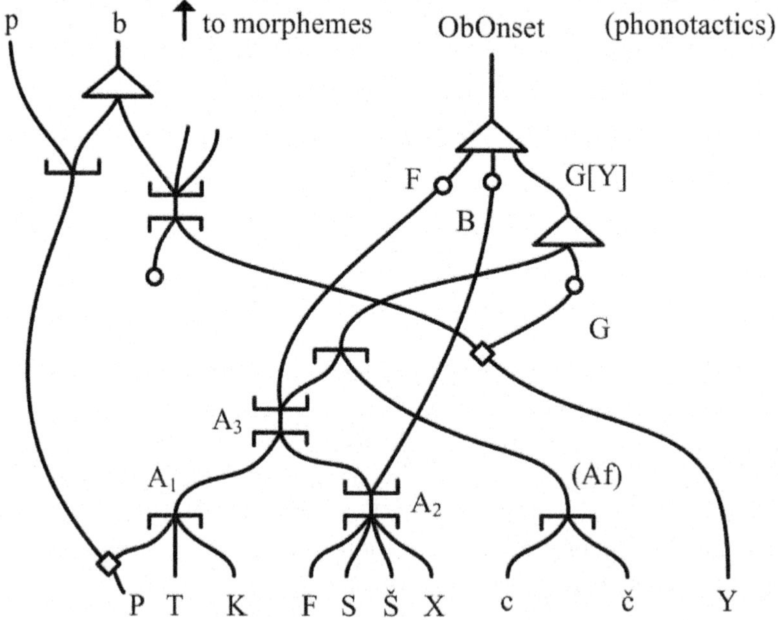

Figure 4.8: Russian obstruent onsets generalized.

4.5   Some Theoretical Considerations

4.5.1 From (Archi)phoneme to Hypophoneme

In relational network terms, a hypophoneme is simply a relation from the phonotactics in the eventual direction of phonetic output via the hypophonotactics, and ultimately the motor cortex and articulators. Hypophonemes are roughly equivalent in function to phonemic features. They identify phonemes or, more properly, elements of contrast that distinguish between morphemes. In Figure 4.8, the line leading down at P is a hypophonemic relation. In Table 4.4, slightly modified and repeated for convenience as Table 4.7, we summarize the hypophonemes and the (archi)phonemes to which they are related.

Not all of Table 4.7 is included in our treatment of hypophonotactics. The restrictions on voice contrast are part of the relations from morphology to phonology and need not be repeated in the phonotactics. Similarly, the question of softness involves the sonorants and is thus required of all of the onset clusters and not just the obstruents. Still, there is enough here to make the case for the utility and capability of a relational network description.

Table 4.7: Russian obstruents: Factoring out voice and softness

	Lb	Ap	Fr	Do	Voice	softness
Cl	P	T		K		
Gr		$c^{a,b}$	$\check{c}^{a,b}$		[Y]	[']
Sp	F	S	$\check{S}^{b}$	X^{c}		

Key: a = not contrastive for voice; b = not contrastive for softness; c = marginally contrastive for voice and softness.

We begin with A_1, the set of stops. As seen in Figure 4.8, a set is described by an OR relation, and all other relations involved are unordered AND relations (including diamonds). That is, P is related to Cl and Lb, both being active at the same time. A_1 is repeated algebraically in (21a) and with hypophonemic elaboration in (21b). A quick examination of (21b) shows that the hypophoneme Cl or oral closure is repeated in each parenthetical grouping. It may be factored out, so to speak, and distributed over the set of articulator hypophonemes. By this method, (21b) is simplified mechanically in (21c). A preliminary relational network description of the set of stops equivalent to (21b) is given in Figure 4.9(a), with a simplified graph equivalent to (21c) given in Figure 4.9(b).

(21) a. A_1 / P, T, K
    b. A_1 / (Cl & Lb), (Cl & Ap), (Cl & Do)
    c. A_1 / Cl & (Lb, Ap, Do)

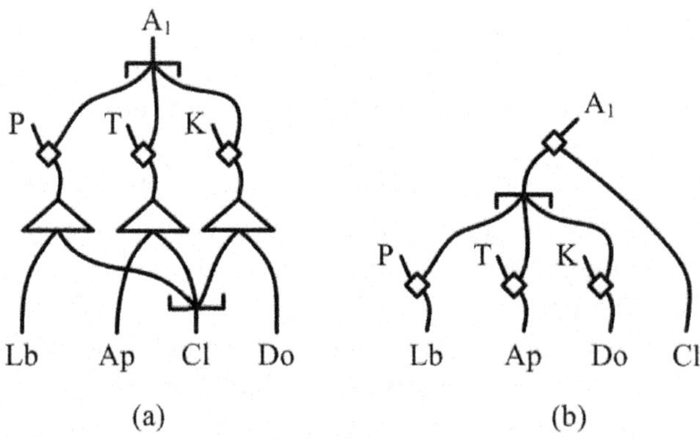

Figure 4.9: (Archi)phonemes to hypophonemes: Preliminary (a) and simplified (b).

A quick inspection shows that Figure 4.9(b) is much simpler and more general than Figure 4.9(a): the three AND nodes below the diamonds and all the lines and nodes leading down from them are gone. The only relation in Figure 4.9(b) that is absent in Figure 4.9(a) is the diamond near the top. It relates to the hypophoneme Cl. The effect of the three AND nodes is given by the one diamond node.

Much the same can be done with the sets of fricatives and affricates. We present the algebraic statements and simplifications in (22) and (23) and the relational network equivalents in Figure 4.10. As the direction of analysis is clear, there is no need to go through the preliminary relational network descriptions. Here, we present just the simplified versions.

(22) a. A_2 / F, S, Š, X
    b. A_2 / (Sp & Lb), (Sp & Ap), (Sp & Fr), (Sp & Do)
    c. A_2 / Sp & (Lb, Ap, Fr, Do)

(23) a. Af / c, č
    b. Af / (Gr & Ap), (Gr & Fr)
    c. Af / Gr (Ap, Fr)

Next, we merge Figure 4.9 and Figure 4.10 with Figure 4.8 to make the unified diagram in Figure 4.11. In the context of this one unified description, we can provide successful answers to a large number of theoretical questions and avoid the kinds of problems that surround underspecification and feature geometry.

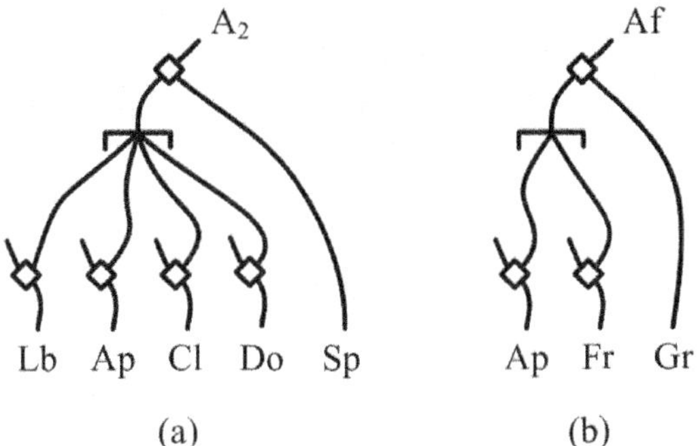

Figure 4.10: (Archi)phonemes to hypophonemes: Fricatives (a), and affricates (b).

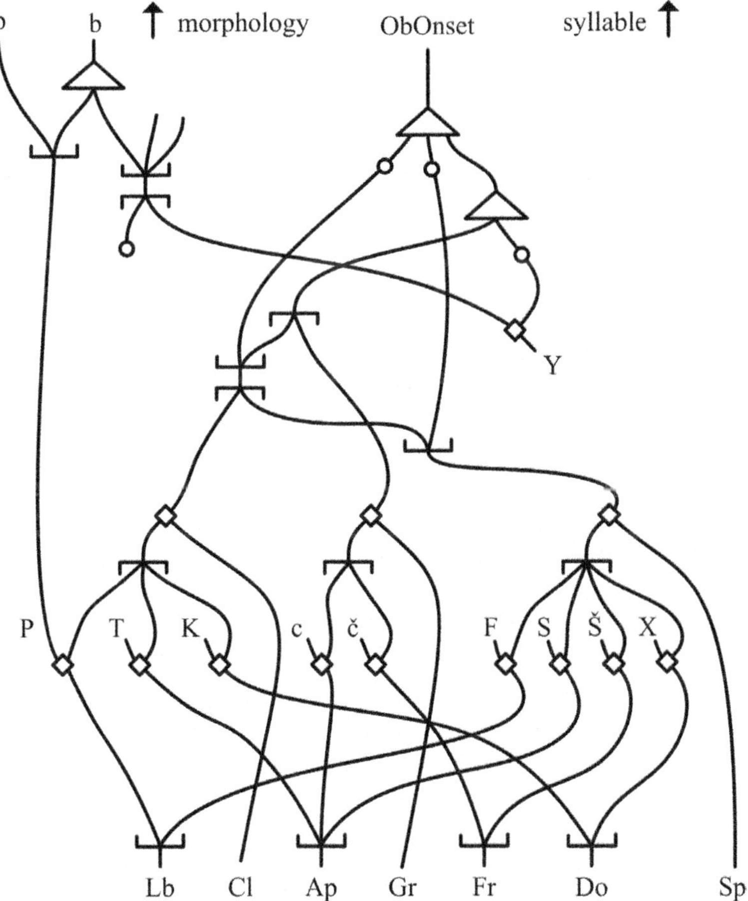

Figure 4.11: Russian obstruent onsets: Morphemes to hypophonemes.

In Figure 4.11 there are quite a few lines that appear to intersect without nodes. This type of formalization would be prohibited in Chomskyan linguistics and may be confusing to someone used to that approach. RNT has no such prohibition, because these apparently intersecting lines do not intersect. The reason for the difference is that Chomsky's models are all two-dimensional, whereas our model in RNT is three-dimensional, and these lines would be skew, like the lines to Ap from T and S at the bottom of Figure 4.11, which cross the lines to Cl and Gr in a two-dimensional drawing.

Figure 4.11 maintains the contrasts that allow native speakers of Russian to distinguish one morpheme from another in the relations from morphology to the diamonds. It also predicts that native speakers should be able to produce and perceive voiced counterparts of c and č, even though they do not occur in native Russian morphemes.

Figure 4.11 incorporates a number of characteristics that phonologists traditionally considered important long before Generative Phonology began. It recognizes the contrastive elements of Russian obstruents in the relations to the diamonds (phononections) from the 'northwest' (NW) and the relations from the diamonds to the 'southeast' (SE). It also makes explicit the difference between phonemes and archiphonemes (cf. Sullivan, 1977). The NW relations are analogous to segmental phonemes and archiphonemes, and the SE relations are analogous to phonemic features. None of these is assumed to exist. The relations in these parts of the description emerge from an exhaustive study of the relations needed to explain the phonology of Russian obstruent onsets.

One characteristic of the RNT approach to Russian phonology (and to phonology in general) needs expansion here. That is the concept of a dependent phoneme (cf. Sullivan, 2005). Phonemic voice (Y) in Figure 4.11 is called a dependent phoneme. Consider both parts of that phrase. Voice is a phoneme here. That is, it is represented by a 1–3–2 diamond with relations to a class of morphemes to the NW, to a single hypophoneme Y to the SE, and to the phonotactics to the NE. Those three relations on the phonemic stratum make it a phoneme. However, its occurrence is restricted to a single position in the obstruent chain and is dependent on the occurrence of an obstruent archiphoneme in final position of the chain. Phonemic softness in Russian is another such dependent phoneme. Again, the existence of dependent phonemes is an emergent property of a relational network description of Russian phonology.

There are other advantages to the network depicted in Figure 4.11. These become clear against the backdrop of two proposals in Generative Phonology which have caused as much controversy as enlightenment: underspecification and feature geometry.[8] A relational network approach avoids the problematic consequences of their assumptions.

4.5.2 Underspecification, Feature Geometry, and a Metatheoretical Discussion

The roots of underspecification can be traced back to JCH (1953). Their idea was to minimize the number of distinctive features that had to be specified for each phoneme of a language, so each one would be uniquely defined. This characteristic of JCH (1953) was not a major consideration in Halle (1959), which rejected phonemic contrast, but it found its way back into Generative Phonology in the Feature Minimization Principle (Archangeli, 1984, p. 50): 'A grammar is most highly valued when underlying representations include the minimal number of features necessary to make different the phonemes of the language.' In practice, this means that the phonologist should always choose the approach that reduces the number of features specified per segment to a minimum. This is easy enough to say, but it leaves a lot to be determined.

Feature geometry represents a principled approach to the problem of feature assignment in a generative framework. To begin with, it looks like an expansion of the approach in JCH (1953), which asked feature assignment questions in different orders, depending on where in the string you were and what the answers to previous questions were. Just as an obvious example, if you have already had the answer [+ vocalic] in Russian, you do not ask whether the segment is strident (a sibilant), because stridency never contrasts for vowels. Similarly, you do not ask whether a vowel is voiced – all Russian vowels are voiced.

But feature geometry has a particularly generative orientation. The features are nodes on a universal feature tree. If the answer to a particular feature question is yes [+], that is the gateway to one path. If the answer to that question is no [−], that is the gateway to another path. And so on, until all features have been assigned. Depending on which path(s) on the feature geometry tree are taken, you do not have to identify the values of all features explicitly. All the values for the features on the branches not taken are presumably predictable and are assigned redundantly. However, to quote from Sullivan on drawbacks to underspecification and feature geometry:

> There are [...] problems with both theories. The feature sets are presumably universal. It seems reasonable to expect that feature trees are also universal. Still, the history of [Chomskyan phonology] has a series of disputes over the number and inventory of features. Similarly, there are disputes over the nature, number, and placement of nodes on FG's feature tree.
>
> Underspecification has its own problems. For example, the interplay between contrast and the transparency of intervening segments to feature spread is 'not fully understood' (Roca, 1994: 76). There is

an ongoing discussion of the relative merits of radical vs. constrained underspecification. Worse, given binary marking and 18 features, the average number of features per segment should be a little over 4 ($\log_2 18$). Few descriptions are anywhere near that figure. In none of these cases is there an obvious way out within [Chomskyan phonology]. (1998a, p. 56)

Note that while Archangeli (1984) approaches this minimum (of a little over four features per segment), we have not checked to see about any compensatory cost involved in added rules.[9]

A clear way out, as well as an explanation for the underspecification/ feature geometry problems, is inherent in Figure 4.11. Each diamond at the row near the bottom of Figure 4.11 is an intersection of either a phoneme or an archiphoneme with Russian syllable onset structure. Their functional relations (to the NW) serve to identify (or help to identify) a class of morphemes. The relations to the SE are their formal relations to hypophonemes (i.e., phonemic features). Note that in Figure 4.11 each diamond is related to exactly one phonemic feature, the feature specifying articulator. Above each set of diamonds is an OR node, above which is another diamond. That diamond is related downward (SW) to the three sets of obstruent classes, and also SE to the manner features (Cl, Gr, Sp), sometimes called class features. Each diamond is also related upward (NE) to a unique distribution of obstruent onset positions. So, in effect, the manner features identify a class of obstruent phonemes and their distributional properties. Phonemic voice is a cluster prosody, and the phonotactics provides it with only one place of potential realization in the onset cluster. We now have a description that provides a single hypophoneme (or phonemic feature) for each (archi) phoneme. We suggest that this is the irreducible minimum. The important point is that this irreducible minimum emerged from a mechanical simplification of a generalized relational network description of the obstruent onset of the Russian syllable. That is, it is emergent knowledge, requiring no additional mechanisms or assumptions. At the same time, it suggests the source of the problems faced by underspecification and feature geometry and provides an answer to them.

Figure 4.11 minimizes the number of features per phoneme by relating portions of the cluster architecture to predictable or determined features. This architecture, derived from the syllable structure of Russian, could be said to be the feature geometry tree for that language.[10] Few languages have a syllable structure as intricate as that of Russian, though some are more complex. Indeed, the structure of the Russian syllable may well be unique. So, if the relation to hypophonemes is drawn from the possibly unique syllable structure of Russian, the feature geometry tree for Russian could be specific to Russian, and there is no reason to expect that the feature geometry tree for any other language will be identical to that for Russian. The distribution of relations to hypophonemes could differ as well as the order of relations to hypophonemes. And not all the contrasts that can be established for Russian can be established for languages as closely related as Ukrainian and Polish. Thus, it is likely that the assumption of universality for the features and the feature geometry tree is the source of feature geometry problems.

Possible objections could still be raised to this line of reasoning. One may ask, for example: what about Polynesian-type languages, which may have only CV syllables and a minimal number of contrasts (e.g., 18 consonants and five vowels)? What would their feature geometry tree(s) look like? The real question is why we should worry about it. Once we have given up the idea that the set of contrasting features must be universal and assigned by a universal feature geometry tree, the problem disappears. We should just worry about the set of contrasts that can be established for a particular language and use only that set of features required to describe such contrasts minimally. Beyond that, mechanical simplification will finish the description.

4.6   Conclusion

A relational network description is easily able to provide a generalized description of the complex obstruent onset clusters of Russian. An irreducible one hypophoneme per phoneme relation defines the contrasts. This triumph of underspecification emerges from the generalized description without additional assumptions or mechanisms. The work of minimizing phoneme-to-feature specification is the job that the feature geometry tree was supposed to do in the generative framework, but it ran into difficulties and disputes. The generalized relational network description produces the desired result and answers the theoretical disagreements, while showing that they largely resulted from adherence to a fruitless, *a priori* dictum.

Notes

1. Mainly because of the insistence that the features be binary and universal.
2. Sullivan is indebted to Peter Reich (University of Toronto) for reminding him to cast off Halle's restrictions when doing a more complete syllable description. Reich pointed out quite forcefully that these restrictions are not justified in Halle (1959), simply assumed. They are also artifacts of what was then Generative Phonology.
3. The purpose was simply to show that a relational network description could do everything Halle claimed for Russian phonology and more.
4. In fact, a generalized onset obstruent cluster does accommodate all of them.

5.   Sullivan, for instance, has heard many examples among native Russian speakers, and his former teacher, Prof. Aleksandr Vasil'evič Isačenko, noted that some of these obstruents occur 'with correct pronunciation in the names of cities in Soviet Central Asia' (personal communication – note, aforementioned is now former Soviet Central Asia).

6.   The question mark before tč is intended to indicate that this cluster may be a spelling pronunciation.

7.   For a discussion of tactic pattern errors, see Chapter 8. Note also the lack of softness in the cluster.

8.   For a more detailed discussion, see Sullivan (1998a).

9.   We are grateful to Caroline Wiltshire of the University of Florida for reminding us of this.

10.   If we ignore that it is actually a reticulum rather than a tree, mathematically speaking.

5 An RNT Approach to the Polish Genitive

5.1 What's in a Case?

Confiteor Deo Omnipotenti, chanted the chorus of altar boys in training. The year was 1949, the Mass was in Latin, and a bunch of American boys at St. Mary's Church in Newington, Connecticut, were reciting the Confiteor, the confession of sins. One of the older boys – perhaps Dickie Charbonniere – asked, 'What's *Deo Omnipotenti*? Because I thought it was *Deus Omnipotens*.' Father Mucha replied, 'Oh, we're saying "I confess *to* God Almighty," so *Deo Omnipotenti* is the dative case of *Deus Omnipotens*. Different endings.' Wally Maselek, Tommy Arusiewicz, and Billy Sullivan were not surprised by words taking different endings here and there. Some of the others grumbled. Yet all memorized the forms.

Father Mucha's explanation presupposed a morphological definition of case focused on the ending, not much of an advance over the ancient Greek definition, which he would have seen in seminary. Nearly twenty years later, Sullivan was in a linguistics class given by a Bloomfieldian structuralist who was asked for a definition of case. The professor responded that it was a noun or pronoun that was syntactically marked. The same kind of syntactic definition is found in Wikipedia today: 'Case is a grammatical category whose value reflects the grammatical function performed by a noun or pronoun in a phrase, clause, or sentence' (Grammatical case).

Case was missing from the first twenty-plus years of Chomsky's output (cf. Chomsky, 1980), but one of his early adherents, Charles Fillmore (1968), introduced a definition of case into generative theory to some success, though Chomsky disapproved of his methods.[1] Fillmore's cases came from semantic frames, making his version of cases conceptually closer to Halliday's semantic role relations rather than to grammatical cases – though Halliday (1967/1968) recognizes both semantic roles and grammatical cases (see also Halliday & Matthiessen, 2014). Certainly, case has been characterized from a variety of viewpoints and, not surprisingly, each definition is characteristic of the theory under which it was produced. While each of them has something commendable, no one has done it all – not even Jakobson's (1971a [1958], 1984 [1936]) overarching morpho-semantic definition (skipping over syntax and discourse). A full description is still lacking.

Polish is a less studied language with a rich case system, and the genitive case presents several interesting features for linguistic description, especially if discourse, cognitive, and explicitly semantic considerations are incorporated. The analysis we set forth below incorporates previous insights to provide an integrated relational network approach that fully defines the genitive case in Polish. Beyond that, this chapter illustrates a more general approach to defining cases across languages.

5.2   Previous Descriptions of the Polish Case System

A fair amount of descriptive work has been done on case in Polish, but progress has been remarkably scant since Schenker's (1964) contributions. More recent materials have addressed the broader topic of Polish nominal morphology. Relevant work published in English is sparse, including even Polish teaching grammars. Among the latter, the volumes by Schenker (1973) and Swan (2002) offer extensive coverage of nominal inflections, desinence forms, and even morphophonemic alternation, with additional focus on how the forms are related to paradigms. However, beyond mention of which generalizations are useful regarding the relations between gender and paradigms, these works overlook semantic considerations.

A handful of specifically linguistic investigations can also be found. A formal study by Zeldes (2007) relates suffixes and morphophonemics, with useful notions for the teaching of Polish. From a different angle, Dąbrowska (2001) offers cognitively interesting insights into children's acquisition of competing forms of the genitive singular masculine. However, neither of these articles is concerned with semantic factors, while other linguistically oriented studies are even further from the issue at hand.

Also worth mentioning are general grammars of Polish, ranging from the encyclopedic Grzegorczykowa, Laskowski, & Wróbel (1998) through Wróbel's (2001) detailed volume, to Strutyński (1997), which adds morphophonemics to Wróbel's format. Other grammars pay specific attention to inflection. For example, Bańko (2004) provides a morphotactic discussion on how to analyze a lexeme into stem and ending and how to synthesize a lexeme from stem and ending. Another volume by Tokarski (2001), often cited by other Polish grammarians, focuses on case forms, their distribution across paradigms, and the verbs that command each case. This leads to lists of the kinds of information that different cases communicate. However, even these accounts remain a long way from the semantic analyses provided by Jakobson (1971a [1958], 1984 [1936]) and Schenker (1964), to which we now turn.

Noting similarities at the phonetic and semantic levels, Jakobson (1971a [1958], 1984 [1936]) systematized distinctive semantic features for which the cases can be marked in the process of identifying their *Gesamtbedeutungen* ('base meanings'). His analysis begins with the forms of the desinences, and then considers the neutralizations between them as well as the syntactic constructions framing each case. Thereupon, Jakobson concludes that there are eight cases that apply to the Russian noun. Jakobson operated on the principle of binary marking, which required the identification of a maximum of three distinctive semantic features, thus $2^3 = 8$. Jakobson (1984 [1936]) provides a better developed, more elegant description of case than Jakobson (1971a [1958]).

Polish is quite closely related to Russian. By Jakobson's criteria for identifying cases, Polish has only six, not eight.[2] Yet the patterns of alternation and neutralization are parallel. For example, both accusative and dative can communicate movement toward the object (directionality). Dative and locative singular are never formally distinct in feminine declensions. Also, locative only occurs on a noun that is the object of a preposition. Moreover, contrasts can be found among Schenker's (and Jakobson's) considerations for distinguishing cases. For example, if a preposition commands both accusative and locative, as in *v dom* 'into the house' and *v dome* 'in the house', the one is directional and the other is not, as reflected in the semantic feature marking. A summary description of Schenker's analysis is given in Table 5.1.

Table 5.1: Distinctive features of Polish cases per Schenker (1964)

	Quantifying	Directional	Marginal
Nominative	-	-	-
Accusative	-	+	-
Genitive	+	-	-
Locative	+		+
Dative	-	+	+
Instrumental	-	-	+

Schenker arrived at a brilliant synthesis of the effects of the relations between several different and sometimes widely dispersed subsystems of the Polish linguistic system. However, his analysis jumped from morphology to semantics, barely touching syntax and never considering discourse. For better or worse, Schenker's (1964) work was built directly on Jakobson's (1984 [1936]) model, with all its advantages and limitations. In both descriptions, many shades or even distinct colors of meaning are subsumed into the *Gesamtbedeutung* complexes. Taken strictly, this ignores any cognitive extensions of the semantics. This fact, together with the relatively truncated consideration of syntax and the complete lack of semology/discourse input, limits the scope of these pioneering efforts. The alternative descriptions we offer below retain the strong points of their excellent analyses while bridging some of their gaps.

5.3   Case under the Lens of RNT

We do not intend to provide an *a priori* definition of case according to RNT. To repeat a critical point, there are no items in RNT in the sense of traditional definitions, whether it be a grammatical concept like a morpheme, defined as the smallest stretch of sound that conveys meaning, or a real-world entity like a table, defined as a piece of furniture with a flat surface on four legs. Rather, each distinctive pattern of morphological information is considered a point in a network which relates meaning and sound and whose nature depends on the relationships it subsumes.

However, the theoretical apparatus behind RNT allows us to describe cases in a particular language based on linguistic facts. Case assignment proves an interesting exploration from a relational perspective, as the theory is able to tie together relevant morphological, syntactic, cognitive, and discourse (sememic) phenomena, thus offering a unified, cross-level description.

The goal here is to describe the sets of functional, formal, and tactic relations that pertain to the genitive case in Polish. We begin with a verbal description of this form's relations as implied by typically occurring examples, and gradually construct a network that accounts for genitive case assignment in general.

5.4   Overview of the Relations of the Polish Genitive

The examples from which we draw our description of the Polish genitive are given in Table 5.2, which contains typical information about all the relations that the Polish genitive contracts. Moving from left to right, we see the nominative forms (NOM) of nine typical nouns modified by the demonstrative *ten* 'this, that'; a typical syntactic FRAME in which genitive appears; the genitive forms (GEN) of the noun-adjective phrases; the sememic role (ROLE) played by the genitive in this particular frame and where that role arose (origin); and, finally, the FORM related specifically to the genitive for adjectival or nominal stems. The first five nouns are singular, the last four are plural. In order, the nouns are *siostra* 'sister', *Pani* 'lady', *brat* 'brother', *dziecko* 'child', *tytoń* 'tobacco', *kobiety* 'women', *rzeczy* 'things', *języki* 'languages/tongues', *uczniowie* 'pupils (m)'.

Table 5.2: Forms, frames, and functions of the Polish genitive

NOM	FRAME	GEN	ROLE / origin	FORM	
				Adj	Noun
ta siostra 'that sister'	*poszli do* ___ 'they went to'	*tej siostry*	LOC & GOAL / semantics	ej	y / i
ta Pani 'that lady'		*tej Pani*			
ten brat 'that brother'	*poszedł tu od* ___ 'he arrived from'	*tego brata*	SOURCE / semantics	ego	a
to dziecko 'that child'	*była koło* ___ 'she was near'	*tego dziecka*	PROXIMITY / semantics		
ten tytoń 'that tobacco'	*kawałek* ___ 'a piece of'	*tego tytoniu*	PARTITIVITY / semantics		u
te kobiety 'those women'	*mam książki* ___ 'I have the books of'	*tych kobiet*	POSSESSOR / semantics	ych	ø
te rzeczy 'those things'	*nie widzę* ___ 'I don't see'	*tych rzeczy*	neg. PATIENT / semology, syntax		y
te języki 'those languages'	*uczę się* ___ 'I'm studying'	*tych języków*	GOAL / semantics		ów
ci uczniowie 'those pupils'	*otóż zdjęcie* ___ 'here are the photographs'	*tych uczniów tych uczni*	POSSESSOR / semantics PART / semantics		i/ów

Table 5.2 summarizes how syntactic frames, functional origins, and morphemic forms occur in Polish. For example, *poszli do tej siostry* 'they went to that sister' has the noun as the object of the preposition *do*, which communicates movement toward an object, a locative GOAL.[3] *Poszedł tu od tego brata* 'he came from that brother' has the noun as the object of the preposition *od*, which communicates the opposite of *do*, that is, movement away from an object, a locative SOURCE. *Była koło tego dziecka* 'she was near that child' has yet another preposition, *koło* 'near, around', which communicates PROXIMITY. *Kawałek tego tytoniu* 'a bit of that tobacco' communicates PARTITIVITY. In *mam książki tych kobiet* 'I have those women's books', the genitive case communicates POSSESSION. It might also communicate POSSESSION in *otóż zdjęcie tych uczni(ów)* 'here are those pupils' photos'. However, this might equally be interpreted as 'here are the photos of those pupils', meaning the photos contain the images of the students. We consider this latter interpretation as the PART function – where

the images can be considered 'part' of the students – overlapping with, but different from, PARTITIVITY.[4] Non-locative GOAL appears in *uczę się tych języków* 'I'm studying those languages'. Finally, syntax directly contributes in *nie widzę tych rzeczy* 'I don't see those things'. The PATIENT, which is a semotactic relation to an act, is normally realized as the accusative direct object of the verb; but when the clause is negated, the PATIENT is still realized as the direct object, though it is in the genitive case.

As the form column shows in Table 5.2, there are three genitive endings for nouns in the singular (*y/i, a, u*) and another three for nouns in the plural (*y/i, ów, ø*). Adjectives provide three genitive endings: *ej* for feminine singular, *ego* for masculine/neuter singular, and (*y/i*)*ch* in the plural. Numerals provide other genitives and some nouns exhibit the characteristics of mixed declensions, which we ignore for space considerations. Notwithstanding, these examples suffice to show that the genitive case can be realized by multiple endings.

5.5   The Syntactic Relations of Case

In RNT, tactic relations may be upward, toward higher-level constructs, or downward, toward lower-level ones. The upward tactic relations define the element's range, whereas the lower tactic relations define its domain. With respect to syntax, case has relations to both hierarchically dominant and hierarchically subordinate syntactic relations.

Consider first the subordinate relations. *Idzie do domu* 'he's going home' shows the noun as the object of the preposition *do*, which governs the genitive, and the noun has a genitive ending. If we have the noun modified by the demonstrative, *ten dom* 'that house', both noun and demonstrative appear in the genitive: *do tego domu* 'to that house'. If we add an adjective or two (e.g., *stary* 'old' and *drogi* 'expensive'), we find that the adjectives are also in the genitive case: *do tego drogiego starego domu* 'to that expensive old house'. The inference is clear: case is related to and dominates the entire noun phrase.[5]

Now consider the relations to hierarchically dominant syntactic complexes. Noun phrases in whatever case can appear as objects of prepositions, as post-nominal qualifiers, or even in a direct relation to a clause. All these observations can be jointly captured in abstract notation networks, including AND, OR, and diamond nodes. In the figures below, labels correspond to the categories in Table 5.2. We turn now to the actual RNT definition of genitive case in Polish.

5.6   An RNT Description of Relations of the Polish Genitive

5.6.1 The Functional Relations of the Polish Genitive

The functional relations of the Polish genitive are described in Figure 5.1. The sememes across the top are distinct semologically and cognitively, though their relations to the semotactics are not shown. Still, they are realized as genitive case in the lexotactics. This is represented graphically by their convergence at the upward OR node that leads downward to Genitive at the bottom of Figure 5.1. This type of relation is traditionally called neutralization (i.e., suspension of a distinction or contrast). Evidence for it can be found at any stratal boundary. Remember, however, that there are no stratal boundaries separate from the network. Instead, it is the occurrence of neutralizations as indicated in the diagram in Figure 5.1, together with other local subnetworks, that constitutes the boundary.

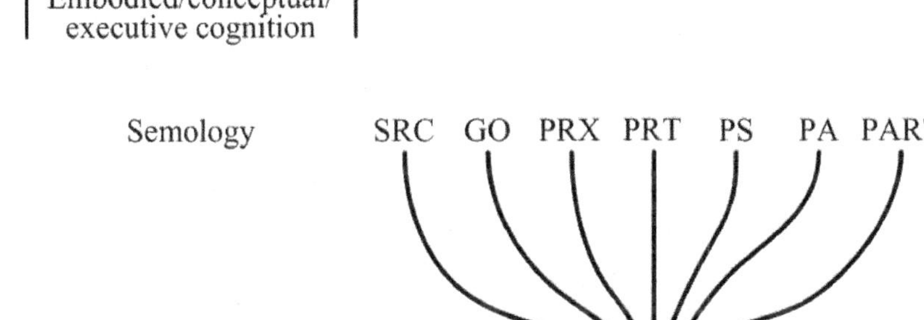

Figure 5.1: Functional relations of the Polish genitive.

Key: SRC = SOURCE; GO = GOAL; PRX = PROXIMITY; PRT = PARTITIVITY; PS = POSSESSOR; PA = PATIENT; PART = PART.

As much as anything in this abbreviated account can, the diagram in Figure 5.1 represents the meanings of genitive in Polish. Its full semantic impact is only reached by the network extending upward from the top of Figure 5.1, which is beyond our present scope. We turn now to the formal relations of the genitive.

5.6.2 The Formal Relations of the Polish Genitive

The formal relations of the Polish Genitive are depicted in Figure 5.2. Here, 'formal' relations should be understood in the sense of relations to phonetic form.

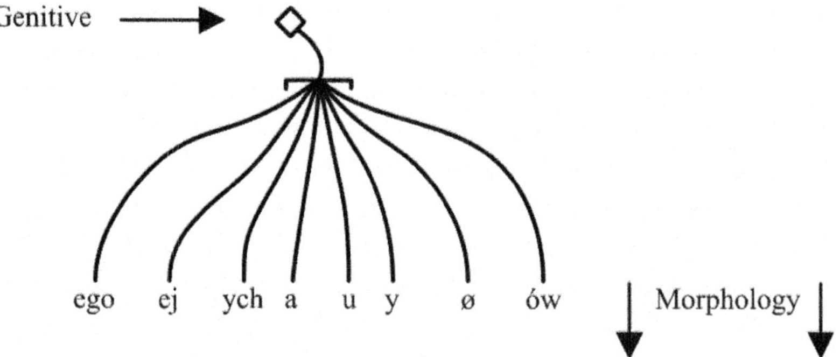

Figure 5.2: Formal relations of the Polish genitive.

As outlined in Table 5.2, there are eight forms that communicate the Polish genitive, when appended to a nominal or adjectival stem.[6] These endings represent the morphological case Genitive. The diagram in Figure 5.2 shows them as a set of lines down from the OR node below the Genitive diamond. This is traditionally called a (morphological) diversification, because all of the endings are related to and realize a single point in the syntax.

We turn now to the lexotactic network of the Polish genitive, the central part of Polish syntax.

5.6.3 The Lexotactic Relations of the Polish genitive

The lexotactic relations of the Polish genitive are given in Figure 5.3.

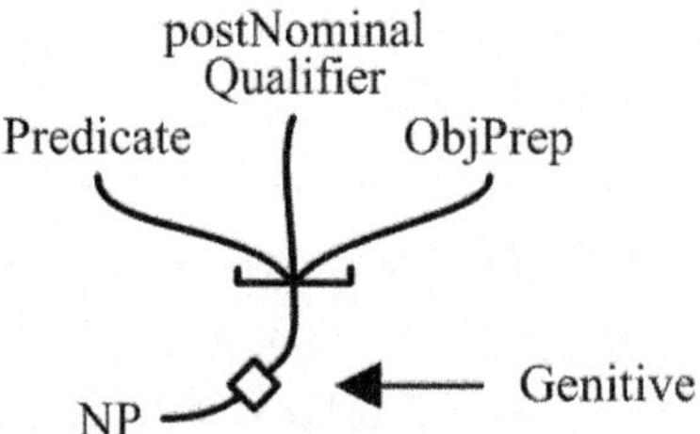

Figure 5.3: Lexotactic relations of the Polish genitive.

The diagram in Figure 5.3 provides us with the relations of the Polish genitive to the hierarchically superior lexotactic networks which govern it (certain prepositional phrases, post-nominal qualifiers, and direct objects of negated verbs). These constitute its range. Figure 5.3 also provides us with a relation to the hierarchically subordinate lexotactic networks – i.e., noun phrase and pronoun (not shown). These constitute its domain.

5.7   An Integrated Description of the Polish Genitive and its Implementation

Three pieces of the definition of the genitive case in Polish are now complete. Three steps remain: putting the pieces together, explaining how they account for the genitive, and showing how the morphology sorts out the details. Putting the pieces together is simple, as the diamond labeled Genitive appears in each of the three diagrams. This is the point at which the three diagrams come together. Everything is connected to Genitive, which is the label on the diamond in Figure 5.4. All other nodes in Figure 5.4 are OR nodes; remember that the diamond is shorthand for two AND nodes back to back, one facing upward and the other facing downward.

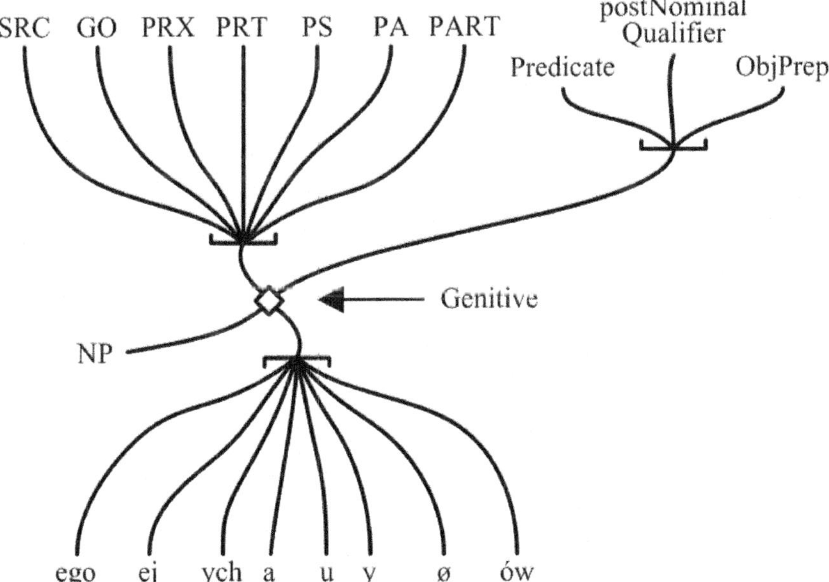

Figure 5.4: The genitive case in Polish.

In this example we focus on encoding a single predication. All of the participants in the predication and their relations to the act (the lines for the role relations or spatiotemporal relations they contract) are activated simultaneously in the semotactics. Activation is sent from the semotactics to the lexotactics (syntax of lexemes). One task of the lexotactics is to sequence the subsequent output across the clause. The participants themselves are realized syntactically as noun phrases or pronouns (ignored for simplicity), with a diamond for each noun or adjective. The structure of the clause is above and to the right of the rightmost upward OR node in Figure 5.4. When the linear position of the clause appropriate to the sememic role related to a particular noun phrase is reached, the line down from the OR at the upper right is activated. Meanwhile, the line down from the upward OR directly above the diamond is already active, as is the diamond that pertains to the noun realizing the participant. We are assuming that the sememic role here is SOURCE or POSSESSOR, for example. So the two lines from the NE and NW of the diamond labeled Genitive are active. Activation is thus sent down the SW line to allow the noun phrase to be encoded, and at the same time activation is sent down the line to the SE from the diamond. When this passes through the downward OR, it spreads activation to all the lines radiating from it. That is, signals are sent to every possible genitive case form in the morphotactics. Of course, a particular noun relates to only one genitive in the singular and only one in the plural. Only one is the correct form. This looks extremely complicated: how do we prevent the realization of the incorrect endings?

The RNT answer is that the morphology can sort it all out, by accomplishing several things. It must make sure that every noun and adjective in that particular noun phrase gets the appropriate genitive case form, and that the appropriate genitive form is suffixed to each stem in the noun phrase, providing the appropriate case ending.[7] This is in fact reasonable. The only interest that the syntax has is assigning the case. It is as if the lexotactics shouts to the morphotactics: 'Give me a genitive on this set of adjectives and nouns.' The syntax does not care which ending appears with a given adjective or noun during encoding; that is a problem for the morphology. Nor does it care what the form of the ending is during decoding; it only needs to recognize that it is a genitive. And it can let the semotactics sort out which sememic role is being communicated.

All of this indicates that the role of the syntax in case marking is straightforward, if not quite simple – assuming that the morphology can sort things out, as we show below.

5.8   Sorting out the Morphology of Case

The morphotactic network that provides the correct case form and makes sure it is an ending is given in Figure 5.5. The diagram shows a section of the morphology that includes a part of the morphotactics and some of the lexomorphemic realizational relations relevant to the morphology of nouns in Polish. Its focus is on the realization of genitive (G) with feminine (*a*-stem) nouns, using the lexeme *kobiet* 'woman'. In addition to the realizational relation of *kobiet*, Figure 5.5 has six lexomorphemic relations. Reading from left to right, they are five cases and plural number (pl). The cases are instrumental (I), dative (D), locative (L), genitive (G), and accusative (A). Polish also has a nominative (N), which is treated somewhat differently from the other cases. We return to N below. The lexomorphemic case relations attach to the NW side of the morphemic diamonds at the bottom. At the same time, the AND node labeled other Nominal Declensions (ND) is part of the morphotactics or syntax of morphemes. All of its lines attach at or near the bottom to the NE sides of the morphemic diamonds.

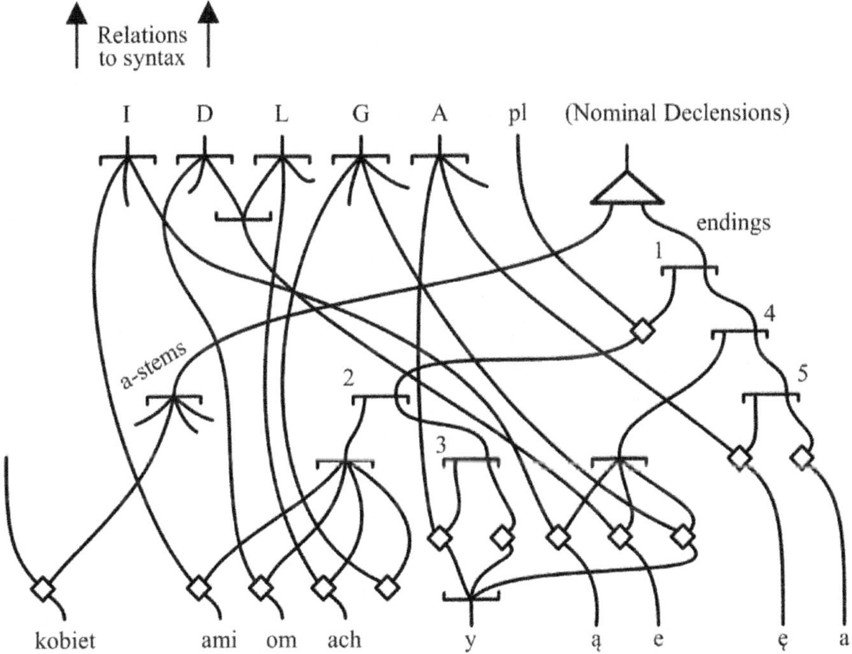

Figure 5.5: The morphological network for the a-stem declension.

Consider first the lexomorphemic relations dealing with case. The OR node labeled G is the OR node at the bottom of Figure 5.4. Each case has a similar OR node related to a set of endings, with distinct singular and plural forms. In the *a*-stem declension the forms are usually labeled *y* (if singular) and ø (zero in plural). Note the two lines from G attached to diamonds. One is related to the upward OR above *y* via the line from the SE side of the diamond. The other line from G connects to a two-sided diamond, which has no line from the SE side. It sends no signal to the phonology during encoding and therefore results in a zero ending. This shows as well as anything the unreal nature of the labels as opposed to the network of relations.[8]

To recapitulate: the syntax, having received an appropriate activation from the semology, spreads activation to G, resulting in activation to all possible genitive forms, in particular to the two lines in Figure 5.5 (y, ø). Now we show how the morphotactic network sorts all this out.

Begin with the ordered AND labeled Nominal Declensions (ND). All Polish lexemes are realized by a stem (the left-hand line from ND) followed by an ending (the right-hand line). Note that the case activation from Figure 5.4 is simultaneous with the entire NP. The ND node in the morphotactics sequences the form of the genitive case after the stem, taking care of one discrepancy in the encoding of case in the lexotactics, and explicitly specifies stem-ending sequence in the network.

Now consider the choice between the two forms of the genitive that apply to this declension. Only one can be realized. The line labeled 'endings' reaches an ordered OR node 1 that is related to all the diamonds by which cases are realized in this declension. The ordering recognizes that plural endings are marked vs. non-plural (singular).[9] If the line labeled 'pl' is activated, then the left-hand branch of 1 must be taken. The activation spreads to another ordered OR at 2. Its left hand leads to the oblique cases (I, D, L, G), all of which receive activation via their NE sides. Yet, since only G has activation via the NW branch, it is the only one that succeeds (with zero further output) and sends positive feedback up the network on both lines. All activations to other cases fade.[10]

In parallel fashion, if pl is not active, activation spreads down the right-hand (singular) branch of endings, where it reaches another ordered OR at 4, which is related to the NE sides of the oblique cases. Again, only G has provided its diamond with NW activation, resulting in activation along the line from the SE branch, ultimately producing the y ending.[11]

5.9 Conclusion

Previous treatments of case showed definitions based on semantics, semology, syntax, morphology, or some combination thereof, depending on their underlying theoretical assumptions. Our comment at the time was that each definition had some insight to offer and that RNT could incorporate those insights. We have illustrated our point by modeling the genitive case in Polish (Figure 5.4), and the role of the morphotactics in correct form assignment (Figure 5.5). The combination of these two networks, together with the implementation of spreading activation, surely results in a more complex description than those offered by preceding accounts; but the key point is that our RNT approach covers all the ground they contemplate while incorporating additional details. Thus, the relative complexity of our reticular treatment reflects the size of the task undertaken rather than theory-internal intricacies. Indeed, that numerous key aspects of the Polish genitive can be made explicit in only two figures attests to the modeling potential of relational networks.

Notes

1. During a seminar at the LSA Summer Institute in 1975, Chomsky was asked what he thought of Fillmore's case grammar. His answer was that it was all right if it could be handled in the lexicon. Case only came to Generative Syntax five years later.

2. To the standard six (nominative, accusative, genitive, locative/prepositional, dative, instrumental), Jakobson's (1971a [1958]) analysis of Russian adds a second locative and a second genitive.

3. For discussion on the semantic relations of prepositions in a parallel situation in Russian, see Sullivan (1998b).

4. See discussion of PART in Sullivan (1998b) and Bennett (1975).

5. Or the pronoun, ignored here for space considerations.

6. If we count ø (zero) as a form, for which see Jakobson (1971b [1939]).

7. Cf. Note 3.

8. Note we do not claim that this network exists in a human brain, only that the brain captures the logic underlying this network, i.e., the logic by which this network was adduced.

9. Jakobson's characterization of Russian cases holds up well in Polish, though with some differences in detail, as might be expected (cf. Schenker 1964, and Note 2).

10. The double activations to ø also fade after sending the positive feedback signaling success.

11. If no oblique case is provided by the lexotactics, activation proceeds along the right-hand branch down from 4, reaching another ordered OR at 5. In the absence of any activation of A, i.e., lacking the occurrence of any marked case, activation proceeds down the right-hand branch from 5. It reaches a two-sided diamond which provides the completely unmarked nominative singular case ending.

6 An RNT Approach to Spanish Pronominal Clitics and Verb Endings

6.1 Introduction

Pronominal clitics and verb endings play a distinguishing role in Spanish morphology. The former constitute units intermediate between independent words and bound morphemes. They can fulfill independent grammatical functions (e.g., as direct or indirect objects), but they have no phonological autonomy (i.e., they are always unstressed and typically pronounced in the same tone group as the verb). For their part, Spanish verb endings are desinences which necessarily express PERSON and NUMBER and which, optionally, may also express MOOD, TENSE, and ASPECT – here referred to as verb characteristics. These two sets of features may be realized by a single morpheme (E. García, 1975, 2009). Pronominal clitics in combination with an inflected verb are illustrated in italics in sentence (1) below. All examples in this chapter are authentic texts taken from *Corpus de referencia del español actual* (CREA) (Real Academia Española).

> (1) Una hora después del partido del miércoles, el técnico Francisco
> Maturana ya tenía elegidos a los reemplazantes de los expulsados
> Perea y Ricardo Pérez; así *nos lo confesó* ('He confessed it to us').
> (CREA, Clarín, 03/07/1987: Intimidad de los rivales)

In (1), *nos* and *lo* are clitics acting as indirect and direct objects, respectively. The verb ending *-ó* realizes several semantic features of the main verb, including 'third person singular', 'indicative mood', 'past tense', and 'perfective aspect'.

While differing in form and function, Spanish clitics and verb endings share several attributes which warrant their joint treatment. Semantically, both types of unit realize features pertaining to at least six common categories (see section 6.3.1).[1] Morphemically, they are all monomorphemic units.[2] Morphotactically, they all occur either attached to or in the immediate proximity of the verb. While endings are always suffixed to the verb, clitics may occur either before the verb – when the latter is in the indicative or in virtually all uses of the subjunctive – or after the verb – when the latter is in the infinitive, imperative, or gerundial form, or in the subjunctive when conveying polite orders (Fernández Soriano, 1999).

E. García (2009) refers to the morphological link between a clitic and its associated verb as a verb complex, and considers that the verb's ending is the grammatical heart of such a structure. The bond between a clitic and a verb indicates that the referent of the former is a participant of the event denoted by the latter. In a verb complex, verb endings are privileged in that they are the only form possessing inflectional properties.

This chapter takes a relational network approach toward describing Spanish pronominal clitics and verb endings within a single model, considering the verb complex as an inclusive network which brings together semantic, morphemic, and morphotactic patterns.[3]

6.2   Previous Descriptions

Previous studies have shown and discussed other distinctive properties of Spanish pronominal clitics. For instance, the same clitic cannot attach to the same verbal form more than once – e.g., the cluster *me me* is ungrammatical (E. García, 2009). Also, successive clitics always occur in a fixed order (Enrique-Arias, 2005). Furthermore, no variety of Spanish admits the cluster *le lo*, even though cognate forms can be thus arranged in typologically close languages, such as French. In Spanish, the successive combination of two third person singular clitics in the dative and accusative cases, respectively, results in a cluster headed by the so-called 'spurious *se*'; instead of *le/s lo dije* 'I told it to him/her/them', Spanish systematically opts for *se lo dije* (Piera & Varela, 1999).[4] Interestingly, some clitic clusters are acceptable only when certain interpretive conditions apply. For example, *me le* is unacceptable when the direct object and the subject refer to different entities (e.g., *me le propusiste* 'You proposed me to him'), but it proves acceptable when such constituents are co-referential (e.g., *me le propuse* 'I proposed myself to him') (Bello, 1980; Bonet, 1994; Haspelmath, 2004).

Accounting for the conditions which render a cluster acceptable or unacceptable has become a focus of interest for functional linguists (for a discussion, see E. García, 2009) and a theoretical challenge to formal grammarians (e.g., Harris, 1996). In addition, Spanish clitics and verb endings have been studied in the functional-cognitive literature with emphasis on their syntacto-pragmatic (Belloro, 2007), compositional-interpretive (E. García, 2009), stylistic (Aijón Oliva & Serrano, 2010), and variational (Martínez, 2010) aspects.

However, formal accounts of the connections underlying Spanish clitics and verb endings have been very limited. To the best of our knowledge, the only network-based model of these two systems has been proposed by Castel (2012). Drawing on the Communicative Mind Model (Fawcett, 2011, 2013), Castel uses systemic-functional categories to characterize relevant connections. Noting that extant systemic-functional models have not provided explicit visualizations of the meaning-form interface, he makes a valuable contribution by offering the first network-based account of the interstratal relationships of exponence, filling, and componence, as defined in Fawcett (2000). Specifically, he addresses the domain of Spanish clitics and verb endings, on the basis of E. García's (1975) classical description. Castel's approach is illustrated in Figure 6.1 (Castel, 2012, p. 172), which captures the relationships among the semantic and form-level representations involved in the production of *me le regalo* 'I give myself to him as a gift / I surrender to him'.

Figure 6.1 illustrates three types of relationships: among semantic categories, governed by the node 'Ev0'; among form categories, governed by the node 'Cl'; and among both types of categories, represented by connections between terminal semantic and form categories. Despite its useful insights into meaning-form mappings, Castel's innovative approach presents at least four descriptive assumptions which can be improved in the quest for cognitive plausibility, namely: (1) unidirectionality (the model accounts for production but not for comprehension); (2) node uniformity (all nodes process information in the same way); (3) syntactic slot-filling (ordering depends on a linear sequence of slots which may be filled or empty); and (4) representational redundancy (the same information is represented multiple times in the network). In what follows, we show how these limitations can be overcome through a relational network description.

6.3   Spanish Clitics and Verb Endings from a Relational Network Perspective

The full Spanish clitic paradigm is made up of 11 units, namely: *me, nos, te, os, le, les, lo, los, la, las,* and *se,* presented in relation to their semantic features in Tables 6.1–6.5. On the other hand, Spanish verb endings constitute a closed class of bound morphemes, encompassing numerous regular and irregular forms. Following the convention adopted by E. García (1975), we will here use the endings of the first conjugation of the present indicative as a synecdoche representing the endings of all moods, tenses, and conjugation types. Therefore, the verb-ending paradigm considered in the present analysis comprises six units, namely: *-o, -s, -ø, -mos, -is, -n.*

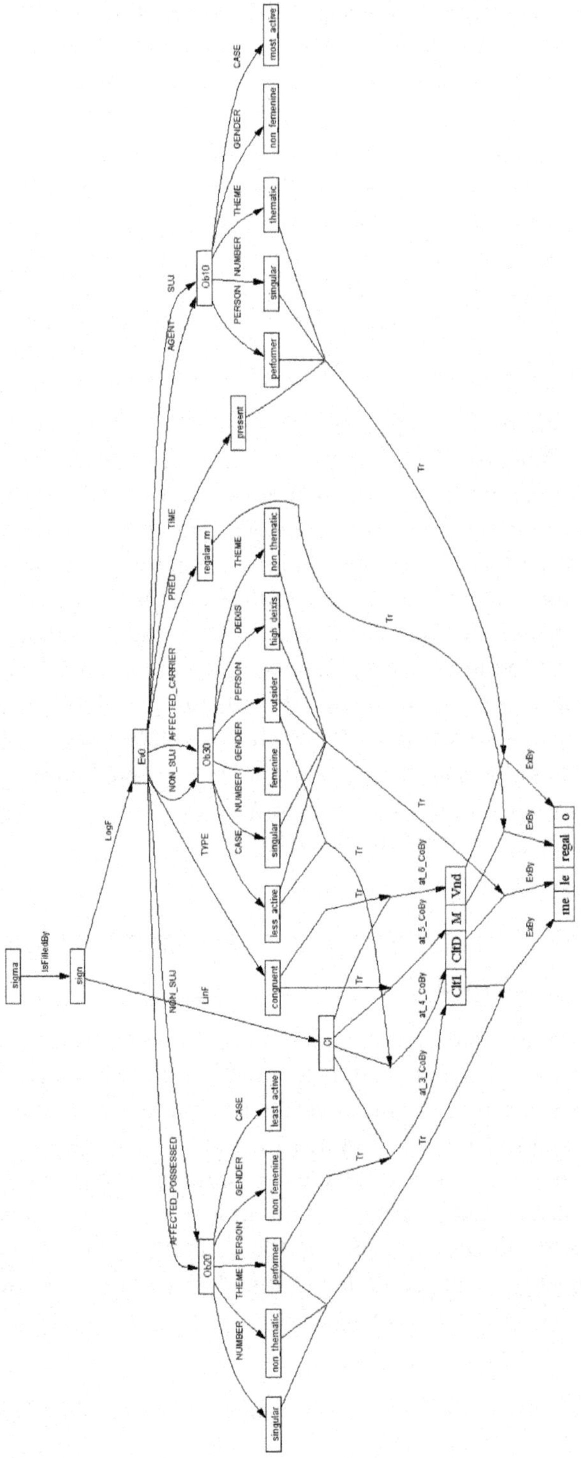

Figure 6.1: Network account of *me le regalo* in terms of Castel (2012, p. 172).

6.3.1 Relationships within and between the Semantic and Morphemic Strata

The morphemic units for the systems of clitics and verb endings are linked to common semantic categories. Consider example (2), in which a man named Porta talks to a woman named Bárbara:

(2)   Porta quería saber si tenía algún amante, pero Bárbara no picó […]
      – Sólo contigo – se burló ella.
      – No me has contestado.
      – No tengo por qué darte explicaciones.
      – Yo no *te las pido* ('I do not ask you for them'). (CREA, *Matar para vivir*)

The clitics (*te*, *las*) and the verb ending (*-o*) in example (2) realize various semantic features (cf. E. García, 1975; Mendikoetxea, 1999; Castel, 2012). First, *-o* refers to the male 'speaker', *te* refers to the female 'hearer', and *las* alludes to *explicaciones* ('explanations') – namely, another participant not directly involved in the conversation (i.e., 'other'). Second, *te* and *-o* realize the feature 'singular', whereas *las* realizes the feature 'plural'. Third, *te* and *las* express the feature 'feminine', but *-o* points to a 'non-feminine' entity. Fourth, the participants realized by the clitics and the verb ending in the sentence have different degrees of activity, ranging from 'most active' (*-o*, in the nominative case) to 'less active' (*te*, in the dative case) to 'least active' (*las*, in the accusative case). Also, the clitic *las* has a greater deictic load than *te* and *-o* – unlike the latter, the deixis of *las* cannot be established by the mere recognition of who is speaking to whom. Thus, *las* may be said to expound the feature 'high deixis'. Finally, as proposed by E. García (1975), verb endings tend to bear a greater thematic focus than clitics. In this case, *-o* is 'thematic', while *te* and *-o* are 'non-thematic'.[5]

In a specific context, a given pronominal clitic or verb ending realizes a constellation of semantic features pertaining to six categories: THEMATIC STATUS, NUMBER, GENDER, PERSON, DEIXIS, and CASE (cf. E. García, 1975). Each of these categories comprises either two or three semantic features. Yet, a given clitic or verb ending used in a specific context will realize only one of the features included in each system, as described further below. Thus, in the RNT framework, the basic semantic relationships for Spanish pronominal clitics and verb endings can be represented with downward unordered OR nodes, as shown in Figure 6.2.

Not every morphemic unit of the clitic and verb-ending systems can realize every semantic feature given above. Tables 6.1–6.5, adapted from Castel (2012, p. 165), list which semantic features clitics and verb endings necessarily or optionally express.

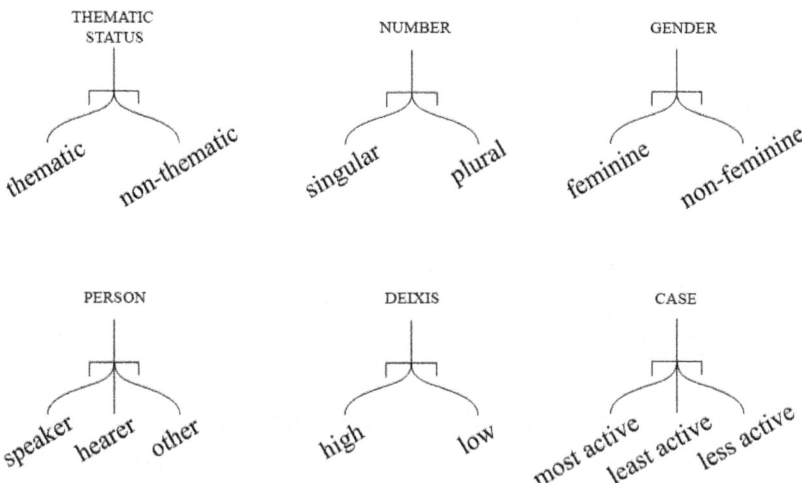

Figure 6.2: Semantic systems involved in Spanish pronominal clitics and verb endings.

Table 6.1: Semantic features of PERSON and THEMATIC STATUS realized by Spanish clitics and verb endings (adapted from Castel, 2012)

		THEMATIC STATUS	
		'thematic'	'non-thematic'
PERSON	'speaker'	*-o, -mos*	*me, nos*
	'hearer'	*-s, -is*	*te, os*
	'other'	*-ø, -n*	*le(s), lo(s), la(s)*
		se	

Table 6.2: Semantic features of PERSON and NUMBER realized by Spanish clitics and verb endings (adapted from Castel, 2012)

		NUMBER	
		'singular'	'plural'
PERSON	'speaker'	*-o, me*	*-mos, nos*
	'hearer'	*-s, te*	*-is, os*
	'other'	*-ø, le, lo, la*	*-n, les, los, las*
		se	

Table 6.3: Semantic features of PERSON and GENDER realized by Spanish clitics and verb endings (adapted from Castel, 2012)

		GENDER	
		'feminine'	'non-feminine'
PERSON	'other'	*la, las*	*lo, los*
		-ø,-n, se, le, les	
	'speaker'	*-o, me, -mos, nos*	
	'hearer'	*-s, te, -is, os*	

Table 6.4: Semantic features of PERSON and DEIXIS realized by Spanish clitics and verb endings (adapted from Castel, 2012)

		DEIXIS	
		'high deixis'	'low deixis'
PERSON	'speaker'		
	'hearer'		
	'other'	*-ø, -n, le(s), lo(s), la(s)*	*se*

Table 6.5: Semantic features of PERSON and CASE realized by Spanish clitics and verb endings (adapted from Castel, 2012)[6]

		CASE		
		'most active'	'less active'	'least active'
PERSON	'other'		*le(s)*	*lo(s), la(s)*
		-ø, -n, se		
	'speaker'	*-o, -mos, me, nos*		
	'hearer'	*-s, -is, te, os*		

Tables 6.1–6.5 make explicit a functional distinction between the *meanings* some forms necessarily express in every context and the *messages* some of them may implicitly convey in a specific context. The distinction between meaning and message, as captured by E. García (1975, 2009), is motivated for this particular part of Spanish grammar and may thus be considered an emergent property relevant to the description of Spanish pronominal clitics and verb endings in particular. The contrast is illustrated in example (3), where the feature 'feminine' is a meaning of the clitic *la* (and *las*) in any context, but it is an implicit message conveyed by the clitic *le* in an example like (3) – notice that *le* does not explicitly convey gender, and may thus be used in reference to masculine or feminine referents in context.

> (3)   […] ella no lo quería recibir porque ella pensaba que yo le iba a pedir a cambio, alguna cosa una cosa mala, pues […] Entonces le di el reloj y *le di la carta* ('I gave it to her'). (CREA, CSHC-87 Entrevista 60)

Similarly, the ending *-o* always realizes the meanings 'speaker', 'singular', and 'thematic'. Yet, depending on the context, it will also expound the implicit messages 'feminine' or 'non-feminine', on the one hand, and 'most active', 'less active', or 'least active', on the other. Consider example (4), uttered by a woman in reference to a man called Andrés:

> (4)   Si he de lanzarle un dardo a Andrés, que al menos valga la pena el hombre por el que *se lo lanzo* ('I throw it to him').
> – ¿Has pensado en el foso medieval como un símbolo de libertad? – le pregunto.
> – No. Pero estoy abierto a pensarlo, si me convences.
> – ¿Sabes, Javier, que a nosotras las mujeres nos han enseñado a temerle a la soledad? (CREA, *Antigua vida mía*)

In this case, the ending *-o* conveys the *messages* 'feminine' and 'most active'. The latter feature can only be inferred by virtue of the participant role structure implied by the process LANZ [THROW], which indicates that the obligatory participant ACTOR (some of whose semantic features are replicated by *-o*, in reference to the female speaker) will have a more active role than the obligatory participant BENEFICIARY (expounded by *se*, in reference to Andrés).

So far, we have seen that the Spanish clitic and verb-ending systems involve different types of connections between their semantic and morphemic representations. As shown in Figure 6.2, each semantic category is organized as a series of disjunctions between its relevant features. Also, whereas some of those features are necessarily evoked by a given clitic or verb ending as meanings, others can only be implied as messages. Finally, in a specific context of use, each clitic and verb ending realizes six semantic features simultaneously. All these varied connections are formally captured in Figure 6.3, where the thick lines represent the connections active in processing *se lo lanzo* (i.e., *se*, *lo*, and *-o*). While Figure 6.3 more comprehensively illustrates the possibilities for connections in the network, we offer as well Figure 6.4 for *se lo lanzo*, showing the active connections (thick lines) only to ease visualization. Non-active connections are omitted from following figures for the same reason.

The network in Figure 6.3 captures all the connections between the semantic and morphemic representations for each system, while Figure 6.4 focuses specifically on those activated for *se lo lanzo*. Each semantic category (e.g., THEMATIC STATUS, NUMBER) and feature (e.g., 'thematic',

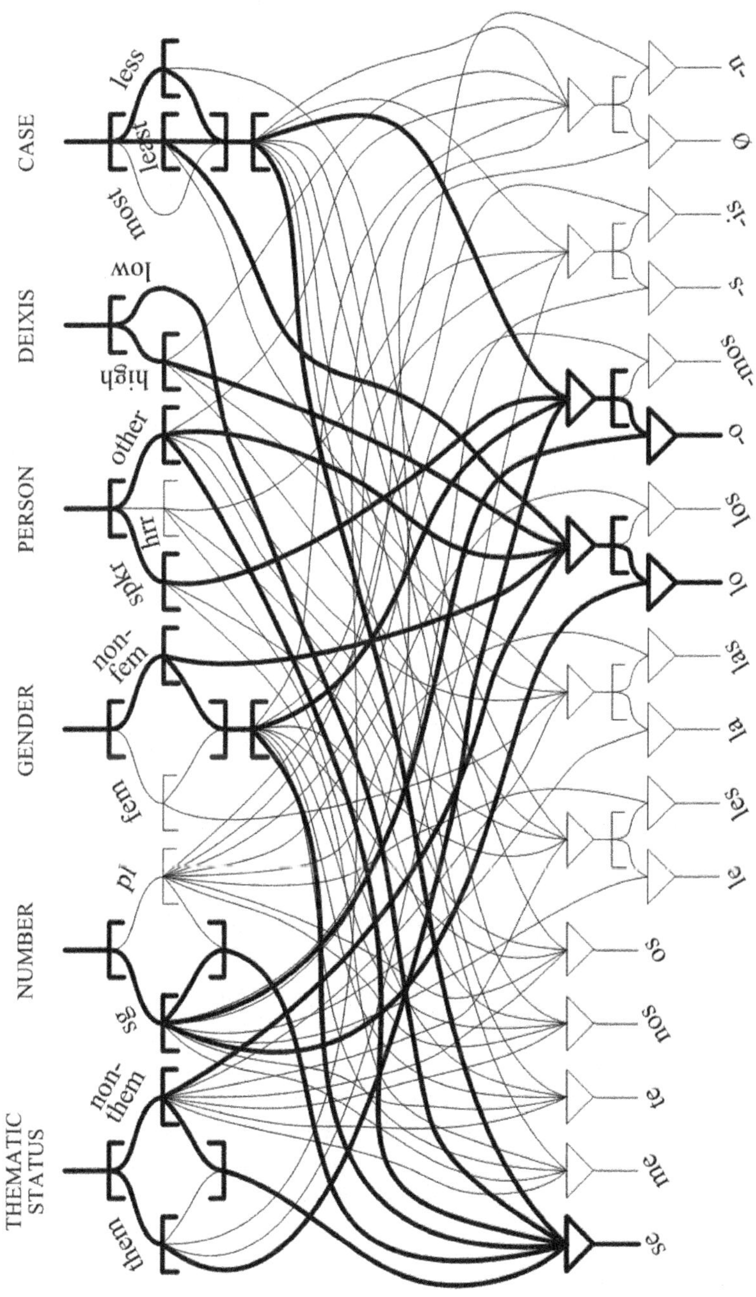

Figure 6.3: Semantic and morphemic representations of the Spanish pronominal clitic and verb-ending systems with active connections for *se lo lanzo* indicated.[7]

'non-thematic', 'singular', 'plural') is represented by a downward unordered OR node, indicating that they can be connected with multiple morphemic representations in both systems. Morphemic elements are represented by upward unordered AND nodes, since the semantic features they evoke or can evoke are activated simultaneously rather than sequentially. For example, the clitic *se* in *se lo lanzo* (example (4)) simultaneously activates the features 'thematic', 'singular', 'non-feminine', 'other', 'low deixis', and 'less active' (Figures 6.3 and 6.4). Each possible constellation of semantic features involves a specific pattern of connections leading to the activation of its corresponding morphemic realization.

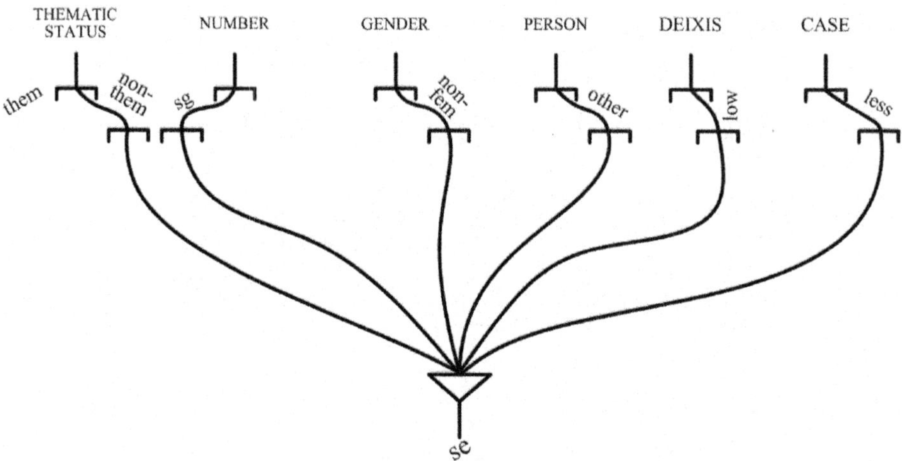

Figure 6.4: Semantic and morphemic representations of the Spanish pronominal clitic and verb-ending systems with only active connections for *se lo lanzo* indicated (cf. Figure 6.3).

Furthermore, this network formalizes the distinction between (explicit) meanings and (implicit) messages (Figures 6.3 and 6.4). Meanings are represented by downward unordered OR nodes stemming directly from their corresponding semantic category label. On the other hand, messages are represented by complex OR node structures in which an upward unordered OR node can be activated by either of its incoming lines so as to then activate a downward unordered OR node which will, in turn, send further activation to a specific clitic or verb ending. This relational distinction, which captures an emergent property of the systems at hand, is exemplified in Figure 6.5, with reference to NUMBER.

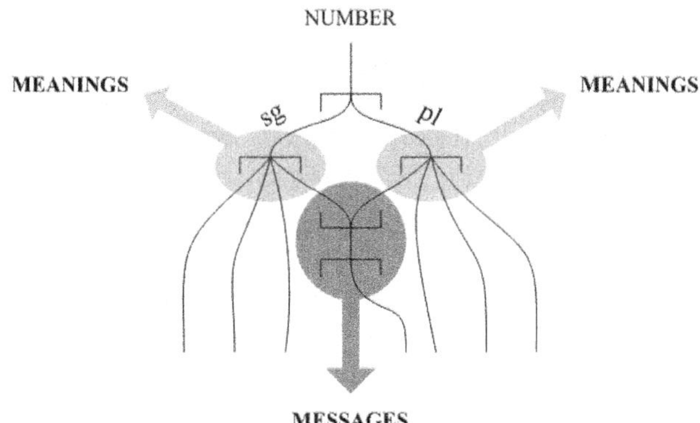

Figure 6.5: Relational distinction between meanings and messages. Light gray shows connections for meanings: features necessarily activated in the processing of a given clitic or verb ending, irrespective of context (e.g., 'singular' in *me*, 'plural' in *nos*). Dark gray shows connections for messages: features that may be exclusively implied by a given clitic or verb ending in a specific context of use (e.g., *se* may imply 'singular' or 'plural').

6.3.2 Integrating the Morphotactics with the Corresponding Sememes

The network in Figure 6.3 (like its simplified version in Figure 6.4) does not specify the morphotactic constraints of the Spanish clitic and verb-ending systems. Of course, it is not the case that any clitic can occur in any position. For example, the pseudo-sentence *lo se lanzo* violates the morphotactic restriction that *se* cannot occur after another clitic. If, as postulated within RNT, all linguistic information is relational, then morphotactic patterns and restrictions must also be characterized as networks of relationships among different nodes. The relational network in Figure 6.6 represents the main connections involved in the morphotactics of the Spanish clitic and verb-ending systems in relation to a specific example. Here again, the connections active in the processing of the sentence *se lo lanzo* are drawn with thicker lines.

Actually, Figure 6.6 presents a partial morphotactic network for the two systems. It includes ordering constraints for the indicative and subjunctive moods only, and it omits several other details.[8] Notwithstanding, it elegantly accounts for several key aspects of the two systems' morphotactics. The downward ordered AND node at the top of the figure indicates that (for the indicative and subjunctive moods) morphological representations are always activated in this sequence: (a) clitics, (b) verb stems, (c) characteristics, and (d) verb endings. In processing the sentence *se lo lanzo* (indicated by thick lines), the first downward ordered AND stemming from the connection for clitics shows that the form *se* is activated first and that the form *lo* is activated afterwards – the downward OR nodes represent other possible but presently inactive morphotactic patterns. The connection for verb stems leads to a downward unordered OR node which can then activate any verb stem – the network pictured includes only the stem *lanz* for illustration. The connection for characteristics leads to another downward unordered OR which presently results in the activation of ø. This means that in processing the sentence in question there is no morphemic form which on its own realizes the semantic features 'mood', 'tense', and 'aspect' (i.e., the verb's characteristics). Such values are all realized by the ending *-o*. Finally, the downward unordered OR for verb endings leads to the activation of *-o*. Note that all morphemic units in the network are represented by upward unordered OR nodes, indicating that one and the same morpheme may be activated by different connections – i.e., it may be activated in different structural positions.

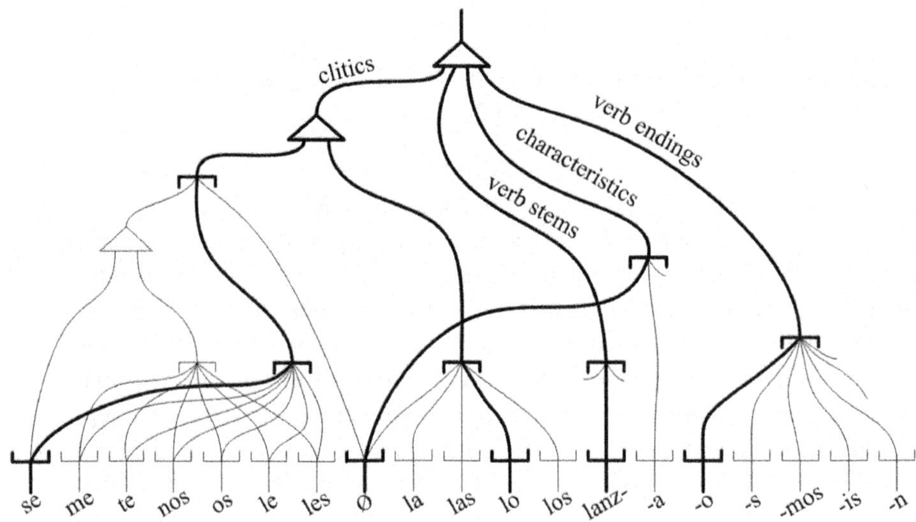

Figure 6.6: A morphotactic network for Spanish pronominal clitics and verb endings with active connections for *se lo lanzo* indicated.

Now, the networks in Figures 6.3 (simplified as Figure 6.4) and 6.6 do not operate separately; rather, activation flows through them at the same time in the processing of a given sentence. In this sense, Figure 6.7 illustrates the integration of both networks – though here only the semantic connections of the clitic *se* are included.

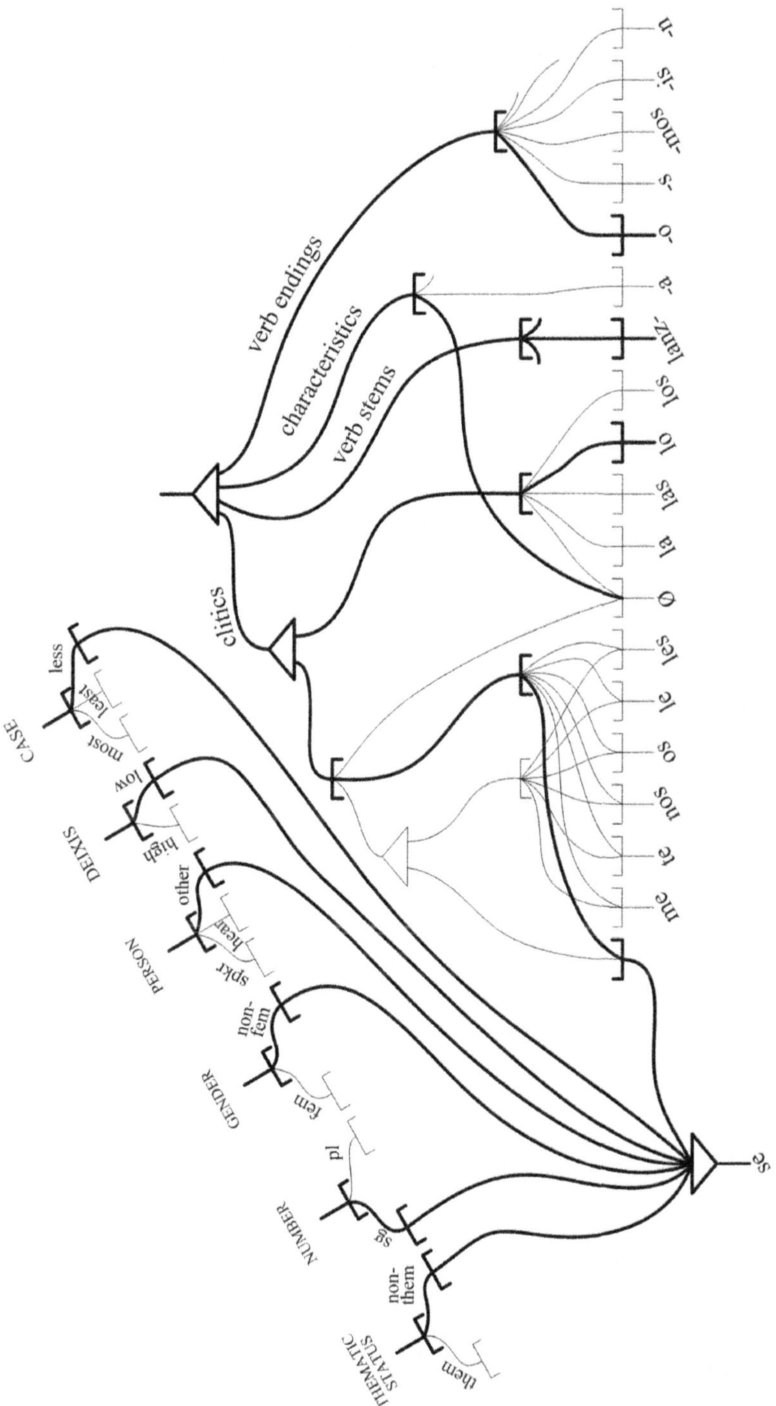

Figure 6.7: An integrative RNT model of clitic *se* in the context of *se lo lanzo*.[9]

6.4   Key Features of the Relational Network Analysis

The relational networks above have several distinctive features and overcome some of the descriptive limitations of the reticular approach presented in Castel (2012). First, the networks in Figures 6.3–6.7 are bidirectional in nature. As the abstract notation indicates, they can be traveled downwards (for production processes) and upwards (for comprehension processes), regardless of the orientation of the nodes involved. Hence, they constitute descriptions of the cognitive structures operative not only in the conveyance of meanings and the implication of messages by the speaker, but also in the interpretation of such semantic representations by the hearer.[10]

Second, the networks reflect the fact that the relationships within the clitic and verb-ending systems are not monolithic. Four distinct types of connections have been identified in different portions of the systems: (1) the relationships between a semantic category and its associated features are disjunctive (e.g., between GENDER and 'feminine' and 'non-feminine'), thus involving OR nodes; (2) whereas explicit, context-independent meanings involve simple downward OR nodes, implicit, context-dependent messages call for complex disjunctive relationships in which an upward OR node is then connected to a downward OR node; (3) the relationships representing morphotactic patterns are sequential conjunctions (e.g., the mother node in Figure 6.6, determining the serial order of 'clitics', 'verb stems', 'characteristics', and 'verb endings'), thus involving ordered AND nodes; and (4) the relationships established between a constellation of semantic features and the morphemic representation realizing it in a specific context of use are simultaneous conjunctions (e.g., each set of semantic activations converging in the upward unordered AND nodes appearing at the bottom of Figure 6.3, cf. Figure 6.4), thus involving unordered AND nodes.

Third, the networks formalize a connectionist account of morphotactics which does away with rules, transformations, displacement operations, and other constructs of questionable cognitive plausibility (Lamb, 1999). The present model characterizes the morphotactics of clitics and verb endings by virtue of connections and spreading activation traveling along those connections. Consequently, the semantic, morphotactic, and morphemic representations of both systems are processed by the same type of cognitive mechanism: flows of dynamic signals leading to the concerted activation of specific patterns of nodes. As regards the morphotactics, what determines the relative order of the representations in sentence processing is the specific pattern of sequential and disjunctive connections in the morphotactic network. In such a network, the activation of each ordered AND node triggers multiple obligatory sequential connections, whereas OR nodes lead to several paradigmatic options within the clitic and verb-ending systems.

Fourth, the networks lack nodes redundantly representing the same information. For instance, the fact that a given semantic feature (e.g., 'singular') is activated in the processing of different morphemic representations (e.g., *se*, *lo*, and *-o*) is modeled by the presence of multiple differential connections leading from the former to the latter. In other words, the realization of the same information by different units is represented via constellations of relationships specific to each of those units. If each morphemic representation were connected to its own (redundant) set of features in the semantic system, there would be no reason to postulate a distinction between the semantic, syntactic, and morphemic strata.

Lastly, the relational networks presented in this chapter – as well as any other relational network – include no symbols or static objects in their structure. In RNT terms, the individual's cognitive system consists only of relationships; thus, the relational network models presented for the Spanish clitic and verb-ending systems are purely connectionist.

6.5   Conclusion

Overall, this RNT analysis addresses some of the drawbacks found in Castel (2012) and provides an efficient account of Spanish clitics and verb endings in a unified description. Specifically, a formal distinction has been proposed among the varied types of relationships allowing for information processing in relevant systems. Level-specific differences in connectivity have been detected between: (a) semantic categories and features (downward OR nodes); (b) context-independent meanings and context-dependent messages (simple vs. complex OR node structures); (c) morphotactic patterns and morphemic representations (downward ordered AND nodes); and (d) semantic features and morphemic representations (upward unordered AND nodes).

The present model accounts for both production and comprehension processes, and offers a clearer discrimination among connection types. It is freed of *a priori* constructs unlikely to correspond to actual cognitive processes. RNT presupposes no rules or filled/empty slots in its conception of syntax, as it characterizes morphotactics via the same type of connectionist constructs used to account for other relationships. In this sense, rather than positing ontologically different mechanisms for semantics and the linguistic system (including syntax and morphology), a relational network approach characterizes all relevant relationships by means of connections and spreading activation through them. Finally, this approach avoids redundancy, considering that each feature is represented only once, where one and the same node may be activated in processing varied lexemic/morphemic representations, even within the same sentence. RNT seems to possess two advantages in this regard. On the one hand, it constitutes a more elegant account, as the same observational domain is characterized with greater representational economy. On the other hand, it seems more linguistically plausible. If each morphemic representation were actually connected to its own redundant representation in the semantic system, there would be no reason to postulate a separate and unified semantic system in the first place. The very idea of realization, a key concept in RNT, seeks to reflect two aspects of language structure: (1) the fact that one and the same constellation of semantic features may be expressed, at least partially, through different morphemic or syntactic units (diversification); and (2) the fact that different constellations of features may be expressed by the same morphemic or syntactic unit (neutralization).

More generally, our RNT treatment presents a crucial conceptual difference relative to the approach followed by Castel (2012) and other systemic-functional models positing an ontological distinction between meaning and form potentials, such that the mechanisms operating in different strata may depend on different cognitive organizations and operations. Moreover, in such accounts (e.g., Fawcett, 2011, 2013), instances of meaning and form are handled by modules different from those representing meaning and form potentials, respectively. On the contrary, RNT does not make such ontological distinctions, as linguistic instances are activated within the linguistic potentials. In other words, in an RNT account, an instance (of meaning or form) is nothing but the constellation of (potential) representations effectively active in a given context of use.

Furthermore, while different cognitive theories about language are rooted in different conceptions of the human mind, the RNT model has as its goal operational, developmental, and neurological plausibility. In this sense, it strives to be more realistic about actual human linguistic processing, and differs, for example, from the Communicative Mind Model, which assumes that a model's cognitive plausibility depends on whether its mechanisms can be emulated by a computer:

> Indeed, it is probably time for linguists to reconsider our traditional assumptions about what makes a model 'elegant' [...] [I]t may be that we should not condemn as 'inelegant' or 'uneconomical' rules that the conscious human mind finds somewhat difficult to implement, but which can be performed by a computer in a moment – and also, some might wish to add, whose analogues in the human brain can similarly be performed in a trice and, moreover, without requiring conscious attention. (Fawcett, 2003, p.13)

Unlike the Communicative Mind Model, RNT posits a connectionist, parallel-distributed conception of mental processes, in line with current trends in cognitive science (see Gazzaniga, 2009).

However, the present account is not without limitations of its own. Crucially, the networks proposed do not handle all possible clitic and verb-ending patterns. It would be interesting to expand this description to include gerundial and imperative forms, for example. Also, further analyses could be conducted to develop networks capable of handling textual phenomena beyond the production of individual sentences (e.g., the establishment of cohesive ties between clitics and noun phrases as multi-sentential texts unfold in real time). Moreover, theoretical debates may ensue regarding how the data have been handled (see, e.g., Note 4), though RNT assumptions and notational conventions allow for alternative accounts of the linguistic facts. While these issues could be addressed in future research, our work demonstrates that a relational network approach can afford a plausible, integrative description of the functional organization of Spanish pronominal clitics and verb endings.

Notes

1. However, the relationships between clitics and verb endings to each of these semantic categories are not exactly the same.
2. The values of MOOD, TENSE, and ASPECT in verbs may be expressed by separate morphemes.
3. In its terminology, the description we set forth follows E. García's (1975, 2009) functional treatment of Spanish clitics. Note, however, that despite broad architectural commonalities, the stratal distinctions assumed by her model do not exactly mirror the ones adduced here (see Chapter 1, Figure 1.2).
4. The spurious *se* is an interesting aspect of Spanish grammar. Several authors (e.g., Aissen & Rivas, 1975; Fernández Soriano, 1999) have advanced conflicting views on the nature of the spurious *se* (i.e., the systematic use of *se lo* instead of the non-occurring cluster **le lo*). The present model accounts for such a cluster at the morphotactic level (Figure 6.6), with additional restrictions coming from the semantic stratum (Figure 6.7), a solution consistent with the framework advanced by E. García (1975, 2009). Thus, in our analysis the impossibility of processing the cluster **le lo* follows from the same principles underlying the acceptable use of other clitics, whether in isolation or in clusters, as E. García describes:

   > *se lo* is easier to process than *le lo*, for the diversification of the references allows the two 3rd ps participants to be identified in the cognitively most economic order, i.e. first the Central, and then the Peripheral participant [...] It is neither conventional use nor morpho-phonological dissimilation that makes **le lo* yield to *se lo*: *se lo* is preferable to *le lo* for essentially the same reasons that *me presentaste a ella* is preferable to *me le presentaste* in conveying 'You introduced me to her'. (2009, p. 142)

   Yet, there are alternative conceptions of the phenomenon. For example, Bonet (1995) and Harris (1996) propose that this restriction reflects morpho-phonotactic processes, whereas Menn & MacWhinney (1984), Fernández Soriano (1999), and Sharp (2005) conceive of the spurious *se* as an instance of arbitrary morpho-phonological dissimilation. Although this chapter does not seek to contrast opposing theoretical perspectives, note that RNT allows the modeling of divergent conceptions of the same phenomenon.

5. By choosing a particular wording, the speaker ascribes different degrees of interest to the entities involved in the event he or she is construing. The notion of thematic status refers here to how focal a participant is for the process at hand. By realizing features within the systems of PERSON and NUMBER, verb endings denote the participant from whose perspective the event is seen. This privileged position renders such a participant thematic. As in Table 6.1, all verb endings stand in paradigmatic opposition to clitics other than *se*. Thus, the referents of such clitics are non-focal, or non-thematic. The thematic status of *se* must be contextually inferred (for details, see E. García, 1975, 2009). For further details regarding why more than one element may bear thematic status in the Spanish clause, see Gil & García (2010) and A. García & Gil (2011).

6. For justification of the tripartite classification of case, see E. García (1975, 2009).

7. Note that some of the semantic categories shown in the figure (e.g., NUMBER, GENDER) interact with other systems (e.g., the nominal system at large). However, additional connections with those systems are omitted to avoid (over)cluttering. Only connections relevant to pronominal clitics and verb endings are depicted.

8. The figure also omits the connections involved in the processing of clitics and verb endings in the imperative mood and in infinitival and gerundial forms, all of which require clitics to function as suffixes. Neither does the network include the connections needed to account for the processing of patterns like *me le/les (lanzo), te le/ les (lanzas), os le/les (lanzáis)* and *nos le/les (lanzamos)*, in which the direct object and the subject are co-referential (e.g., 'I throw myself to him'). Also, notice that the model presented here refers only to pronominal clitics. Clitics used in impersonal constructions fall outside the scope of this chapter.

9. Note that the AND node for *se* is equivalent to an alternative representation using a 1-3-2 three-way diamond (as in Chapter 2, Figure 2.7b) with an upward OR node on the NW (side 1).

10. Since the alternative narrow notation decomposes bidirectional nodes into pairs of unidirectional nodes running in opposite directions, it would make bidirectionality more obvious. However, abstract notation is presented here for clearer diagramming (see Chapter 2, section 2.4).

7 An RNT Approach to Participants in English Texts

7.1 Venturing into Discourse

In his classic 1968 article on contrastive text analysis, Gleason observed: '[a] fully acceptable sentence impresses a native speaker as fundamentally different from a randomly selected sequence of words […] An acceptable longer discourse also differs fundamentally from a randomly selected series of sentences' (pp. 39–40). One such difference concerns the possibility to identify the participants realized by pronouns. In English, names and an indefinitely large number of noun phrases (NPs) can be used for participants, but there are only four third-person personal pronouns. While the potential for ambiguity is unlimited, reference in discourse is typically understood by competent language users, suggesting that there are patterns of information that allow unambiguous identification of a pronoun's antecedent.

In his discussion, Gleason (1968, p. 41) listed five features that distinguish an acceptable piece of discourse (e.g., a short story, a newspaper article) from an arbitrary series of sentences, clauses, or phrases:

(1) The chain of events which forms the back-bone of a narrative and whose structure controls its overall organization.

(2) The identification of the participants and the indication of their roles in the several events.

(3) The detailing of the attendant circumstances and the indication of the scope of their application. The setting in time is the most frequently specified.

(4) The relation of the observers to the unfolding narrative. 'Observer' is to be taken as including both the narrator and the audience, since a narrative is a device to make the audience in some way observers. Halliday's work (especially in 1967) on theme and rheme, and given and new in English, is a germinal contribution on one aspect of this.

(5) Certain dimensions of the text as text – register, style, and level of redundancy among them. These lie not within the domain of linguistics as such, but astride the boundaries, so that linguists must be joined by others in attacking them.

Features (1) and (3) are extensively covered for Polish texts in Bogdan & Sullivan (2009). This chapter focuses on feature (2). We consider patterns of NP and pronoun usage in English texts by reference to a sample literary passage, and model their interpretive constraints in RNT terms. In doing so, we offer an illustration of how an RNT description works at the discourse level.

7.2   Previous Research: Insights and Gaps

While our treatment of participants in discourse finds its seminal antecedents in the work of Gleason (1968), valuable contributions had been made before him. Some of them emerged from the linguistic efforts of faith-based organizations, whose mission work included the study of diverse, lesser known languages from around the world. In addition to the work supported by the Hartford Seminary Foundation (www.hartsem.edu), of which Gleason was a member, discourse work has been supported by the American Bible Society (ABS, www.americanbible.org) and the Summer Institute of Linguistics, now SIL International (www.sil.org). For example, ABS published the contemporary English version of the Bible, on the basis of a study of speech patterns. Practical and theoretical work on discourse structure has been published by many SIL members, from Kenneth Pike, Evelyn Pike, Eunice Pike, and Robert Longacre, to Ilah Fleming and Shin Ja J. Hwang, to mention a few. In the case of English discourse, groundbreaking contributions came from the hands of systemic-functional linguists like Michael Halliday, Ruqaiya Hasan, Peter Fries, and Michael Cummings. With such eminent scholars laying fertile ground early on, it is difficult to understand why the discourse structure (or semology) of English still proves an elusive phenomenon.

A number of reasons come to mind. First, the ABS and SIL have not been primarily interested in English. Second, the main thrust of their studies is aimed at practical problems. Typically, in the field, their researchers start by analyzing an undescribed language and providing a system of writing for it. They then develop a grammar, a dictionary, and a translation of the Bible, and establish a literacy project. Against these goals, theoretical work takes a back seat (but see Longacre, 1976). Third, systemic-functional linguists have provided a tremendous body of work on English, but it is connected with large-scale systems (text cohesion, information management, communication of meaning, classification of syntactic structures and how they are used, etc.), and their communicative functions. More fine-grained discourse-level features, like the structural management of pronouns, though an important part of text cohesion, have not been the focus of this tradition.[1]

Finally, most linguists working on English over the past 55 years have been trained in the generative framework, which has left apparently indelible marks on their theoretical approach: in a nutshell, language is framed as syntax, and syntax is concerned only with single sentences. Thus, the bulk of linguistic research and publications has long been aimed at exploring details of different generative models. With regard to pronouns, Chomsky (1957) first had an optional transformation that replaced most NPs on a random basis. That was clearly unworkable, and his foundational model, Standard Theory, thus included the A-over-A principle, which was supposed to constrain the identification of a pronoun's antecedent. Eventually, A-over-A developed into the Subjacency principle, which went through more than one incarnation but still made wrong predictions (see Sullivan, 1992). Notwithstanding, some former generative linguists have been drawn into looking at discourse. Langacker (2011), for instance, looks at discourse context to inform the relation of meaning to form. Yet, context is still mostly operationalized at the sentential level.

Thus, while there has certainly been relevant and useful work in the field, a comprehensive discourse-level approach to topics like participant reference is still lacking. Here, relying on RNT, we tie together semantic, sememic, and syntactic aspects of NPs and pronouns in discourse[2] to account for participant usage in an example English narrative text.

7.3   Participant Tracking: A Problem and an Algorithm

Keeping track of multiple participants in narrative discourse does not challenge the reader in a well written text. How is this achieved, considering that there are four third-person personal pronouns in English as against several names and potentially thousands of NPs that could be applied to each participant in a narrative? This question concerns a small but well-contained and important part of what Halliday (2002, p. 8 *et passim*) calls lexical or lexicogrammatical cohesion.[3] As Gleason and other scholars observed, the first mention of a participant in an English text is typically done through a noun, but further references to the same participant are frequently made through a pronoun.[4] As the distance from the first mention increases, there is an increasing likelihood of a noun being used. Below we aim to establish some key factors that motivate the appearance of pronouns and nouns in reference to a previously mentioned participant.

Consider a single male participant. That individual may have several names, and any of them can be used unambiguously to identify him. Many common nouns and an indefinitely large number of descriptive NPs can also be used unambiguously. However, only a few personal pronouns can be used. First- and second-person pronouns present no difficulty since their antecedents are clear, so we ignore them. The third-person personal pronouns of English and their loose communicative functions are given in Table 7.1. The problem is: how do third-personal pronouns unambiguously denote the proper referent?

Table 7.1: Third-person personal pronouns in English and their communicative uses

PRONOUN	MEANING AND FUNCTIONS
they	any plural (generic pronoun in colloquial American English)
it	general inanimate (or personal insult)
she	general female (or special 'feminine' usages)
he	general male (or special 'masculine' usages)

We now describe an algorithm that can elucidate how participants are encoded for proper clarity. The algorithm, presented as an ordered list of rules of thumb, is given in Table 7.2.[5] There are two signals relevant to the discourse units of linguistic paragraphs referenced here and in the analysis: internal cohesion and boundary signals (see section 7.4.2). The rules given are based on the observation that the noun-pronoun alternation contributes not only to paragraph-internal cohesion but at times signals the transition to a new paragraph.

Table 7.2: An algorithm for encoding participant reference

(a)	zero in English is limited to (1) 'absolute' constructions (gerundives, participials, infinitives) or (2) ellipsis, if the information load (chance of error) is negligible;
(b)	a participant appears in a text first as (1) a noun, thereafter as (2) a pronoun, except:
(c)	a new thematic participant must be established with a noun, usually an agentive subject;
(d)	identifiers (appositives or predicate nominatives) must be nouns;
(e)	nouns may be used (1) to create emphasis, (2) to introduce new information, or (3) to avoid confusion or ambiguity;
(f)	with a new topic (usually a new paragraph but perhaps in a pivot[6] sentence) return to (b).

Note that the algorithm can only present tendencies or typical scenarios because of the choices authors have. That is, there are many ways of providing identifiers (d), and (e) notes possibilities for using nouns that are particularly sensitive to discretionary considerations. Editors as well as authors spend a fair amount of time on ensuring clarity (e3), and the latter can decide when they want to provide new information (e2) or create emphasis (e1).

We also suggest two principles for decoding pronominal participant reference: the first choice for pronoun reference is the current thematic participant; the second choice is the nearest noun of appropriate gender. Exclusive of problems with zero (e.g., dangling participles), pronominal ambiguities appear most often where the pronoun is nearer to a non-thematic participant noun than to the thematic participant noun. Below we track these aspects in a specific narrative passage as illustration.

7.4   The Discourse

7.4.1 The Text

The excerpted text occurs early in the novel *Alive!* by Loren D. Estleman (2013). Estleman is a newspaper editor with over 60 novels, collections, and a couple of historical studies and novelizations to his credit. His specialties are hard-boiled detective novels about Amos Walker, in contemporary Detroit, and Deputy Marshal Page Murdock, on the post-Civil War frontier. *Alive!* is third in a series featuring Valentino, a film detective working for the UCLA film preservation program. The excerpt given in (1) is restricted almost entirely to narrative, ignoring all dialogue except for two direct quotations having zero attribution, though there is no question about who speaks. We distinguish the individual participants by the following typographic conventions: all participants, as NPs or pronouns, are in bold; while Valentino appears in regular font style, Ruth is italicized, Broadhead is in small caps, and Fanta is underlined (**Valentino**, ***Ruth***, **Broadhead**, and **<u>Fanta</u>**). Linguistic paragraphs (see below) are numbered.

> (1) Excerpt from *Alive!* with text restricted to main narrative (exclusive of dialogue, exceptions noted).
>
> *pp. 24–25 ...*
>
> Para 1:   ... ***Ruth*** pounced on **him** the moment **he** left the elevator. ***She*** rarely stirred from ***her*** station inside the doughnut-shaped desk where ***she*** served sentry, but ***she*** was a predatory old ***bird*** who swooped down with the power of ***her*** eyes. They were kohl-rimmed, as black as ***her*** hair, and equally inflexible. Age was ***her*** archenemy. ***She*** would attack every wrinkle and gray strand as soon as it surfaced, using all the weapons in ***her*** arsenal. **Broadhead** had speculated there were more poisons on ***her*** dressing table than in all the Japanese gardeners' sheds in Beverly Hills. "I'd be as disinclined to visit one as the other." But for all **his** shudders **he** was the only **man** on campus ***she*** couldn't intimidate.
>
> 'You had a call.'
> **Valentino** never knew from the burnished-steel tone of ***her*** voice if ***she*** thought **he** was at fault for not being there when a call came in or for the call having been made at all. ***Ruth*** was efficient and well-nigh indispensable, but ***she*** was one of those in favor of demolishing the building and eliminating the film program altogether as a frivolous waste of money and young minds. ***She*** tore a pink sheet off ***her*** pad and thrust it at **him**.
>
> [half a page of dialogue]

Para 2:   '*She*'s in there.'
She made the pronoun sound like a vile epithet. **He** had no doubt who ***she*** was.
Ever since **Fanta** had breezed into their lives, ***Ruth*** had behaved like the old herd *leader*, determined to resist challenge from a younger **rival**. The fact that ***Ruth*** had no romantic designs on **Broadhead** didn't enter into it. In *her* world, women typed letters and answered telephones and ran things from behind the camouflage of indentured servitude. The presence of any other **female** in the old power plant was a threat to *her* authority.

Para 3:   … [Then] **Fanta** swept out of **Broadhead**'s office …

pp. 26–28

[two pages of dialogue, and a descriptive passage without third-person interplay, but Ruth and Fanta are the basic speakers, with minor input from Broadhead, and Valentino simply observes]

Para 4:   **Fanta** bent down, gave ***Ruth***'s laminated cheek a pat, and whirled on out. The elevator doors opened at **her** touch. **Valentino** stared at the *secretary*, fascinated despite **his** horror. But ***Ruth***'s expression was as unreadable as a bisque-headed doll's. **He** fled to sanctuary.

7.4.2 A Word on Paragraphing

Gleason (personal communication) also considered that there are structural levels within the semotactics that might be called paragraphs, but he was quick to point out that he was referring to linguistic paragraphs, not to editorial paragraphs. The two differ as much as a letter of the alphabet differs from a phononection. For example, a standard contemporary editorial paragraph is indicated in a dialogue whenever a new speaker takes a turn. For our purposes, however, we must look to discourse-internal signals of paragraphing.

Internal cohesion in the analyzed excerpt shows up in two places: one formal (linguistic) and one conceptual (supralinguistic). The conceptual part is sometimes in the topic of the paragraph or in the scene, which can be spatial or temporal. That is, the paragraph in question is a self-contained part of the tale, or a part of the tale that takes place in a specified place at a specified time in the narrative. None of these parts of the discourse is sharply defined, any more than portions of cognition are. Yet they cohere. With respect to the role of nouns and pronouns in narrative structure, the formal part of internal cohesion is in participant identification, and that sometimes plays a role in signaling that the author has shifted to a new paragraph.

7.4.3 The Text Rendered According to Participant Mention

Below we render the excerpt in section 7.4.1 according to participant mention. To set up the analysis, we focus on participant realization ordered by linguistic paragraph, sentence, and clause. Note that preceding text (a single paragraph with a single participant) follows Valentino's path into the building and up to the offices, all part of his return to work; the paragraph continues as paragraph 1, with additional participants Ruth, Broadhead, and Fanta joining:

(2) Excerpt from *Alive!* with text rendered according to participant mention by paragraph, sentence and clause.

pp. 24–25

Para 1

1 a **_Ruth_** pounced on **him**
  b the moment **he** left the elevator.

2 a **_She_** rarely stirred from **_her_** station inside the doughnut-shaped desk
  b where **_she_** served sentry,
  c but **_she_** was a predatory old **_bird_**
  d who swooped down with the power of **_her_** eyes.

3 They were kohl-rimmed, as black as **_her_** hair, and equally inflexible.

4 Age was **_her_** archenemy.

5 a **_She_** would attack every wrinkle and gray strand as soon as it surfaced,
  b using all the weapons in **_her_** arsenal.

6 **Broadhead** had speculated there were more poisons on **_her_** dressing table than …

7 But for all **his** shudders **he** was the only **man** on campus **_she_** couldn't intimidate.

8 'You had a call.'

9 a **Valentino** never knew from the burnished-steel tone of **_her_** voice
  b if **_she_** thought
  c **he** was at fault for not being there …

10 a **_Ruth_** was efficient and well-nigh indispensable,
  b but **_she_** was one of those in favor of demolishing the building …

11 **_She_** tore a pink sheet off **_her_** pad and thrust it at **him**.
[half a page of dialogue, Ruth does most of the talking.]

Para 2

12 '**_She_**'s in there.'

13 **_She_** made the pronoun sound like a vile epithet.

14 **He** had no doubt who **_she_** was.

15 a Ever since **<u>Fanta</u>** had breezed into their lives,

    b   **Ruth** had behaved like the old herd *leader*,

    c   determined to resist challenge from a younger **rival**.

16   The fact that **Ruth** had no romantic designs on Broadhead didn't enter into it.

17   In *her* world, women typed letters …

18   The presence of any other **female** in the old power plant was a threat to *her* authority.

Para 3

19   [Then] **Fanta** swept out of Broadhead's office …

pp. 26–28

[two pages of dialogue, and a descriptive passage without third-person interplay, but Ruth and Fanta are the basic speakers, with minor input from Broadhead, and Valentino simply observes]

Para 4

20   **Fanta** bent down, gave **Ruth**'s laminated cheek a pat, and whirled on out.

21   The elevator doors opened at **her** touch.

22   **Valentino** stared at the *secretary*, fascinated despite **his** horror.

23   But **Ruth**'s expression was as unreadable as a bisque-headed doll's.

24   **He** fled to sanctuary.

Table 7.3 presents the participant mentions together with their justification according to the algorithm presented in Table 7.2.

Table 7.3: The participant mentions analyzed according to the algorithm

¶	Sentence and clause	Participants				Justification from Table 7.2
		Ruth	*Valentino*	*Broadhead*	*Fanta*	
1	1a	Ruth				b1
			him			b2
	b		he			b2
	2a	she				b2
		her				b2
	b	she				b2
	c	she				b2
		bird				e2
	d	her				b2
	3	her				b2
	4	her				b2
	5a	she				b2
	b	Ø				a1

¶	SENTENCE AND CLAUSE	PARTICIPANTS				JUSTIFICATION FROM TABLE 7.2
		Ruth	*Valentino*	*Broadhead*	*Fanta*	
		her				b2
	6			Broadhead		b1
		her				b2
	7			his		b2
				he		b2
				man		d
		she				b2
	8	Ø				a2
	9a		Valentino			c
		her				b2
	b	she				b2
	c		he			b2
	10a	Ruth				c
	b	she				b2
	11	she				b2
		her				b2
			him			b2
2	12	Ø				a2
					she	e2
	13	she				b2
	14		he			b2
					she	e1
	15a				Fanta	b1
	b	Ruth				c
		leader				e2
	c	Ø				a2
					rival	e2
	16	Ruth				e1, e3
				Broadhead		b1
	17	her				b2
	18	her				b2
3	19				Fanta	b1, c
				Broadhead		b1
4	20				Fanta	b1, c
		Ruth				b1
	21				her	b2
	22		Valentino			b1, c
		secretary				e1
			Ø			a1
			his			d
	23	Ruth				e1, e3
	24		he			b2

7.4.4 Commentary on the Analysis

This narrative is easy enough to follow but a bit more difficult to categorize clearly with respect to justification because of its discontinuous nature: the narrative is interrupted several times by dialogue. Though the dialogue is important relative to the nature of and relationships among the participants, we ignore it to foreground noun-pronoun alternation through the flow of narrative. Let us look at that narrative, one paragraph at a time.

The excerpt omits the beginning of Paragraph 1, a lengthy narrative section focused solely on Valentino's progress from his car through the walkways and stairways to his office in the old power plant building at UCLA. There is a good bit of description of the surroundings but no other character for him to interact with. The first such opportunity arises when he enters the office and is confronted by Ruth, where our excerpt picks up. As indicated in Table 7.3, Ruth immediately becomes the thematic participant. All occurrences of *she/her* in sentences 1–9 refer unambiguously to Ruth. This is, of course, almost trivial, given the lack of any other female character in this paragraph. Yet, it does show that the chain of pronominal referents corresponding to a single participant can be quite long. Distance alone does not seem to evoke the repetition of name or NP. The same observation holds for the *him/he* in reference to Valentino in sentence 1, which carries back to the preceding text.

In sentence 2c we have a classifying clause that assigns Ruth to the category *bird*. This provides us with an image on which we can build our picture of this character. Sentences 6–7 provide a flashback on Valentino's faculty colleague Broadhead, providing insight into his character as well as Ruth's. The flashback is marked by a pluperfect tense that provides a temporal shift, and Broadhead becomes the thematic participant. Moreover, his strength of character is emphasized by the use of a (nominal) identifier: he is not just a member of the set of men on campus unintimidated by Ruth, but the only one. His moral fiber makes him superior not only to her, but also to Valentino, the Ruth-fearing protagonist.

There is a case of ellipsis in sentence 8. The chance of error here is zero, both because of the setting (only two characters, one providing the narrative point of view), and because of the action described later, in sentence 11, where Ruth passes Valentino the telephone message. Valentino becomes the thematic participant in 9a and Ruth replaces him in that discourse role in 10a.

Considering that all third-person pronouns refer to the current thematic participant, in the event of potential ambiguity, and that in the absence of thematic status and potential ambiguity, reference is to the nearest name or noun of appropriate gender, to this point, that generalization holds through for 22 clauses in 11 sentences.

Paragraph 2 opens in sentence 12 with another case of ellipsis with zero chance of error, establishing Ruth as the thematic participant in this paragraph.[7] Sentence 13 then has a pronoun that refers to the ellipsis. Because of the topic shift and Estleman's generally careful alignment of topical-temporal-spatial shifts and paragraph structure, we do not connect this section of the narrative with paragraph 1.

In sentence 12 we have an interesting pronominal usage. Ruth's statement in that sentence should have the name of the person in Broadhead's office. The deliberate use of a pronoun when a name is appropriate is usually felt to be insulting. Estleman characterizes the pronoun as 'a vile epithet', rendering the intent unmistakable. In sentence 14, Estleman doubles down, repeating the insulting usage for emphasis. These are cases when our algorithm predicts noun usages, but the insulting intent supersedes in a reasonable case of author's choice.

In sentences 15–16 we have another descriptive insert, providing a bit more history on the two women. Four nouns appear in five tokens in rapid succession: *Fanta, Ruth, leader, rival*, and once again *Ruth*. All participants are female, so the need to keep them correctly attributed is clear. *Fanta* in sentence 15 is her first non-insulting appearance in the paragraph, making the noun appropriate. We do not claim thematic participant status for any of the four nouns, because the paragraph concerns all of them and describes their relations. *Leader* and *rival*, also in sentence 15, are assigned to e2, supplying additional information in the form of category characteristics. *Ruth* in sentence 16 is emphatic (e1) and disambiguating (e3).

Paragraph 3 has only one narrative sentence (19). It introduces an extended dialogue in which Valentino does not take part. We witness it through his eyes and ears. There is no ambiguity to account for. The narrative portion is remarkable only for the re-entry of Fanta and Broadhead as names the first time these participants appear in the new paragraph. There is no thematic participant established, as the conversation is back-and-forth between the two of them and Ruth, without a dominant individual.

Paragraph 4 has a couple of points of interest. Fanta breaks off the ongoing conversation. In sentence 20 she becomes the thematic participant and performs three actions in a row (bending down, patting Ruth's cheek, and whirling out). Ruth is named on her first appearance but is otherwise passive in the paragraph. As subsequent text makes clear, the pronoun *her* in sentence 21 can only refer to Fanta, the thematic participant.

Valentino appears as a noun in sentence 22. Here there is a double motivation. It is his first appearance in the paragraph and he is established as the thematic participant, as the action shifts to him. *His* in sentence 22 and *he* in sentence 24 refer to Valentino. Also in sentence 22, *secretary* realizes Ruth. A noun is needed for disambiguation. Yet, the use of the noun instead of her name dehumanizes her – she is reduced to a position in the office. This supplements her object status in sentence 20, where she is reduced to a laminated cheek, the direct object of Fanta's condescending goodbye pat.

In sentence 23 the name *Ruth* again appears, humanized once more in Valentino's eyes, if still a mystery to him. Which subcategory of (e) in the algorithm dominates here is unclear. Of course, the noun avoids any ambiguity, though that seems to be incidental. The rehumanization may be as much to provide insight into Valentino as into Ruth. Their relationship has lasted through three novels in the series, though its development has been slow.

7.4.5 Summary of the Analysis

In sum, while the examples in this excerpt are not copious, they suffice to illustrate our observations and provide a skeleton for an RNT description of participant structure realization. Gleason's basic observation (first time noun, then pronouns) is validated here. The re-entry of nouns for disambiguation is also validated, though this practice is not as common as might be expected. Much more is going on. First, nominals are used to communicate new information about a participant. This observation is compatible with the understanding of information management and lexical cohesion in Systemic-Functional Grammar, even if the particular point is not made explicitly. Still, it should be verified empirically. Next, the use of nominals to establish a thematic participant is an important observation, as is the recognition of the importance of thematic participants in decoding. That is, in the absence of contextual information to the contrary and given a choice between the nearest possible nominal participant and the thematic participant, a particular pronoun points at the thematic participant. This point will also have to be verified empirically (cf. section 7.6). The generalization of first appearance of a participant as a nominal in a paragraph seems to be original with us and possibly controversial. It requires empirical verification, too.

The excerpt has three features the algorithm does not cover. First is the insult use of a pronoun in sentence 12. This presents no problem. There is more than one way to incorporate it, but our present idea is to assign it to e2, new information. The insult tells us something immediate about Ruth and her feelings about Fanta, but it presages just how annoying Fanta can be.

Next is the use of an elliptical occurrence of Ruth as the thematic participant in sentence 8. This was unexpected, since our present treatment is not concerned with the specifics of zero realizations. It will require further study, once we have gathered enough examples to adduce a pattern.

Finally, consider how the algorithm might apply to examples like (3) and (4), in which *he* refers to *John*.

(3) After John returned home, he ate dinner.
(4) After he returned home, John ate dinner.

While both sentences are fully grammatical, previous accounts (e.g., Chomsky's Subjacency principle) would allow (3) but rule out (4). This distinction is unacceptable, because both sentence types occur. However, they are not exactly identical in meaning and they are appropriate to different discourse contexts.

In fact, the discourse explanation is quite straightforward. Sentence (3) is fully covered by the algorithm under b, all other things being equal. That is, *John* is b1, *he* is b2. Other things may be in play in a particular case, but b1/b2 always holds. Conversely, (4) is also covered by the algorithm, but we must adduce a context to provide a specific description, always remembering that other possibilities exist. In short, sentence (4) is not discourse-initial, so the pronoun is most likely just an ordinary b2. We suspect the occurrence of *John* is intended to establish a thematic participant, beginning with his eating dinner and continuing from there.

Since we have no body of spontaneously produced examples in context, our discussion ends here. This preliminary analysis covers enough ground to inform our intended relational network description of participant reference, as described below.

7.5   A Relational Network Description of Participant Reference

A full relational network description of the noun-pronoun alternation requires modeling semantic, semological, and syntactic levels operative in both production and comprehension. Our basic outline description includes as much of each as is needed for understanding the core of this linguistic phenomenon, without any assumptions about ideal novelists and their ideal consumers. That is, what we present below must be integrated into the rest of the relevant individuals' linguistic systems, a task far beyond our present scope. We return to our simplified description now.

Let us first consider the relationship between embodied/conceptual/executive cognition (hereafter, cognition), semology, and syntax. If we accept the materials in talks and in written form from authors like Rex Stout, Loren Estleman, Poul Anderson, Roger Zelazny, and Isaac Asimov, an author must contemplate multiple issues before the word processor is booted up, the first sheet of paper is rolled into the typewriter, or even before pencil is set to paper. This includes the cast of characters, most with carefully chosen names and biographies; the setting in some detail; and at least an outline of the plot. All of this is present in the author's cognitive system at the same time. None of it is laid out in linear fashion. Laying things out in linear fashion is part of the artistry of composition: how much to reveal and when is critical for effective narrative.

In RNT, this cognitive mass must have inputs to the author's linguistic system for many types of things as authors create their stories. These include the participants, the acts they engage in, and the roles they play in relation to the acts. The primary semotactic structure involved is that of predication, in which participants are related to acts and the roles each participant plays relative to an act are specified. Predications are grouped into paragraphs and linearized or sequenced over the course of the paragraph, as the story is developed.

Now consider the syntax, the next step after semotactic sequencing and structuring are established. Predications are related to phrases, clauses, and sentences in the lexotactics. Acts are realized as one kind of verb-like lexeme or another, and role relations are realized as position in the clause or phrase, grammatical prepositions, or sometimes case in English. Of course, in other languages, the case realization might play a much larger part in the syntactic realization than clause position (e.g., in Polish) or no part at all (e.g., in Chinese). The participants are realized as names or NPs or pronouns. Since case plays such a small role in English, we do not go into the morphology here.

The relational network description presented below proceeds from cognition to semology to syntax, with a focus on the noun-pronoun realization of two participants, Ruth and Fanta, who have many realizations in the short passage. We look at their occurrence in the excerpt as participants 1 (Ruth) and 2 (Fanta), respectively. In the entire excerpt, participant 1 has six realizations: one name, three more nominals (noun or NP), two pronominals. Participant 2 has five realizations: one name, two nominals (one noun and one special use of a pronoun as an insulting substitute for the name), and two pronominals. These realizations are summarized in Table 7.4. Together they constitute the input-output conditions of the larger noun-pronoun alternation that we describe below.

Table 7.4: Realizations of participants 1 and 2

PARTICIPANT	NAME	NOUN (PHRASE)	PRONOUN
1	Ruth	bird	
		leader	she/her
		secretary	
2	Fanta	*She*	
		rival	

The descriptions provided in the sections and figures below focus specifically on that portion of the excerpt presented and analyzed in the commentary on paragraphs 3 and 4 in section 7.4.4, which concerns the two female participants. It is a network that could be constructed by the author during composition or by a reader during comprehension, so it is in that way moot with regard to encoding or decoding. However, as it stands, it is not general with regard to some kind of generic English text. It would be easy enough to construct a hypothetical template from this description, but we decline to do that at this point. We do not have all possible English discourses at hand, the way we had all possible Russian syllables at hand for a generalized description of Russian obstruent onsets (Chapter 4), or all possible Spanish clitics for a generalized account of Spanish clitics and verb endings (Chapter 6). Still, a preliminary description should suffice to test inferences drawn from it and see whether the description is accurate.

Thus a preliminary relational network description is given considering paragraphs 3 and 4 in the passage. Our description extends from the planning stage in cognition, where all is simultaneously present, to the semotactics, where the predication relates the participants and their roles to the sequenced acts. From the semotactics the participants are realized as different nominal lexemes or as pronouns, according to the relations from discourse (paragraphing, thematization). We begin with cogno-sememic realization, continue with a semotactic fragment, and conclude with semo-lexemic realization and a fragment of lexotactics.

7.5.1 Cognition to Semology

Figure 7.1 models the initial stage of composition behind paragraphs 3 and 4 in the Estleman excerpt. The cloud to the left represents the cognitive plan of operation. It includes four human participants (Valentino, Ruth, Broadhead, and Fanta) and one object participant (Ruth's cheek). Again, here our focus is on the two female participants. Though they are identified by name in the cognition representation, as the author knew which was which and what their actions would be, they are simply labeled participants number 1 and 2 in the semotactics, with the cheek labeled 3. Sentence 20 has no other participants. By the time they reach the lexotactics, they are realized as name, noun, or pronoun.[8]

7.5.2 Semotactics

Figure 7.2 provides a portion of a possible semotactic network for the clause *Fanta ... gave Ruth's laminated cheek a pat* (sentence 20) in its discourse context, that is, in relation to its paragraph. We begin at the top, with the node

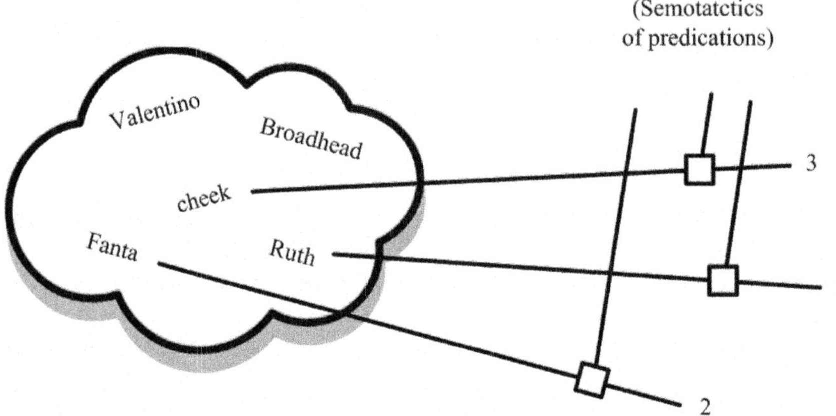

Figure 7.1: Cognition to semotactics for three participants.

labeled Paragraph (¶). This node is related to an obligatory first predication. Now a paragraph must have at least one predication. It may have more,
but additional ones will be structurally optional. So the second line down
from ¶ is optional. It is related to an AND node that is optionally related
to a sequence of predications and obligatorily related to a paragraph-final
predication. Of course, a great deal of detail has been left out in the interest of space and clarity. In any case, we can summarize this portion of the
semotactics algebraically as in (5), where IPr stands for Initial Predication,
FPr stands for Final Predication, and superscript n stands for an unspecified
number.

(5)   ¶ / IPr [[Pr^n] FPr]

Note in Figure 7.2 that the initial predication has a semo-lexemic relation
labeled New ¶. When this line is activated during encoding, it triggers the
realization of participants as nouns (see Figure 7.3).

Up to now, the network is couched in fairly general terms. Its lower
portion relates to the clause under consideration. The sememes labeled in
parentheses (namely, *give*, *pat*, and *cheek*) are not relevant to participant
realization in the lexotactics as in Figure 7.3 and are ignored henceforth.
Note that the act sememe, *give*, is dominated by the agentive (Ag) sememe,
which is participant 2. As it happens, participant 2 is also the thematic participant θ, which relates to the lexotactics in Figure 7.3. *Give* dominates the
Patient (Pa) and Recipient (Rc) networks. Pa is of no interest to the lexotactic network in Figure 7.3. Neither is the Rc network, except that participant 1 is the Possessor (Ps) of the Pa (3). Below we address the syntactic
aspects of the network.

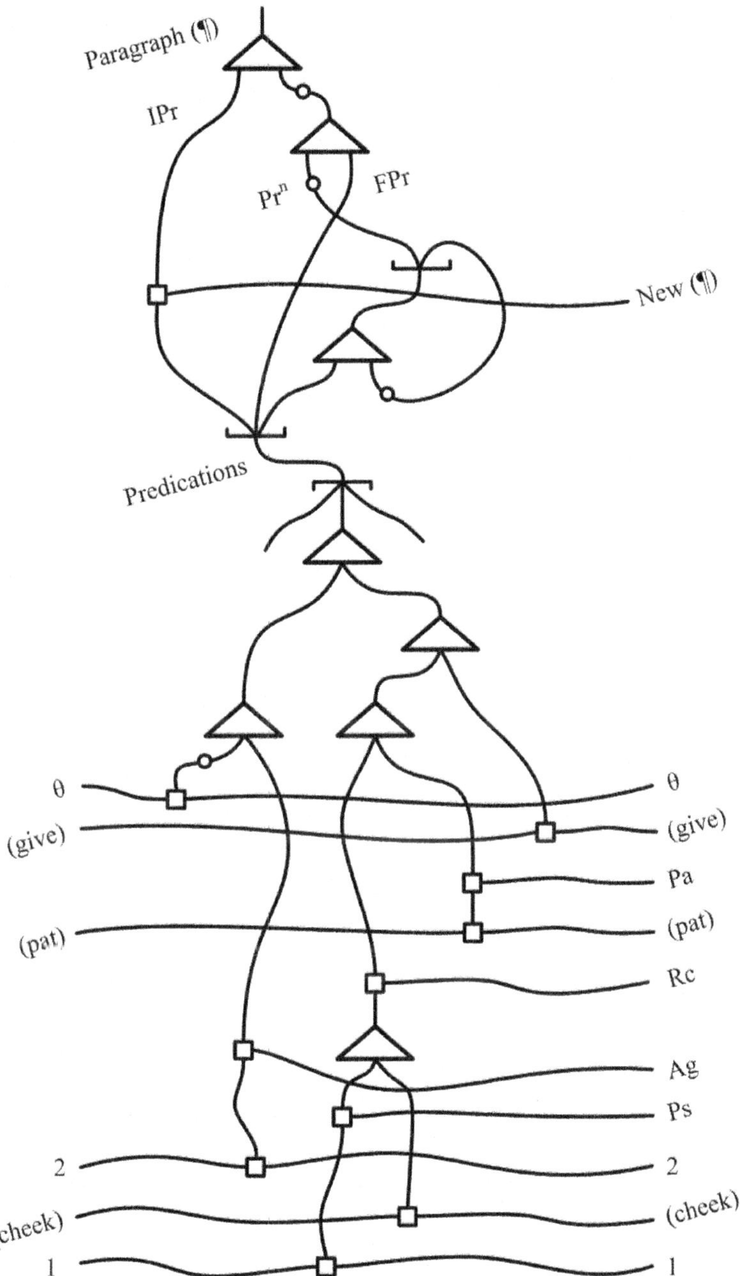

Figure 7.2: Semotactic network for *Fanta ... gave Ruth's laminated cheek a pat* in discourse context (paragraph-initial).

Key: IPr = initial predication; Pr^n = intermediate predications; FPr = final predication; θ = thematic participant; Pa= patient; Rc = recipient; Ag = agent; Ps = possessor.

7.5.3 Syntax

Consider first the semo-lexemic inputs to the lexotactics. There are six semo-lexemic inputs at the upper left of the diagram in Figure 7.3 that require a nominal realization. At the bottom are the two participants of interest in our excerpted clause. Within the entire excerpt, including all four paragraphs, participant 1 is related to the name *Ruth* and to the nouns *bird, leader,* and *secretary.* Participant 2 is related to the name *Fanta,* the noun *rival,* to the pronoun *She,* used by Ruth as an insult in her refusal to pronounce *Fanta*'s name, and to the pronoun *her.*

Now consider the tactic network defining the realization of participants as nouns, NPs, or pronouns, and how it relates to some of the semolexemic relations that provide the inputs under which the choices are made. Again we begin with the top of the diagram in Figure 7.3. The ordered OR node at the top relates the realizations to a marked-unmarked dichotomy, in which a pronominal realization is the unmarked, default realization (see b2 in Table 7.2). The marked left-hand branch leads to a diamond, which is activated by any of the cognitive or semotactic relations that demand a nominal realization. Below the diamond is another ordered OR node. The marked branch of this OR is activated by one of the three cognitive relations listed on the left side of Figure 7.3. These functions normally require an NP rather than a name. The unmarked branch leads to another OR. This time the marked choice leads to the names of the participants. If a name is not available, an NP may be used via the right-hand branch. Similarly, if input that usually requires an NP is present and the circumstances are right, a name can still be used. In short, Figure 7.3 covers the most frequent distribution of NPs vs. names, but there is more to be said. A full specification of the lexotactic network has yet to be described and the implications concerning 'most frequent distribution' should be verified.

Each participant has several possible realizations. The lexotactics must choose between them, just as the morphotactics must choose between the various forms for Polish genitive in Chapter 5. There is insufficient information to allow this range of specification here, but it is possible to illustrate the simpler situation with the names. Suppose the lexotactic path leads to Name. Activation would proceed down both branches of the OR node, activating the diamonds at *Ruth* and *Fanta.* But if this is a text involving participant 1 only, then only *Ruth* would get the activation necessary to provide output to the morphemic stratum. The activation from Name to *Fanta* would simply fade.

This brings us to another potential anomaly. Start from the network at the top of Figure 7.2. The semotactics would send activation down the ¶ line to the diamond related to 'first time (paragraph)' in Figure 7.3. Then,

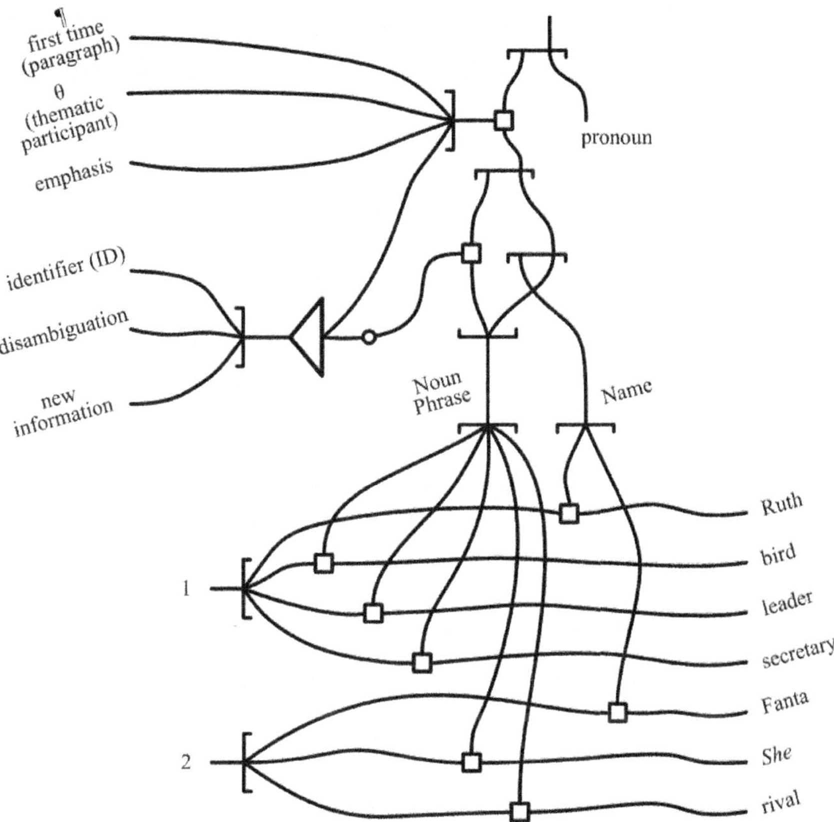

Figure 7.3: Lexotactic network for participant realization.

since participant 1 (Ruth) is the thematic participant in the first predication of the paragraph, another stream of activation would spread via θ from Figure 7.2 to the same diamond in Figure 7.3. This would be a double or redundant input. But this is no problem. Further activation lower down in Figure 7.3 requires activation from the semotactics and from higher in the lexotactics. Once that is supplied, output is made from the diamond and everything proceeds as usual. Any double or extra input to one side of the diamond would simply fade, thus having no effect.

It is also possible to provide a description of the possible decoding process, but we leave that description aside, awaiting empirical results for disambiguation as outlined in section 7.6 as well as other considerations. Having completed our relational network description, we turn now to consider future research.

7.6   Future Research

Before outlining steps that should be taken to expand the description provided herein, it would be a good idea to test some inferences that can be adduced from it. These include areas like ambiguity of pronominal reference, NP vs. name distribution, and noun-pronoun distribution itself. As an example, consider a test of ambiguity.

Such a test could proceed as follows. First, take the original excerpt. We know from the published text what pronouns the author and the editors considered unambiguous. We should verify this by having native speakers identify which participant each third-person pronoun refers to. Then we could rewrite the original text, using only nouns or NPs. Let native speakers then substitute pronouns wherever they feel they are needed. Next, run the same test with only pronouns and ask the subjects to put nouns in, wherever they feel the need. This test can be run with a list of the names or NPs used in the original text or without such a list. The results of each of these tests could be compared to the predictions in the description, and the comparison could be used to guide the direction of further research as well as refinement of the network. This test could be applied to the excerpt considered here, or another narrative text containing varied participants.

7.7   Conclusion

This chapter has offered an algorithm accounting for noun and pronoun distribution in a text and illustrated its application with a focus on participant realization. A complex description in words covering several pages can be rendered in a few relational networks. The description accounts for a minuscule portion of the phenomena systemic-functionalists refer to as cohesion in a text, but it is a portion of cohesion that seems to have been largely overlooked, except for Gleason's provocative comments. It also shows places where other portions of semotactics and lexotactics can be related to the noun-pronoun alternation – e.g., where the first mention in a new paragraph occurs after the initial predication.

The main shortcoming of the present study is its limited size and the amount of material left out. Notwithstanding, it succesfully captures key aspects of its modeling domain and proves compatible with the systemic-functional framework. A great deal of future research will be along the lines of providing an RNT formalization of well described materials.

Notes

1. This is just a very general overview of the systemic-functional work. Cohesion has a central place in Halliday's writings from Halliday (1967/1968) on, including, of course, Halliday & Hasan's *Cohesion in English* (1976). To get a good idea of the scope of Halliday's work, see Webster's collection of Halliday's works over five decades in core areas of Systemic-Functional Linguistics (Halliday, 2009).

2. We focus on noun/noun phrase-pronoun alternation and do not provide an integrated description of the zero alternative, but we touch on a couple of usages that appear in our excerpt.

3. For several discussions of such types of cohesion, see Hasan & Fries (1995).

4. But see his treatment of Kâte and Adamawa Fulani texts (Gleason, 1968, pp. 53–54).

5. This algorithm and its application in teaching composition was presented as applied to a different text at the annual forum of the Polish Association for the Study of English (PASE) in 2001, but no formalized description was presented (cf. Sullivan, 2004). An oral presentation was given, again with a different text, at LACUS Forum 42 in 2015, without the teaching applications but with a formalized description.

6. The term 'pivot', heard in the 1970s and understood as applying to a certain type of grammatical object in Chinese, is used here for a parallel type of clause in discourse. In a sentence like *I ordered Sam to eat lunch,* Sam is the patient of *order* AND the agent of *eat.* If not realized by a noun, Chinese grammar requires a pronoun here, because of the way the participant pivots between two predicates. A pivot sentence is a sentence that acts as the final sentence of one paragraph and the initial sentence of the next. No pivot sentences occur in our excerpt.

7. This use of ellipsis to establish a thematic participant at the paragraph boundary is the first such case we have run across and requires some analysis. In the absence of other examples, there is no possibility of establishing a pattern that would underlie a generalization. Any suggestions at this point would be pure speculation.

8. In fact, these realizations must be dealt with first in the semotactics. But this would require a much more extensive network to contemplate all relevant phenomena. Thus we restrict this realization to the semo-lexemic nections in the interest of simplification and space considerations.

8 An RNT Approach to Speech Errors in English and Polish

8.1 Introduction

Like other linguistic theories, RNT focuses on describing normal language processes leading to the successful production of the speaker's intended utterance. However, the theory can also account for multiple types of speech errors that frequently occur in ordinary speech. Here we examine four of the most common types, namely, timing errors (including anticipation, perseveration, and spoonerisms), structural or tactic pattern errors, unintended blends, and substitutions.

The errors are drawn from a large corpus of natural speech samples which, as shown by context or self-correction, did not match the speaker's intended utterance. The corpus contains Polish and English examples collected in Poland and the United States, respectively. Interestingly, the model proposed is capable of handling errors across these very different languages.

Our analysis fits well with the five-strata model introduced in Chapter 1, as adopted in the present descriptive applications and in previous works.[1] Moreover, it offers insights into the model's architecture and dynamic coordination during language use. Processing details elucidated include spreading activation, the linearization of unordered emes, asynchronies in the system, and competition among potential realizations. Thus, in addition to offering cognitively plausible explanations for common speech errors, we find specific support for an RNT model of dynamic language processing.

8.2 The Five-strata Model

For the reader's convenience, Figure 8.1 reproduces the five-strata model presented in Chapter 1 (Figure 1.2).

Figure 8.1 shows the linguistic system connecting embodied/conceptual/executive cognition (hereafter, cognition) with the systems for the production and perception of speech sounds. It constitutes a relational network with five strata. Recall that each stratum defines its constituent emes (or contrastive elements) and involves a generalized (not necessarily optimized) tactic pattern specifying the emes' structural relations. Each tactic pattern has realizational relations to adjacent tactic patterns, or to cognition (in the case of semology), or to the sound production and perception

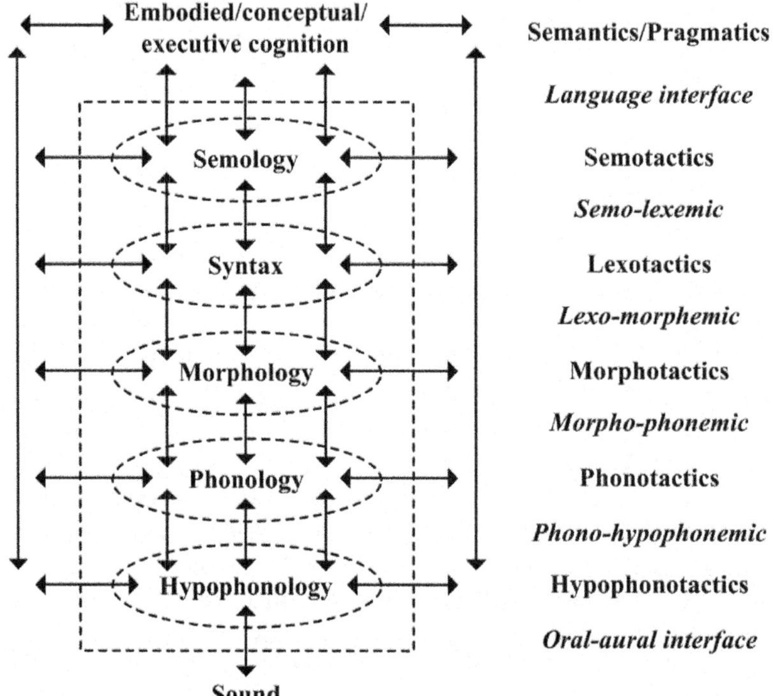

Figure 8.1: A five-strata model of the linguistic system, relative to embodied/conceptual/ executive cognition.

systems (in the case of hypophonology). Encoding generally begins with inputs to semology from cognition. These inputs are in the form of spreading activation traversing the system from top to bottom. Soon after semological processing begins, spreading activation ignites syntactic mechanisms through realizational relations; thereupon, activation further spreads through realizational relations to morphological networks, and so on through the system. At this point semological and syntactic processing may still be going on. In the context of such loosely-yoked parallel processing, each stratum may also take random rest periods or be modulated by signals from other neurocognitive systems. Disruptions of inter- and intra-stratal synchrony or competition among possible realizations are the main causes of speech errors.

8.3   Step-wise Linearization

The system produces well formed utterances when the output of each stratum is correctly linearized. We consider that material in the cognitive architecture is organized hierarchically, not in strict linear sequence. For example, when you start telling a familiar or pre-planned story, you have the entire tale in your memory. What comes out of your mouth is a linear chain of sounds corresponding to successive syllables. Yet, it is not just the syllables that are in sequence. The story must make sense to the listeners. This means that the events must be framed in coherent order, the clauses that communicate events must provide properly patterned forms, and the chain of morphemes must be realized in (not necessarily coterminous) language-specific syllables. The question at once arises: where did the linearization take place? We propose that linearization occurs dynamically at different processing stages during encoding. This position seems elegant in that it avoids additional assumptions and ad hoc mechanisms.

The key to the RNT explanation is in the tactic-realizational distinction within the system's architecture and the cooperation between tactic patterns and realizational relations during production and reception. Input from cognition is realized as sememes, which are grouped, unsequenced, into predications. Predications are sequenced across linguistic paragraphs. Sememes are realized as lexemes and the lexemes are sequenced across clauses in the lexotactics (cf. Chapter 7, section 7.5). Lexemes are realized as (unsequenced) morphemes, and the morphemes are sequenced in the morphotactics. Perhaps the most readily understood example would be the connection between morphology and phonology. A morpheme is realized as a group of phonemes and the morpheme-sized groupings of phonemes are then sequenced into syllables in the phonotactics. We return to the effect of stepwise sequencing below.

In sum, during the encoding process, sequencing is gradually imposed on successive processing patterns. What emerges as sound, then, is a linear output. While a principled account of decoding could be provided using the same constructs, here we focus on production in order to explain the emergence of speech errors.

8.4   Earlier Research on Speech Errors

Fromkin (1971, 1973) studied what has been termed 'anomalous utterances'. She argued that they are not anomalous and sought to explain their occurrence; but that was in the Chomskyan era between the apparent success of the *Aspects* model (Standard Theory) and the revision that took place during the Extended Standard Theory period. At that time, as for mainstream linguists now, the current model was supposed to account for 'all and only' the grammatical sentences of a language. All the twists and turns of Chomsky's theories were attempts to prevent the production of ungrammatical sentences. In short, the only valid data was error-free and structural. Fromkin's work was on errors produced during performance and was therefore deemed uninteresting, in the jargon of the day. Her attempt to find an explanation within the Chomskyan framework was doomed from the start, and even if successful, it would have been ignored.

The work of Peter Reich and Gary Dell during the 1970s and 1980s is more significant. Reich's earliest work, never published separately, deals with phono-hypophonemic timing errors. It was extended to include morpho-phonemic timing errors (Dell & Reich, 1977), and Reich (1985) brought in cognition to deal with unintended puns. Dell (1986) expanded the scope to include semo-lexemic timing errors. Yet, neither Reich nor Dell incorporated all linguistic strata as well as cognition, though they made extensive use of spreading activation in a relational network model.[2]

The analysis presented here, based on a wide range of speech errors, covers all the ground that Fromkin's work covered and it also encompasses later work of Dell and Reich on English, extending it both in that language and in Polish. Notably, speech errors in two very different languages can be explained using a single set of constructs.

8.5   Data Collection and Corpus

We define speech errors rather broadly as output that is compatible with the speaker's linguistic system but not with his or her intended utterance. In compiling our corpus, we determined the intended output on the basis of the context of the erroneous utterance or by the speaker's self-correction. On some occasions the speaker was asked what he or she intended to say, in order to verify our interpretation or distinguish between two possible intended utterances.

We gathered examples of four different error types: timing errors, structural errors, unintended blends, and substitutions. Timing errors include transpositions, like the classic slip by the Rev. Dr. Spooner ('… a toast to our queer old Dean'), but also anticipation and perseveration errors. Structural errors are usually the result of misordering within a single tactic pattern (*kordła* for [Polish] *kołdra* 'quilt'). Blends like *brunch* and *carmageddon* (referring to a hundred-plus car pileup on a California highway) are coined deliberately on a daily basis; but the same kind of output is evident in inadvertent utterances, like *a formal prosecutor* instead of the intended *a former federal prosecutor*, where the material in bold is omitted. Substitutions are also common, as in 'he traveled *east* to Jericho', written of a man setting out from Baghdad. Our review of the different types of errors in the corpus found these four types to be by far the most common (Sullivan & Tsiang, in press a).

At present, the corpus comprises several thousand examples, mainly in Polish and English. Data collection began in Poland in 2010. Sullivan was teaching a broad-based university linguistics course involving cognition, encoding-decoding, and relational networks. He challenged his students to adduce a network from spoken output and test the resulting system against patterned errors. The students recorded spontaneous speech samples and transcribed instances that they considered anomalous, along with any context they could provide. They could also supply their best guess as to what was intended. Written sources, including text messages, were also acceptable, provided they were tagged as such. These students were enthusiastic and the examples they submitted created the core of the corpus. For example, a radio announcer said *Pamiętajcie, palenie **raka** powoduje **tytoń*** 'Remember, smoking a crab leads to tobacco' instead of the standard *palenie tytoniu powoduje raka* 'smoking tobacco leads to cancer', the warning then written on each pack of cigarettes sold in Poland. Like the famous example produced by Rev. Dr. Spooner, this constituted a spoonerism – though syntactic (or, more precisely, semo-lexemic) rather than phonological (actually, morpho-phonemic) in nature.

In addition to the student submissions, Sullivan collected data himself, mainly in Polish. In the US, Tsiang joined the project and the corpus of English examples soon grew to match its Polish counterpart.[3] It quickly became evident that many errors were not due to timing disregulations. Additional error types included structural or tactic pattern errors, unintended blends, and substitutions. Examples of redundancies were also submitted, but these provide fewer insights into the linguistic system and are therefore less interesting to our present purpose, so we omit them here.[4] We take the four main error types in order, after a short exposition of the underlying theory.

8.6   Theoretical Background

The key to many of these speech errors is found in anataxis, often mistaken for metathesis. Metathesis is well known in historical linguistics. It is a historical shift whereby a vowel and liquid change places – e.g., Fr. *Roland* < Lat. *Orlandus*, or Cz. *král* 'king' < Gm. *Karl* (*der Grosse*) 'Charlemagne'. A similar phenomenon can be noted synchronically, but as it lacks the historical association, it is better labeled anataxis.[5]

A well known Russian example can be seen in simple number phrases: *pjat' rublej* 'five rubles' but *rublej pjat'* 'about five rubles'. The traditional description is to accept *pjat' rublej* as the base and derive *rublej pjat'* from it by promoting the noun to first position. This parallels the historical promotion of the liquid *r* in *Karl* to prevocalic position in *král*. But the historical shift is only visible in retrospect; the resulting form is fixed, always *král*, whereas the Russian number phrases are productive. For accounts of anataxis problems in general and their manifestation in Russian number phrases, see Sullivan (2000) and Sullivan (2010), respectively.

Following a relational network approach, the assumption presented in Sullivan (2010) is that number expressions of this sort are related to an unordered AND node in the semotactics, as shown in Figure 8.2. This AND is related to a set of countables and the set of simple numerals, along with an optional relation to the sememe proximate (Prx). In the lexotactics, the syntax of simple number phrases is given by a two-place ordered AND node. The first branch is related to an ordered OR node. The left-hand (marked) branch of this OR is active when Prx is signaled from the semotactics. The line is then related to the noun, which is realized first. The right-hand (unmarked) branch of the OR is related to the simple numerals. In the absence of Prx activation, the numeral is realized first. The second branch of the ordered AND node is related to an unordered OR, which is related to the simple numerals and the countable nouns. Whatever is not realized in first position is realized in second position. Noun-number is not derived from number-noun and there is no *re*ordering, since they were never ordered to begin with.

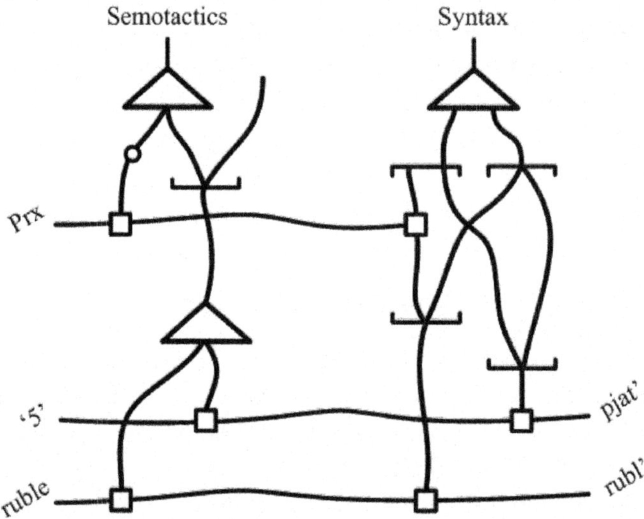

Figure 8.2: Anataxis in Russian number phrases.

In this study, how the sequencing occurs is at least part of an RNT explanation for all speech error types, except for substitutions: two emes unsequenced at the input to a tactic pattern are then sequenced in the output from that tactic pattern to the next lower stratum. This is where certain types of errors arise.

8.7   Four Kinds of Speech Errors

8.7.1 Timing Errors

Timing errors include anticipation, perseveration, and spoonerisms. We focus here on the latter as the clearest examples. A set of English and Polish spoonerisms is provided in Table 8.1.

Table 8.1: Spoonerisms in Polish and English

STRATA	POLISH	ENGLISH
Cogno-sememic	***Wystaw język*** i ***otwórz buzię*** ('stick out tongue and open mouth')	(none reported)
Semo-lexemic	palenie ***raka*** powoduje ***tytoń*** ('smoking a crab leads to tobacco')	Many changes are a result ***in*** a shift ***of*** upper arctic circulation
Lexo-morphemic	med***nik*** vsad***nyj*** ('mounted bronze')	you'll need the ***com***mission of the ***per***mittee
Morpho-phonemic	wa***l***czyć ta***ń***ca ('fight a waltz')	***th***eroid ***st***erapy
Phono-hypophonemic	sa***let***ytarny ('satellite')	***f***eautiful ***b***erry (beautiful fairy)

In the Polish cogno-sememic example, a doctor's request intended to initiate a physical examination is represented by a two-act text, probably related to a common cognitive scheme (e.g., LET'S GET STARTED) and repeated a dozen times a day. Each act is represented by a predication, but the order of the two predications is the reverse of what was intended. The result is a humorous impossibility. It happened that no clear case of a cogno-sememic spoonerism was reported for English.

We described the Polish semo-lexemic spoonerism in section 8.5. The important thing to note is that the spoonerized elements are both patients (sememic Pa) of acts, even though one comes out as the post-nominal genitive case complement of a deverbal nominalization and the other comes out as the accusative direct object of a finite verb. The sememic functions remain intact. Just the lexotactic realizations are reversed, and even so the morphological realizations are appropriate.

The English semo-lexemic spoonerism is between the prepositions in the two qualifying phrases. The intended *result **of** a shift **in** upper arctic circulation* is unremarkable linguistically. What we observed was almost incoherent. English prepositions are prototypically centered in spatial or temporal geometry. Here their semotactic functions are undisturbed but the lexotactic linearization places them as prepositions in the wrong phrases.

Next are the lexo-morphemic spoonerisms. We include a solitary Russian example in the present corpus. The title of Pushkin's beautiful and lyrical but tragic tale of Sankt-Peterburg (the original name of St. Petersburg) is *Mednyj vsadnik* ('The Bronze Horseman'). The form observed had the adjectival suffix *nyj* spoonerized with the nominal agentive suffix *nik*.[6] In the English example, spoken by historian Michael Beschloss, instead of intended ***permission of the committee***, the two prefixes are spoonerized. But note: as these examples show, it is two prefixes or two suffixes, not a prefix and a suffix.

The two morpho-phonemic examples are interesting in different ways. The Polish example was supposed to be *tańczyć walca* ('dance a waltz'), but the accented syllables are spoonerized. ***Theroid sterapy*** (instead of steroid therapy) shows the spoonerism of accented initial-syllable onsets, where one is only a single consonant and the other a cluster.

The Polish form produced for intended *saletytarny*, ('satellite [adj.]') shows a phono-hypophonemic spoonerism. It is exemplary. It shows the manner of articulation (oral closure, laterality) spoonerized between two adjacent apical consonants. In the English example, manner of articulation (here oral closure and spirant friction) is again spoonerized between two adjacent labial consonants.

The examples gathered arise at each of the five interfaces between the cognitive input and the hypophonemic output. If the upper stratum provides no linear order to the lower stratum's emes, leaving that task to the lower stratum's tactic pattern, it is easy to spot the characteristics of the error: the spoonerized emes are found in the appropriate relation of the same kind of lower-stratum complex (e.g., verbal complements or syllable onsets), except that the complex is not the appropriate one. Examples of perseveration and anticipation (not included here) are similarly patterned.

8.7.2 Structural or Tactic Pattern Errors

The structural relations in our model (Figure 8.1) are described in the tactic patterns (TPs). Each stratum has its own TP, which structures and linearizes the stratum's emes. While TP errors are also a result of misordering, timing errors imply more extensive structure. Consider a spoonerism between the onsets of two successive accented syllables. English and Polish permit only one major accent per phonological word. It follows that a spoonerism between the onsets of two accented syllables must be part of the encoding of two phonological words, including any unaccented syllables in them. But a TP error in the phonotactics might jumble the order of phonemes in a single syllable. Every phoneme would be in an appropriate spot for its phoneme class, just not in the right position. A representative set of TP errors is given in Table 8.2.

Table 8.2: Tactic pattern errors in Polish and English

Stratum	Polish	English
Semotactic	*za umarłość* ('after having been dead')	my mom is hotter than me
Lexotactic	*matkę już nie boli głowa* ('mother no longer has a headache')	They *just* don't make mistakes, they justify them.
Morphotactic	*za umarłość* ('after having been dead')	derivating
Phonotactic	*kordła* ('quilt')	[skæt]
Hypophonotactic	*letny* ('summer')	[wɛlti]

The first Polish error, *za umarłość* ('after having been dead') for *po śmierci* ('after death'), is both semotactically and morphotactically erroneous. *Za* in Polish is not used in the temporal sense 'after' when the object is a point in time, only when it is a period of time – hence the awkward gloss. *Po* 'after' is correct. We return to the morphotactic error below.

The English semotactic error requires some background. A British reality TV show was entitled 'Hotter than my daughter'. However, the show's title was misremembered by a radio host as 'My Mom is Hotter than Me'. Both titles communicate the same situation, but the intended title indicates the mother's point of view and the host's version indicates the daughter's point of view. So the same cognitive input was realized by an apt but incorrect semotactic pattern.

The Polish lexotactic error in *matkę już nie boli głowa* is the anomalous accusative case on *matkę*. It should be dative *matce*. The accusative normally communicates Pa (patient) and the dative communicates Exp (experiencer). The two are not far apart in the context of a sensory verb, so the error is understandable. When asked point blank which case it ought to be, Poles had some difficulty with the answer, often repeating both versions of the sentence several times and sometimes failing to come up with a definitive answer.

The English lexotactic error shows confusion in the position of the adverb *just*, which normally appears before verbs, though adverbs may occur elsewhere. This sentence has three potential slots for it, and *just* landed in the first one. It is syntactically well formed but clearly erroneous in context.

The Polish morphotactic error returns us to the semotactic example, considering now the word *umarłość*. *Umarł* is the past-tense stem of *umrzeć* 'die', which is etymologically related to *śmierć* 'death'. *Umarł* '[he] died' is also the base of the past tense and of the adjectival past participle *umarły* 'dead'. A state noun can be derived from an adjective with the addition of the suffix *ość*. So *umarłość* should mean something like 'the state of having died', which sounds very much like *śmierć* 'death'. The problem is that *umarłość* is not a Polish lexeme,[7] hence a morphotactic error. English *derivating* in place of *deriving* is a parallel case.

The phonotactic errors are also interesting. The English speaker produced [skæt] in place of [stæk]. Both are valid words and syllables with each phoneme realized in a proper stop position. The two stops are not in their appropriate positions for the intended word, however.

The Polish example *kordła* is similar, but a little more complex. This disyllabic phonological word is intended to realize two morphemes: *kołdr+a*. The order of stem before ending in the morphotactics provides the linear order of the *o* and the *a*, which center the two syllables of the phonological word. The morpheme-initial *k* provides the onset to the first syllable. The first place for the realization of the *d* is in onset position of the second syllable. All that is left is sonant positions for *ł* [w] and *r*. The observed form *kordła* has them both in appropriate positions but, as in the English example, not the correct ones.

We now turn to hypophonotactic errors. Errors in articulatory coordination are frequent, and the examples given show two variants of this type of error. Consider first the Polish error. The Polish example *letny* [tnɨ] in place of *letni* [tńi] 'summer (adj)' has a sequence of an apicodental stop followed by an apicodental nasal and a high central vowel. It should be noted that such a sequence is not uncommon in Polish – cf. *okrutny* 'cruel'. We cannot classify this as a perseveration from consonants to vowel, because the place of articulation differs. Nor do we classify it as a substitution, because the *ny*, which would be the substitute, is neither a phonotactic nor a hypophonotactic constituent such as would be available for substitution. In the correct articulation, the oral closure present in the cluster must shift from apicodental to frontodomal, whence the release to a high front vowel is automatically at the nasal's frontal position. In the case of *letny*, the shift of articulator is delayed and in the end never made, so that the release to a high vowel is at the unmarked central place of articulation.

Now consider the English example. Pronouncing *wealthy* requires a shift in tongue articulation. The [l] is articulated with the apex at the roof of the mouth and the sides (latera) of the tongue lowered. Conversely, [θ] is articulated with the sides of the tongue touching the upper jaw (whether teeth or roof of the mouth is unimportant here) and a slit opening at the apex. So articulating [lθ] requires a near-simultaneous raising of the sides of the tongue while lowering the apex from the alveolar ridge to a slit opening. In the articulation of [lt] the error is clear. The sides of the tongue were raised but the slit opening was never formed. This is an example of the kind of hypophonotactic error often called mispronunciation.

8.7.3 Unintended Blends

A representative sample of unintended blends is given in Table 8.3. The stratum to which we assign an unintended blend is determined by the stratum we need to invoke for the explanation. Note that no spontaneous blends were reported in Polish at the sememic and hypophonemic strata, and only one hypophonemic blend was reported for English. We return to possible reasons for this below.

The English sememic blend, *mending bridges*, is a combination of two fixed expressions, each to be understood metaphorically. *Mending fences* repairs a breach in relations, whereas *building bridges* establishes the precondition for having ongoing relations. They are in similar realms of human activity, but one is retrospective, the other prospective. Both might have been activated simultaneously, producing a combined output.

The English syntactic example blends *following Norbert Wiener's footprints* with *walking in Norbert Wiener's shoes*. Both expressions have to do with finding out or understanding where Mr. Wiener is going/has gone. Presumably both were activated and the blend came out with the object that makes the footprints.

Table 8.3: Unintended blends in Polish and English

STRATUM	POLISH	ENGLISH
Sememic	(none reported)	he's all about mending bridges
Lexemic	*dwie margaryty zaproszę*	following Norbert Wiener's shoes
Morphemic	*autopadek*	it makes conferences to other legislation
Phonemic	*mostre*	event[áž]
Hypophonemic	(none reported)	Raker

The Polish example is much more complex syntactically. Clearly a request for two drinks at a bar or restaurant, the problem lies in the verb. First of all, *zaproszę* ('invite') is a perfectly good but simply inappropriate lexical choice here, as it normally takes a human Patient. So this was not analyzed as a substitution. Two possible choices are appropriate here, both requiring *dwie margaryty* in the accusative case: *poproszę o dwie margaryty* 'I ask for two margaritas' and *zamówię dwie margaryty* 'I order two margaritas'. In the first example, the verb takes a prepositional phrase complement and in the other it simply takes a direct object. This shows a lexotactic blend. But there is also a morphemic side to this blend: the prefix of *zamówię* is related to the stem of *poproszę* (*o*), making this a double blend.

Now consider the morphological blends. The English blend appeared in a discussion about the complexity of the Affordable Care Act (Obamacare). The speaker had talked about the length of the act (over 2,000 pages) and added that: 'it makes *conferences* to other legislation', immediately corrected to *constant references*. The Polish example is almost transparent in its meaning by comparison. Part of a news report mentioned a *straszny autopadek*. Accompanying pictures made it clear that it was a *straszny wypadek* 'terrible accident (usually with fatalities)' involving an *autokar* 'tour bus'.

Phonological blends, intended or not, are very common. The English example was clear from context, but the Polish example was clarified by almost immediate correction. We take them in that order. The performance at a Kentucky horse show was to be *eventing dressage* [drɛsáž] but was announced as *event* [áž]. We consider this error phonological rather than morphological, because of the pseudo-French pronunciation that is carried over from the lexeme *dressage*, which was borrowed from French along with its pronunciation. The Polish example had *mostre* in what should be adjective position, but it is not a Polish lexeme. The speaker clarified it when asked, saying he should have said *mocne* 'strong' and *ostre* 'sharp'.

Our solitary hypophonemic blend is found in the [k] in *Raker*. A TV news anchor tried to introduce a sportscaster named Rafer, who would be speaking about the problems Tiger Woods was having. After laughter at the wrong name, the anchor stated that, when he said *Raker*, he was saying the two names together. If we look at the hypophonemes involved, we have the combination in (1), which looks like a true blend:

$$
\begin{array}{lll}
(1) \quad f & k & g \\
\quad Sp & Cl \leftarrow & Cl \\
\quad Lb & Do \leftarrow & Do \\
\quad \text{-Y} \rightarrow & \text{-Y} & Y
\end{array}
$$

Key: Sp = spirant friction; Lb = labial;
Y = phonemic voice; Cl = oral closure; Do = dorsal.

All of the lexeme *Rafer* is non-contrastively voiced, except for the *f*, which is phonemically unvoiced. Voicing in the pronunciation of *Rafer* must be turned off when the hypophonotactics gets to the *f*. That is, the output [k] in *Raker* gets the Dorsal Closure from the [g] of Tiger and the instruction to turn off automatic voicing from the [f] of Rafer.

The paucity of reported semotactic and hypophonotactic errors should not be taken as proof of their rarity. The result of a sememic blend could well be incomprehensible or simply misunderstood. In the former case, reconstructing the hypothetical parts of the blend would be impossible, and the most probable next step would be for one of the interlocutors to ask for or attempt a clarification. We think that the latter case, misunderstanding, is more interesting. We suspect that most such errors are similarly overlooked at the time of the error, because only one of the two interpretations was intended and only one was understood. Later the misunderstanding becomes clear, and the interlocutors may discover that the intended interpretation differed radically from the one understood. Similarly, we suspect that hypophonotactic errors are simply overlooked or not perceived, even by the more vigilant data collectors.

8.7.4 Substitutions

Substitutions have been studied in different ways. For example, Mayberry (1993) focused on whether the occurrence of a substitution was motivated semantically or phonetically in late first-language acquisition. Miceli *et al.* (1989) dealt with omissions and substitutions of grammatical morphemes in agrammatic patients, and Lombardi (2003) concentrated on substitutions in manner of articulation of dental consonants in second language acquisition. These and other references seem to have two characteristics in common. First, they are very limited in the type of substitution under consideration (lexeme or morpheme or phonemic feature), and their pool of subjects is similarly limited (post-childhood first-language acquisition, second language acquisition, or patients diagnosed with agrammatism). Our interest in substitutions is broader in type and scope. We are concerned with those substitutions that commonly occur in normal speech as slips of the tongue. Our corpus includes substitutions at any level of the human linguistic system as produced by mature native speakers – in our case, native speakers of English or Polish.

A representative sample of English and Polish substitutions is given in Table 8.4. Each error could be called a lexemic substitution, with one exception, to which we return below. We base our classification of the error in the first column on the nature of the substitute that can be adduced.

The cognitive substitutions are exemplified by semantic confusion. The intended Polish expression, ***długo go nie było*** 'he hasn't been here for a long time', begins with an expression of spatial extent. The clause observed had *daleko* 'far from here', an expression of temporal extent: a confusion of time and space. Similarly with the English example, ***ahead of us*** and *behind us* are both expressions of relative spatial position, differing only in order, so the confusion regards relative locus.

Table 8.4: Substitutions in Polish and English

LEVEL/ STRATUM \ LANGUAGE	POLISH		ENGLISH	
	REPORTED	INTENDED	REPORTED	INTENDED
Cognitive	**daleko** *go nie było*	*długo*	**ahead of** us	behind
Sememic	*zjadłbym* **wilka** *z kopytami*	*konia*	taxpayers will have to **weigh** the brunt of these expressions	bear
Lexemic	*znaleźć* **jeden** *język*	*wspólny*	when Christmas is celebrated by millions of Orthodox **religions**	Christians
Morphemic	*płci* **miej**skiej	*męskiej*	I hear 'babe' foot**prints** behind us	steps
Phonemic	*Krzysztof* **Jajnik**	*Janik*	We've seen the use of the N-word, the F-word, the C-/ Sea Wo**rl**d	C-word
Hypophonemic	*czostek*	*czosnek*	Hear how a passenger, th**r**ew sheets to the wind …	**three**

The sememic substitutions are characterized by semotactic constructions replacing what would otherwise be a sememe that encodes a fixed expression. The Polish example, *zjadłbym* **wilka** *z kopytami* 'I could eat a wolf with the hoofs', with *wilka* 'wolf' in place of *konia* 'horse' (as in the proverb), causes no syntactic or morphological problems, but is twice anomalous: the proverb is a semotactic construct and the expression observed is semantically striking, since wolves do not have hoofs. Similarly, the English example has *the taxpayers* **weigh** *the brunt* in place of **bear** *the brunt*. Again a sememe that encodes a fixed expression is semotactically encoded with an incorrect sememe. This one is also semantically striking, because the lexeme *brunt* is normally only collocated with *bear*.

The syntactic substitutions are fine as isolated sentences but were anomalous in context with the substitute in place. In the Polish example, most people have no trouble speaking *jeden* 'one' language; but in the context of a group of people from different countries, the interest lies in finding a common (*wspólny*) language. Similarly, the English example is taken from a discussion about the date when Christmas is celebrated. Citing a certain date as pertaining to *millions of Orthodox Christians* is unremarkable, but applying it to *millions of Orthodox* **religions** is inappropriate.

The Polish morphological example came from a discussion about differences between the sexes. The statement containing *płci* **miejskiej** 'of the municipal sex' followed some comments about *płci żeńskiej* 'of the female sex'. Clearly the appropriate phrase should be *płci* **męskiej** 'of the male sex'. The English morphological example derives from a saying among foreign residents of Poland that crossing a street safely requires you to wait for a 'babe', preferably in a short skirt, so that (male) drivers will stop to watch her as she crosses. Then you can sneak across safely in her wake. Sullivan and his wife Mary were standing at an intersection, waiting for a break in the traffic, when they heard the clip-clop of high heels approaching. Mary said she could 'hear babe foot**prints**'. The juxtaposition of aural *hear* with visual *print* made the error striking.

The Polish phonological example has a coda substitution, but this produces a humorous output. Krzysztof Janik, a Polish politician, has an ordinary Polish surname, but the speaker said *jajnik* 'ovary'. In this context, such an example never fails to get a laugh from a Polish audience. The English phonological example is striking in another way. *C-word* would be the natural member of the set of expletives (X-words?) spoken: the N-word, the F-word, the C-word. All went well until the coda of the final syllable, where the Florida attraction out-competed the X-word for production. What started the competing activation of *Sea World* is a matter of speculation, but it only became the substitute at the final coda.

Finally, consider the hypophonological substitutions. The Polish example, with *czostek* '?' appearing when *czosnek* 'garlic' was intended, can be analyzed in different ways. The difference in realization is given in (2) with both phonemic and predictable, non-contrastive features, the latter in parentheses.

```
(2)  n       t
     Ns      -
     Ap      Ap
     (Cl)    Cl
     (Y)     -
```

Key: Ns = nasal; Ap = apical;
Cl = oral closure; Y = phonemic voice.

The easiest description of this example, depending on where determined features are related to the complexes of contrastive hypophonemes, is a substitution of Cl in place of Ns (nasal). A different substitution analysis and a more complex phono-hypophonotactic structural analysis are possible, and we do not rule either one out. Yet, the simplest explanation remains a hypophonological substitution.

The English example, *hear how a passenger, **threw** sheets to the wind*, could be said to be a phonemic substitution of [u:] for [i:]. But both are long, high vowels, and the only difference between them is the substitution of Lb (labial) for Fr (frontal). Note that we could also argue for a lexical substitution, but according to the general principle of minimal substitute adopted throughout this chapter, *threw* fills the hypophonemic position. Of course, the lexical resemblance could have played a role, though the existence of the fixed expression would seem to operate as a counterweight to that.

In sum, the observation of substitutions at each stratum is borne out.

8.8   Summary of Findings

Recall the characteristics of the linguistic system presented in Figure 8.1. This system has proved useful for describing English and Polish.[8] It has five strata, each with a central tactic pattern. Realizational relations are located between each pair of tactic patterns. Realizational relations also connect the semotactics with the cognitive system and the hypophonotactics with the systems for the production and perception of sound. As we pass through the system from top to bottom, successive tactic patterns impose linear order on the emes of their stratum. Table 8.5 shows the relation between the characteristics of Figure 8.1 and the error types studied herein.

Table 8.5: Error types and linguistic subsystems

	FIVE STRATA	FIVE TPs	TP-REALIZATIONAL INTERSECTION	UNORDERED TO ORDERED
Timing errors	+	+	+	+
TP errors	+	+	+	+
Unintended blends	+	+	+	(+)
Substitutions	+	(+)	(+)	

Timing errors and TP errors support all four characteristics given for the linguistic system in Figure 8.1. Unintended blends support the idea of five strata, five tactic patterns, and the tactic-realizational intersections. Also, they are compatible with a stepwise imposition of order. Substitutions support the idea of five strata. They are compatible with tactic patterns and the tactic-realization intersection at each stratum. The appearance of linear ordering in the output is not relevant to substitutions but the two are not incompatible. So to some degree the descriptive model is validated by substitutions, too.

Previous work (cf. Bogdan & Sullivan, 2009) has focused on the description of the system as it works to encode and decode messages properly. Unlike all branches of Chomskyan linguistics, RNT considers the whole of the linguistic system and the related phonetic and cognitive semantic areas in its purview. Moreover, RNT considers erroneous products of the system in addition to well formed products. The present chapter is a small part of our contribution to that end.[9]

Notes

1. For example, the series of speech error articles by Sullivan and Tsiang (Sullivan, 2011; Sullivan & Tsiang, 2011, 2012, in press a, b, c, d; Tsiang & Sullivan, in press).
2. Smith (2010) provides a fairly good description of Dell's work, but he does not cover the scope of application of spreading activation in the context of a relational network model.
3. Other long-term collectors of English examples were Mary Sullivan and Katarina Starčević.
4. Redundancies and their similarities to and differences from canonical speech errors are discussed in Sullivan & Tsiang (in press c).
5. For an exhaustive taxonomy of anataxis, see Lockwood (1977).
6. A more delicate morphological analysis could be advanced, in which the spoonerism would be between *yj* and *ik*. The argument would remain the same.
7. Though several native informants thought it was a clever neologism, and as a period of time, it is appropriate as an object of temporal *za*.
8. As well as Russian and, to a lesser extent, several other languages.
9. Sullivan and Tsiang are working on a project involving the corpus of speech errors in English, Polish, and some other languages used here and in previous studies, which will enable them to look deeper into the logic underlying the architecture of the linguistic system, and to simulate the production of the errors based on system processing. Insights into decoding will also be considered.

Afterword

I   What We have Done

Throughout this book, we have offered a historical perspective on RNT and relied on it to model a considerable array of linguistic phenomena. From Hjelmslev's early insights into language structure as a network of relationships only, to Lamb's logical formalization and dynamic implementation of this idea, to the quest for neurological plausibility in the late twentieth century (still ongoing), the theory has embraced successive refinements guided by empirical constraints. By minimizing apriorisms and incorporating contributions from various fields, RNT has forged an elegant conceptual and notational apparatus capable of handling myriad details of verbal processing. We have exemplified the theory's potential by treating problems of Russian phonology, Polish cases, Spanish clitics and verb endings, English discourse, and speech errors in English and Polish. These issues cut across virtually all strata of several different languages, highlighting the theory's broad applicability.

II   How RNT Deviates from Mainstream Formal Linguistics

Despite its merits, RNT has remained an underdog in linguistics. Crucially, this is not because its tenets or hypotheses have been falsified or found lacking. Rather, it is because the theory has been largely ignored and has failed to attract a great number of practitioners. To a large extent, such unpopularity reflects how far it stands from mainstream formal theories, in particular from generativist approaches. By way of illustration, we summarize the key differences between RNT and the generative program, with a view to situating the former in a broader epistemological context.

First, since its very inception, Generative Grammar has assumed two key counterfactual idealizations. Speakers/hearers have been conceived as if they were part of a completely homogeneous community and as if they were not affected by memory limitations, distractions, or changes in focus or loss of interest, so that they would not make mistakes in using language. These conceptions are intended to isolate the properties of the language faculty and thus allow their study from a universalist perspective, assuming that the only object of attention in linguistics is idealized competence or knowledge (Eguren & Fernández Soriano, 2004). RNT endorses radically different premises. Crucially, it seeks to account for language production, comprehension, and learning as they occur in actual individuals. In this sense, rather than rejecting the infelicities that occur during language use, the theory frames errors as sources of insight into the system's functional organization (e.g., as we can see in Chapter 8). Moreover, the theory relies heavily on observations of naturally occurring speech. RNT has long sought to describe the linguistic system of a real, communicating human being. The input-output sets include articulatory output, auditory input, and the acoustic phonetic relations between the two, as well as the messages intended by the speaker during encoding and evoked in the hearer during decoding.

Second, generative linguistics has endeavored to study the so-called faculty of language, a 'computational system that is rich and strongly limited in its structure and rigid in its essential operations' (Chomsky, 1986, p. 43). From the early days of phrase structure rules and transformations to more recent (and abstruse) mechanisms introduced in the minimalist program, generative models have been based on serial algorithms operating on finite symbolic units. Such models operate deductively with the intention to produce all and only the grammatical sentences of the language. Inherent in this goal is the assumption that language is composed of concrete, quantifiable objects which can be logically manipulated. On the other hand, RNT envisions the linguistic system as a network of relationships whose nodes may integrate information relevant to distinct linguistic categories, which exist only by virtue of their relationships. Moreover, RNT proposes that serial operations in language go hand in hand with parallel distributed processing. Indeed, different strains of activation are proposed to flow simultaneously in different parts of the language network during verbal production and comprehension. Instead of converting or displacing static symbolic objects, RNT accounts characterize language processes as parallel, coordinated patterns of activation cutting across distributed nodes. To repeat, these nodes do not constitute linguistic objects themselves, exclusive of their relationships.

Third, following early work by Fodor (1983), Generative Grammar has endorsed a modular conception of the mind – although, to be fair, modular assumptions were present since Chomsky's (1957) *Syntactic Structures*. Among other things, that theory posits that the language faculty is a specialized mechanism following domain-specific principles (Chomsky, 1980). While recent reconceptualizations of the language faculty (Chomsky, 2005; Hauser, Chomsky, & Fitch, 2002, 2005) have been seen as a retreat from modularity (Pinker & Jackendoff, 2005), the generative program still posits that it includes human- and language-exclusive subcomponents (namely, recursion or narrow syntax). However, the claim that such subcomponents are distinct from domain-general mechanisms has been acknowledged to constitute a non-testable hypothesis (Hauser, Chomsky, & Fitch, 2005). On the other hand, RNT makes no assumption about its descriptive apparatus involving *sui generis* language mechanisms. Indeed, it seeks compatibility with general principles of neurocognition, in an attempt to integrate its postulates with overarching conceptions of the mind and brain. Thus, successive adjustments in the theory have aimed to include more detailed empirical constraints derived from language or neurocognitive research – which contrasts with the generativist practice of postulating ever more complex ad hoc constructs to safeguard the speculation that grammar relies on modular, domain-specific components.

Fourth, in assuming that language processes are strictly serial, generative models have abandoned all hope of characterizing them as online cognitive mechanisms, implying that certain linguistic operations occur in some sort of temporal vacuum. As Poeppel and Embick argue,

> [t]he tendency in generative syntax, for example, is to speak as if the computations proposed in syntactic analyses need not be regarded as computations that are performed in real time. But why should the null hypothesis be that there is some notion of grammar that is not computed in the brain in real time? This assumption simply makes the link between linguistics and neuroscience harder to bridge, for reasons that are ultimately historical, and not necessarily principled. (2005, p. 106)

Conversely, plausible characterizations of online processing are a key concern of RNT. The very operations of ordered and unordered nodes, together with the presence of excitatory and inhibitory connections, aim to provide dynamic accounts of verbal activity. If anything, RNT needs a better characterization of the temporal aspects of its networks (e.g., by incorporating reaction time and electrophysiological data), but this is certainly different from factoring temporal issues out of a cognitive model.

Fifth, generativists have consistently insisted on a generalization which can produce all 'grammatical' sentences of a language and does not permit the generation of any ungrammatical ones. The definition of grammatical is problematic by virtue of being circular. But if we ignore these problems, it is possible to discover another, very basic difference between generative and relational network theories. In RNT, the tactic patterns define the grammars of each stratum, a generalization supported by language acquisition data. Yet, this and other generalizations in RNT stop short of the all-and-only requirement, for example, as the research on speech errors reported here and in publications of Sullivan and Tsiang demonstrates (see Chapter 8). In RNT terms, tactic patterns are generalized, but not optimized, which allows individuals to take different paths and stop at different points.

On the question of tactic pattern generalization and improved resulting simplicity, two more points can be raised. To begin with, even after years of trying, generativists have never been able to agree on a simplicity metric. Peter Reich (1973) developed one for RNT. A workable metric permits us to determine the limits of simplification – i.e., when a simplification at one stratum causes a complication at another stratum that is greater than the original savings. Sullivan (1969) encountered just such a situation when drawing diagrams for his dissertation on phonology and inflectional morphology in Russian.[1] He was able to show that the morphotactic relations needed for a Jakobson one-stem description of the Russian verb were simpler than those needed for a traditional two-stem description. But he also found that the additional phonological structures needed to incorporate the resulting non-productive morphophonemic alternations exceeded the savings in the morphology. The lesson, in short, is to stop optimizing when you reach the point of diminishing returns.

Finally, Generative Grammar has been mostly dismissive of a conversation with neuroscience. As we noted in the Introduction and repeat here, Chomsky himself has claimed that '[w]e don't know nearly enough about the brain for cognitive science to take it seriously' (cited in Feldman, 2006, p. xi), adding that 'researchers in fields outside linguistics should adopt a wait-and-see attitude as [...] intradisciplinary issues are sorted out' (cited in Hauser, Chomsky, & Fitch, 2005, p. 183). On the contrary, RNT frames neuroscientific data as a key source of empirical constraints to incorporate in language models. In this way, it deviates from the disciplinary isolationism favored by staunch generativists, recognizing that a realistic model of language cannot be informed only by logical formalisms.

In sum, RNT is at odds with several key tenets of mainstream linguistics in general, and the generativist tradition, in particular. Crucially, the specific tenets endorsed by RNT are motivated by empirical reasons rather than *a priori* commitments. This, in addition to the theory's permeability to interdisciplinary developments and its compatibility with the findings of cognitive and neurological research, highlights the underexploited potential of the theory in the larger context of linguistics.

III   Prospects for Development

Despite its long history, RNT has been far from sufficiently developed. Fortunately, the theory is laden with possibilities for breakthroughs in many respects. Here we briefly address four of them: (a) the description of particular languages; (b) the establishment of links with Systemic-Functional Linguistics; (c) the deployment of platforms for computational implementations; and (d) the exploration of more fine-grained, multidimensional links with neuroscience.

First, no theory has yet been used to construct a fully exhaustive grammar of any given language. Though the practical problems of this exercise would most likely exceed the benefits, RNT has the reach to provide such a grammar. Extant work attests to the theory's modeling potential. Lamb (e.g., in 1966a, 1980, 1999, and in many of his papers collected in Webster [2004]), as well as Sullivan (1980) have offered detailed treatments of isolated features of English, such as declarative clause syntax and its interaction with semology, obviating the need for movement. For his own part, Lockwood (1972) outlined a general relational characterization of Czech and a detailed relational network treatment of markedness in the Bulgarian vowel system (1969). More work has been conducted on other languages. Sullivan (1998b) describes the semology and syntax (and some morphology) of preposition-case pairings in Russian, while Bogdan & Sullivan (2009) treat tense and aspect in Polish, including phenomena at the semantic, discourse, syntactic, and morphological levels. Recent studies touch on various aspects of Russian (Sullivan & Bogdan, in press) as well as speech errors in English and Polish (Sullivan & Tsiang, cf. Chapter 8, note 1). More efforts must be made in this direction, perhaps by relying on extant accounts from compatible frameworks (see Chapter 6).[2] Systemic-Functional Grammar is a good case in point.

Let us expand on this thought. Despite having relatively different central interests, RNT proves widely compatible with Systemic-Functional Linguistics. The affinities between the two approaches have been highlighted both in publications (Gil, 2013; Halliday, Lamb, & Regan, 1988; Lamb, 2013; and see Chapter 6) and at scholarly meetings (such as the Connecting Paths conference, held in Hong Kong in 2010). Indeed, in the third edition of the classic introduction to Systemic-Functional Grammar, Halliday & Matthiessen (2004, p. 24) state that the 'relation between semantic choice and what goes on in the brain' can be understood in RNT terms. Valuable seeds could be sown by integrating the exhaustive descriptions available in the systemic-functional literature with the neurocognitive framework afforded by RNT.

Also, additional progress could be made by exploring the theory's potential for computational implementation. This would allow the examination of hypotheses on the nodes' dynamic interactions during specific language processes. For those interested in this possibility, an initial effort can be found in the Ph.D. dissertation by Harrison (2000). Moreover, the Neurocognitive Linguistics Lab software[3] offers a user-friendly platform to test and visualize real-time processes in relational networks. Explorations of RNT based on these and other computational resources could yield original insights into language organization and function.

Finally, the question remains whether any relational network diagram is neurologically plausible. While possible neural correlates have been proposed for RNT constructs (Chapter 3), it cannot be assumed that the networks proposed to model specific linguistic phenomena are straightforwardly implemented by the brain. So far, neurological evidence has been used as a source of constraints that the theory has to satisfy in its quest for plausibility. However, relational networks are blind to myriad aspects of brain structure and function that directly impact cognitive processes, such as the accumulation and flow of specific types of neurotransmitters in different circuits, the role of cortico-subcortical loops in handling excitatory and inhibitory mechanisms, and the relationship between linguistic and non-linguistic systems (e.g., executive functions, social cognition). Thus, more extensively elaborated and multidimensional bridges must be forged with neuroscience in order for RNT to expand and refine its present theoretical apparatus.

IV   A Parting Word

As shown in Part I, RNT offers a logically, cognitively, and neurologically sound framework to characterize organizational and functional properties of language. Its key distinguishing feature is that it operates with relationships only; there are no items separate from the nodes that symbolize relationships. The multiple language problems addressed in Part II attest to the theory's modeling potential and elegance: a handful of well-defined constructs suffices to account for linguistic phenomena across numerous strata in different languages. We hope that this book will help the theory gain the visibility it deserves. Whether such prospective attention leads to greater acceptance, widespread fine-tuning, or even outright rejection remains to be seen. The point is that a full-blown neurocognitive theory rooted in structural linguistics should become better known among researchers in the field. We believe that both professional and aspiring linguists (as well as scholars in related disciplines) may capitalize on the insights derived therefrom.

Notes

1.   Sullivan was aware of Reich's simplicity metric, because Reich had presented it at a working seminar at Yale during the late 1960s.
2.   As a practical matter, more descriptive linguists working in RNT on languages other than English would be a major contribution to these efforts.
3.   The software is available for free download at <https://bitbucket.org/kulibali/neurocogling/wiki/Home>.

Appendix: An interview with Sydney Lamb

Introduction

Professor Sydney Lamb is arguably one of the most underrated linguists of our time. He is the creator of RNT; he was the founder of the linguistics department at Rice University; his name has long been an entry in the *Encyclopaedia Britannica*; and he has been recently recognized as one of three luminaries in the field of language to have graduated from Yale University.[1] Any linguistics scholar with such credentials should require no introduction to those operating within the discipline. Yet, somehow, most of Lamb's work and ideas remain largely unknown to both professional and aspiring linguists.

Perhaps because of such lack of recognition, not many interviews with Professor Lamb have been made available in academic circles. Only three can be easily found in relevant media. The first one was initially published by Herman Parret in 1974 and more recently re-edited as a chapter in *Language & Reality* (Webster, 2004). Given the development of the theory at the time this interview took place, no reference is made to its neurological implementation. The second one, which was conducted via e-mail in 1998 and published the following year in a Chinese journal by Cheng (1999), deals with broad generalities of RNT and offers no information that is not already available in its neurocognitive manifesto, *Pathways of the Brain* (Lamb, 1999). The third one was actually not a single interview but a series of interviews conducted by J. Paul Sank and aired in Life-Net News & Radio. These were divided into ten MP3 files – each dealing with a separate question. Both Cheng's and Sank's interviews can be found online at http://www.ruf.rice.edu/~lngbrain/.

Although somewhat outdated and even sketchy at times, such interviews can be seen as suggested preliminary readings to the present one, insofar as it avoids questions dealing with points already covered in them. Moreover, this interview might serve as a companion – or even an appendix – to Lamb's *Pathways of the Brain*, since it seeks to offer more precision regarding some of the topics the book addresses.

Without further introduction, what follows is the full transcription of an oral semistructured interview granted to Dr. Adolfo M. García by Professor Lamb on November 5, 2011, on the occasion of his scholarly visit to Argentina. The questions have been organized in three parts. Part I deals with Lamb's influences and his conception of language. Part II addresses some technical aspects of RNT. Finally, Part III is devoted to a discussion of the applications, limitations, and prospects of Lamb's proposals. Part II, in particular, presupposes some technical knowledge of relational networks. The other two are aimed at general audiences. This text will hopefully raise interest in, and divulge the views of, one of the foremost thinkers in the field. To this end, endnotes have been copiously used as references to various texts where specific ideas of Professor Lamb are explained in greater detail.[2]

I   Influences and Conception of Language

1. Professor Lamb, thanks for granting me this interview. I would like to begin by asking you who your main influences in linguistics have been.

First, I think I would mention Louis Hjelmslev, the Danish linguist. I never worked with him, but I read his *Prolegomena to a Theory of Language* (Hjelmslev, 1961 [1943]),[3] to which I was introduced by one of my Russian professors at the University of California, Berkeley, Francis Whitfield. He is the one who translated Hjelmslev's *Prolegomena* into English from the Danish. And he also introduced me to linguistic theory, which I found to be very fascinating. Up to that point I had been planning to specialize in Slavic linguistics, which I now find particularly boring [*laughs*]. I was also influenced by another professor, Murray Emeneau, a fine gentleman who just died a couple of years ago at the age of about one hundred. And there was Mary Haas, the great American Indian language specialist.[4]

I must also mention Charles Hockett. I actually met him back in my days as a student, when I attended the Linguistic Institute held at the University of Chicago. (In the US we have Linguistic Institutes every summer, though nowadays they are held every other year.) Hockett was one of the (visiting) faculty members that year. I read his theoretical writings and I realized he and I were thinking along the same lines, back in the days of the structural linguistics of the mid-1950s. At that same Institute, I also met Floyd Lounsbury, a great anthropologist from Yale. I took a course in Iroquoian languages with him. In that course I was the only student – a very specialized topic, Iroquoian languages. In those days, teachers didn't have any PowerPoints or overhead projectors; instead, they would write things on the blackboard. So he would write things on the blackboard and I would copy them; but since I was the only student, one day he said: 'Why are we doing this? Here, look at my notes!' [*laughs*].

2. You mentioned that Hockett and you were thinking along the same lines. What notions did the two of you share?

In those days, structural linguists were trying to figure out the nature of the phoneme – that was mostly in the 1930s – and then by the time of the late 1940s and early 1950s, the focus was on trying to figure out the nature of the morpheme – the morpheme being a unit intermediate between meaning and phonology. Some people would say that it is a combination of phonemes, but that's not enough. And others would have different theories about it. Hockett was interested in that question and so was I. As a matter of fact, that question is what led me to the discovery of relational networks. Hockett had meanwhile come very close to that. In the early 1960s, he published an article called 'Linguistic Elements and their Relations' (Hockett, 1961), in which he came very close to that same discovery, but he didn't quite get there.

Eventually I got there myself with the help of my other major influence, Michael Halliday. Actually, Halliday and I were influencing each other. We got together one day and I said 'I like your analysis of the English tense system,' and he said 'Well, I like your idea of stratification and realization.' He had been using the term 'exponentiation' and he said 'I'll use the term "realization" instead.' We were trading back and forth.[5]

I met him in 1964, and he showed me his notation for what he was calling systemic networks. At that time I was working on the problem of linguistic elements and their relations, and saw that his network notation was just what I needed to clarify my thinking about linguistic relationships. It was precisely in the fall of 1964 that I came to the discovery that language structure is a relational network. It doesn't have items or objects of any kind; it's all relations. I was aided in that by the help of notation. You know, we don't really think in the abstract. We think with the aid of words, or symbols, or notations of some kind. Now, that language is a system of relations is something that Hjelmslev had already said in his *Prolegomena* (the Danish original was published in 1943), but he had never demonstrated the truth of that idea. It wasn't until we had relational networks as a notation that it could be demonstrated.[6]

3. Are there any contemporary linguists whose work you admire?

Yes. I still admire the work of Michael Halliday. He's about five years older than I am, so he's been like my older brother in linguistics from the very beginning. I saw him most recently one year ago at a conference in China, and he's the linguist whose work I still admire most.

4. For over half a century now, you have been a fervent opponent of Chomsky's views of language. Your writings make it clear which generative theses you consider flawed. However, are there any generative principles or constructs that you agree with?

When I first heard about Generative Grammar and Chomsky, I was in that same Linguistic Institute where I studied with Hockett and Lounsbury. It was probably 1955 when I first heard of Chomsky. He and I both were in agreement that there were certain things about structural linguistics at that time that were misguided and needed to be changed.[7] To that extent, we were in agreement from the very beginning. But his proposals for bringing about that change turned out to be rather flawed, in my opinion.

Still, we were in agreement about some of the things that needed to be changed. For example, in structural linguistics, most people were using a procedural orientation. Instead of talking about linguistic elements and their relations, as Hockett did, they were talking about procedures that could be used, theoretically, to discover the structure of language. But you don't need to state a theory in the form of a discovery procedure. What you really need to do is to say what the relationships are, not how they would be discovered. Chomsky said that, and I was in total agreement. In fact, I was going to write an article about this topic and then I realized that Chomsky had already done it!

So this is where I agree with Chomsky. But I disagree with him on the grounds that he also has procedures in his theory that are undesirable. He didn't have discovery procedures, but he had derivation procedures – procedures for deriving sentences from, essentially, other sentences.[8] For example, in the passive transformation, first you start with a sentence in the active form and then you end up with a sentence in the passive form. That seemed to me wrongheaded. He then introduced the distinction between deep structures and surface structures. That would have been a good idea, if he had done it correctly. But he didn't do it right, because his way of getting from deep structure to surface structure was by a series of procedures. And that's not right. Deep structure is a structure, and surface structure is a structure, and what you need to do is show the relationships between them. And the best way to do that is *not* by means of procedures. Then there was the group from Ohio State – McCawley, Lakoff, and Fillmore – proposing an alternative that maybe we should go from surface structure to deep structure – the so-called Interpretive Semantics. But that was also wrong, because you should do it without a procedure at all. You should have relationships that you could traverse in either direction.

5. Given all this background, what is your definition of language nowadays?

Let me begin by saying that I don't like that kind of question. I know that it's been common for people to try to define language … but aside from that, we have to be clear what it is we are trying to define. The trouble is that the term 'language' has many different meanings; so, which one of those is it that we are trying to focus on? Instead of trying to define language, I try to think of what it is that we're interested in. One thing that we can be interested in is linguistic structure, and we can look at that either in an abstract form – which is what most linguists do – or in a concrete form. If you choose the former, it gets very confusing, so I prefer to look at language in a concrete form, by considering the system that people have in their brains, which makes it possible for them to speak and understand speech. That linguistic system is what I focus on. It is a physical system. Of the many meanings of 'language', that's the one that I choose. I would say that, by way of definition, it is a physical system located in the brain consisting, essentially, in a system of relationships.

Now, let me give you a little contrast. Many people have tried to define language as something used by a social group – the speech community.[9] This leads to all sorts of problems when you try to define it, the main reason being that every member of a speech community actually has his or her own system, which is not exactly the same as that of any other person in the community. So it's impossible to define language as a system used by a group. That is too vague a concept. But you *can* define the individual linguistic system, in terms of the individual's brain.[10]

6. In that sense, one of your main proposals is that the individual linguistic system is not just 'one big system', but that it has internal structure.

It does have internal structure, yes; and it can include knowledge of two or more languages. Usually it includes fragments of knowledge of many languages. And there, too, you have great differences between the systems of different people. Some people maybe know a hundred words of German, along with their English, and then fifty words of Spanish, and so on …

7. Evidently, yours is now a neurolinguistic theory. How do you conceive of neurolinguistics and how did you become interested in it?

First we should discuss what linguistics is. Linguistics, officially, is the science of language. Some researchers study phonology; others focus on semantics; still others work on comparing different languages and describing their respective evolution through time. However, not many people are operating in neurolinguistics, the field which studies how linguistic information is represented in our brain. This is what I'm interested in.

The field of neurolinguistics, a combination of language and brain studies, got started in as early as 1861, we might say. That year, the French doctor Paul Broca, studying people with brain damage, discovered that patients with damage in their frontal lobe were unable to speak, but they were able to understand language. Then, in 1874, Carl Wernicke had a patient who had sustained brain damage in his temporal lobe and couldn't understand, but was able to speak. This began the study of brain damage in relation to language.

My interest in the field, however, was sparked differently. Many years ago, my daughter Sarah was learning how to play the piano. She was six back then. I already had some intuitions as to how our cognitive system actually works, so I asked her: 'Sarah, when you hit that key with your finger, how does your brain tell your finger what key to hit?' She thought about it for a while, and then told me: 'Well, my brain writes a little note and then sends it down to my finger; then my finger reads it and knows what to do.' If you think about it, that doesn't quite make sense. Does the brain have a little pencil in there, and a piece of paper? And how does that piece of paper get down to the finger? And how does the finger read the note on that piece of paper?

We can ask the same question about how people talk. How does your brain tell your tongue what to do when you want to say a particular word? It doesn't write a little note, because there are no papers or pencils inside it. There must be another way. And, of course, there is: it's all done with connections – specifically, nerve connections. There are connections that go from the brain to that finger and move the muscles that make that finger work. In the same way, there are connections going to the muscles in your tongue. If I was going to figure out how language works, I had to do it without symbols. We can't assume that there are little papers with symbols and little eyes to read those symbols, and so on. It just doesn't work that way. That's basically how I got into neurolinguistics.

However, I discovered that language is a system of relationships before I knew anything about the brain. When I was giving presentations on this theory, people kept pointing out that relational networks resembled neuronal networks and asking me whether they were related in any way to brain structures. All I could say then was 'I have no idea!' I didn't know anything about neural networks. So I figured maybe I'd better learn something about the brain.

I was teaching at Yale at that time. I found a neuroscientist who was also working there, called him up, and invited him to have lunch. During that lunch I asked him to explain to me how neurons worked. He started drawing pictures on the paper napkins to show me how neurons are connected, and how impulses travel from one neuron to another … and the more he told me about how neurons work, the more astounded I was, because several aspects corresponded to relational networks, which I was developing on purely linguistic evidence. That was very encouraging. Ever since, I have studied the brain more and more, and I discovered that neural networks actually correspond to relational networks. That's a good thing because, after all, linguistic structure is in our brains.

8. People who are not familiar with neurolinguistics, upon first learning what the field is about, often ask: 'Where exactly in our brains do we have language?' How would you answer such a question?

It's a very interesting question. As it happens, language is not in just one location in the brain. It's all over it. Certain parts of language are mainly represented in specific parts of the brain, however. A lot of linguistic structure is in the left hemisphere; our recognition of speech is pretty much in the temporal lobe; speech articulation is in the frontal lobe, in a certain well-known area. But language is more than that. Think about semantics, for instance. We use language because we mean to say something, and semantics is all over the brain, involving both hemispheres. This makes sense because we use language to talk about everything that we can experience, and everything that we can experience is represented in different parts all over the brain. So we can say that language is widely distributed. When you're using language, you're using all parts of the brain.

9. In addition to this embodied conception of your object of study, what are the main theses of RNT?

First, language is a system of relations. That's the most important one. I came upon this discovery back in the fall of 1964. I still remember the afternoon in my office when I came to that realization. At that time I didn't know anything about the brain, no more than anyone else. But now I would add that the system is embodied in the brain. For the last twenty years I've been studying the brain, and I could see how this relational network, as an abstract system, actually relates to neural structures.

When you look at language in terms of brain structures, you also find that the linguistic system consists of multiple subsystems. That's what the idea of stratification was all about: first you have a phonological stratum, then you have a lexicogrammatical stratum, and at the top you have a sememic stratum – where you have concepts and so on. Now we can, to a certain extent, assign different localities in the brain to these different systems, but not the way you might think. For example, phonology is not in one part of the brain, but in two major parts. There's production phonology in the frontal lobe, and receptive phonology in the temporal lobe. There's also a third part, in the parietal lobe, which is the somatosensory part: in order to control the articulators (the tongue, and the teeth, etc.), you have to know where they are and what they are doing. So, for phonology, we actually have three different areas. Phonology is spread throughout what is called the perisylvian area, but each part of that area has its own unique function.

When you go to the higher levels, they are even harder to localize. The lexicogrammatical system is partly in the frontal lobe, the part of the system which has to do mostly with prepositions, verbs, and syntax – verbs and syntax are very much aligned anyway. The posterior part of the brain is concerned with nouns and adjectives. And then, if you get to the semantic level, it's all over the brain – including the right hemisphere – because what we talk about with language is everything we can experience; and everything we can experience is represented all over the brain.

10. Now, this is perhaps a personal view of mine, but it seems like a proper occasion to ask you. I've always been of the idea that there are parts of our experience – of our mental life, of our emotional life, if you will – that *cannot* be realized linguistically. There seem to be certain concepts, or certain constellations of meaning and experience, that can be perhaps expressed through music or with images, while language doesn't even come close to expressing them. Would you agree with that?

Yes, I agree, absolutely. Certain things are in the brain somewhere, but somehow they are not quite accessible to being expressed in language. That's a topic I'm very interested in. As the saying goes, a picture says more than a thousand words. Actually, a picture, if it's the right picture, can say more than ten thousand words. And there are certain aspects of music that you can't even come close to with words, yes.[11] There are other things you cannot do with words. For example, somebody makes a particularly delicious dish, and you eat it and it's a wonderful experience to eat it, but you cannot describe with words that unique taste it has. But what you *can* do with words is write a recipe so others can prepare that dish and then experience it for themselves.

11. Going back to the history of your theory, is there a difference between Stratificational Grammar and RNT, or are they just alternative labels for one and the same theory?

I would say that the answer is in between those two. Stratificational Theory is what I used to call the theory at first. I made a quasi-publication of it in 1962 – it was published at the University of California but not widely distributed. In that version there were no relational networks. And then, a few years later, *Outline of Stratificational Grammar* (Lamb, 1966a) came out and that's when relational networks were introduced. But I still called it

Stratificational Theory, because the emphasis was on the different strata of linguistic structure. So, the different terms provided different emphases.

Actually, it was Peter Reich, a student of mine, who said 'Why don't we just call it "Relational Network Theory"? Because maybe the most important thing about it is the relational networks and not the strata.' And I decided that he was right. From then on, I've mostly used the term 'Relational Network Theory'. It's a matter of what you want to give emphasis to. So we can say that the term 'Relational Network Theory' is used mainly in relation to the later versions, and 'Stratificational Grammar' with reference to the earlier versions; but in the middle there was a transitional period during which both terms were used. More recently, sometimes we talk about 'Neurocognitive Linguistics', since I started getting serious about how this theory relates to neural structure – that would be in the last twenty years.

12. So, nowadays, would it be fair to say that if I speak about relational networks I would still be talking about an abstract, disembodied theory, whereas if I wanted to make reference to your neurolinguistic theory I should call it Neurocognitive Linguistics? Or could I still use the term 'relational networks' with reference to the neurological implementation of your theory?

You could still use the term 'relational network' because we can show, step by step, how relational networks are related to neurocognitive networks. But relational networks are the more abstract version. It's the same thing with chemistry, and physics, and biochemistry. You can talk about chemistry in more abstract terms without actually talking about atomic structures, or you can get down to a finer level.

13. A few minutes ago you were discussing the impossibility of locating certain linguistic functions in one single, discrete area of the brain. However, we have a lot of clinical evidence coming from cases of the different aphasic syndromes and the double dissociations established between them. Semantic aphasia, for example, affects semantic processing, but not lexicogrammatical or phonological processing. Can we take the selectivity of these syndromes as evidence of the inner architecture of the linguistic system, of which subsystems actually exist within it?

In brief, the answer is yes, we can. We can use this along with other kinds of evidence. The interpretation of a lot of that aphasiological evidence is improved with a good knowledge of linguistics. And we also have other sources of information nowadays … brain imaging, which is very hard to interpret, and there it also helps to have good knowledge of linguistics.

Then there's the technique called transcranial magnetic stimulation ... All these things go together and they tend to reinforce each other as evidence.

Once again, it helps if you have a good knowledge of linguistics. Consider, for example, people who study different kinds of anomia. There are patients with impaired access to words for vegetables – sometimes it's both food and vegetables – but their knowledge of words for animals is perfectly fine. If you show them the picture of an animal, they have no problem, but if you show them the picture of a vegetable, they can't think of the name for it. Some of the people that try to interpret what's going on in the brain in these cases have incurred the mistake of thinking that the semantics of a particular category is located in one part of the brain. Actually, we know that that's not true. We have to recognize the difference between the levels of lexical and semantic representation. And semantics is distributed throughout many parts of the brain. These patients just happen to have problems with some specific areas of that widely distributed system.

14. What is the difference between the notions of 'mind' and 'brain'? How does each of them relate to your conception of the linguistic system of the individual?

We know what the brain is, thanks to the work of neuroanatomists. It is a physical object. The notion of mind is not as clear-cut at all. 'Mind' is a vague word in the English language – and there are similar words in other languages which do not exactly correspond to it – with different meanings to different people. So, it's not at all like the term 'brain'. In my work I avoid using the term 'mind' for just that reason. For one thing, you're not going to be clearly communicative if you use it because it can be interpreted differently. And it means nothing really concrete to anybody, because it's not a concrete thing. So I just stick to the word 'brain'.

15. However, most theories in the field of cognitive linguistics have no biological concerns whatsoever. Does the absence of neurological evidence somehow compromise the validity of disembodied cognitive theories of language (e.g., Langacker's Cognitive Grammar)[12]?

There is an article by Bert Peeters, published about ten years ago, called 'Does Cognitive Linguistics Live Up to its Name?' (Peeters, 2001). And the answer is no. He was talking of Langacker's theory mainly, and Langacker, of course, objected to that article. But Peeters still has a good point. Now, at the beginning I developed my own theory without knowing anything about the brain, but eventually I did look at the brain. When you try to see how to relate Langacker's theory to the brain, there's no obvious way to do that. Even less is there any way to relate Chomsky's theory to the brain. Lakoff has tried to develop a theory based on brain processes, but it's not getting anywhere. It's just too far removed from actual brain structures.

On the other hand, I find a lot of valuable things about Langacker's work. He has some great insights about semantics and other aspects of language. And then there's the people working on Construction Grammar, like Adele Goldberg. She knows nothing about the brain, but she's come up with some very good ideas about syntax. But the jury is out that you cannot ultimately justify a linguistic theory, in my opinion, without eventually going into the brain. What the proponents of disembodied theories could do, so as not to go directly into the brain, is show how their theories relate to RNT, since we already know how relational networks can be implemented in the brain.

II   Technicalities of Relational Network Theory

16. Let us now get more technical and discuss some specific aspects of your relational networks. I have noted that the nodes and lines which characterize relational network notation are very similar to those proposed by McCulloch and Pitts (1943). Did these authors influence your thinking or are such coincidences merely fortuitous?

It's just fortuitous. I didn't know anything about their work until people started pointing out the similarities you mention. You can see that my thinking was parallel to theirs in some aspects; they make use of basic logical distinctions that I was using, too. There are AND and OR nodes in both theories, and in digital electronic networks they do the same thing – Boolean gates and so on. But what we have discovered in relational networks is that the AND and OR distinction is not a basic distinction after all. What we have is a threshold, and the threshold is variable. It can be of any value from zero on up, irrespective of the number of incoming lines into a node. The AND and OR are just special cases: in the case of AND nodes, the threshold coincides with the number of incoming lines, and in the case of the OR node, the threshold is just 1.

17. You propose that the cognitive system does not store symbols or objects of any kind. Instead, you propose that in an individual's cognitive system 'there are only relationships' and that 'all information is in the connectivity.' Would you please elaborate on these ideas? To many scholars, they seem to be the hardest notions to either grasp or accept.

I find it that the only way I can explain it is with the aid of diagrams. Now that we have the Spanish translation of my book[13] – or for those who prefer to read it in the original version – Chapter 4 contains the diagrams I'm making reference to. Once again, the rejection of symbols as the constituting elements of the linguistic system is not based on neurological evidence at all. In *Pathways of the Brain* (Lamb, 1999), I didn't use neurological evidence at all until the theory was fully developed – only in the later chapters do I introduce the brain. But we can say this much in words: if there are symbols in our cognitive system – as Pinker claims, though he ought to know better – how does the brain use them? Does it have little eyes to read the symbols? Are there any other sense organs in the brain? No, the brain does not contain any sense organs! Sense organs are all on the outside of the brain. The brain processes sensory information coming from the outside. There is no way that the brain could use symbols. There must be something else going on. We know from neuroanatomy that the brain consists of connections; there are neurons and their interconnecting fibers, and that's all.

Now, neuroscientists have not been able to tell us anything about how the brain actually works, about how it actually processes information. They can tell us how neurons receive and send activation, how synapses get formed and strengthened, what brings about long-term potentiation, and so on. But they can't tell you the first thing about how language works, for example – or any other cognitive process, for that matter. They're working with the hardware. It's similar to asking an electronic engineer to tell you how the computer translates, or how it calculates the orbits of satellites. They're working in a different area. Relational network linguistics has provided the answer to that question: how the brain processes information. The answer to the basic question of cognitive neuroscience has come from neurocognitive linguistics and nowhere else.

18. In *Pathways of the Brain* you advance the hypothesis that nections are implemented neurologically as cortical minicolumns. Now, in your most recent work, you are also making reference to functional webs *à la* Pulvermüller (2002). What would be the difference between cortical minicolumns and functional webs as the physical implementation of linguistic representations?

The functional web consists of interconnected nodes, and what I'm saying is that each node is implemented in the brain as a cortical column. The functional web is perfectly consistent with this claim. I suggested in *Pathways of the Brain* that the nodes of networks are represented as cortical columns. More recently, since Mountcastle's book[14] on cortical columns has come out, I have a much clearer understanding of them. In *Pathways of the Brain* I also had functional webs, but I didn't use that term. When I talk about the network representation for a lexeme or a morpheme or things like that, all those are also functional webs. Now I find that this is a useful term to make some things clearer.

My contention is that each of the nodes in a functional web would be implemented as a cortical minicolumn or as a bundle of minicolumns. A functional web is distributed over a large area of cortex. If you look at just about any of the diagrams in *Pathways of the Brain*, you're seeing either a functional web or part of a functional web, consisting of multiple nodes linked by interconnecting lines.

Contiguous columns, which form a maxicolumn, are usually in competition with each other since they belong to different functional webs. For example, let's take a phonological web for a syllable – let's say, /kæt/. The final consonant is a /t/. That /t/ will be in contrast with other final consonants, and all of them will be clustered together in a maxicolumn, although each of them can belong to different functional webs. For example, that final /t/ is also part of the functional web for /pæt/, /ræt/, and so on.

So every node is represented by a column. Depending on how much learning has taken place, the columns for a particular node may be represented by a minicolumn, or a maxicolumn, or something in between that we would call a functional column.[15] It could be, and often is the case, that further learning will take place in the future allowing a column to be divided further into smaller functional columns, because you've learned some new distinction.

19. In relational network notation, the same type of node may be used to represent a phoneme, or a demisyllable, or a morpheme, or a lexeme, etc., and you presume that the physical implementation of *any* node is a cortical column, irrespective of the type of linguistic representation that it processes. Are you saying that the same type of biological substrate may suffice to process either a phonetic trait, or a phoneme, or a morpheme, or a lexeme, and so on?

Yes, it's the same basic structure and the same basic process. The node itself, the column, doesn't know what it's doing. It's receiving activation and sending activation out, and what actual function that node turns out to have depends on where it's receiving information from and where it's sending information to.

20. In *Pathways of the Brain* you mention three possible mechanisms that could implement the delay element in ordered AND nodes. Today,

over a decade later, have you been able to rule one of them out, or to offer more precision as to how each of them works?

Yes. In the first place, we shouldn't think that we have to choose between those possibilities. The brain makes use of whatever equipment is available. Probably all three, and maybe even more, are actually in use. There is a clear source for fixed timing, namely the thalamus – and maybe whatever else is involved in brainwaves. You have different frequencies of brainwaves, each of which is an actual clock sending out impulses at fixed intervals. When we are awake and conscious, the thalamus sends signals sweeping through the whole cortex about 40 times per second, so that's providing a regular clock. This kind of timing control probably is involved in many aspects of language.

There's another type of timing control, which uses the 'wait element' as described in *Pathways of the Brain*. The 'wait element' is a device that keeps activation alive by recycling it. We now find in the knowledge of cortical columns that every column has the potential for being a 'wait element', because it can recycle information among its various neurons and keep that information active until it gets turned off by inhibitory neurons.

21. Is there a difference between this notion and that of 'reverberation'?[16]

Reverberation is something different, as it occurs *between* different cortical columns. For example, in an activated functional web, the different columns are sending activation back and forth among one another, which keeps the activation in the web alive. There is also the question of how long the activation is kept alive in actual processing. Maybe it can remain active for as long as we want. If I look at that glass of water and I keep thinking about the glass of water, the reverberation for that functional web will keep going for as long as I keep paying attention to the glass of water. As I keep watching, the web keeps receiving additional activation from my eyes while it stays active.

22. The two types of inhibitory connections recognized within RNT (viz., the one landing on a node and the one landing on a line) closely resemble the two types of inhibitory connections found between cortical neurons (namely, axosomatic and axoaxonic inhibitory connections). Is this a coincidence, or was that distinction actually taken from neuroscience?

This is a really interesting case. It was not imported from neuroscience because I was making that distinction before I knew about neurons. In relational networks we also have inhibitory connections – we have the blocking element. In fact, we have two types of inhibitory connections in narrow notation, both justified purely on linguistic evidence. You could say it's just a coincidence that relational networks have the same two types of inhibitory connections present in the brain. But it's not a coincidence because, after all, language is something that is used by our brains. Of course, you first have to realize that language is a relational structure. Then you can start drawing models of this structure, and those models will be networks. As you refine your knowledge, step by step, you realize that you need two types of inhibitory connections. Only then can you look at the brain to see whether you find correlates of those two types of inhibitory connections.

Some fifteen years ago, when I was teaching classes at Rice, one of my students mentioned that he was taking a course in neuroscience and that there were two kinds of connections between neurons that exactly corresponded to the abstract distinction. It figures: if I'm describing language accurately, and if language really is a system in the brain, then it has to be that way. The linguistic finding that there are two types of inhibitory connections actually amounts to a hypothesis about what the brain must have in it somewhere. Then, when you find that, the hypothesis is confirmed.

23. Now, when it comes to drawing relational networks, how do you decide whether to use one type of inhibitory connection or the other?

It's hard to answer this in the abstract, without any drawings. But consider a case of alternate realizations, where you have the marked case and the unmarked case. There you always have inhibition going to a line. However, if you're talking about something semantic, then it's different. Take, for example, the categorization of CUPS and GLASSES. CUPS and GLASSES would be a case where you have concept nodes in a maxicolumn for DRINKING VESSELS, which then gets subdivided into a part for CUPS and another one for GLASSES. A property like HAVING A HANDLE would be excitatory for CUP but inhibitory for GLASS. There you would be going directly to the node.

24. Could you give us an example of how we process linguistic information in our brains?

Language, as you know, is very complicated. What people would really like to know is how a whole sentence works, but that's just way too complicated. So let's just take one word. I'll tell you about a particular experiment that was done, in which people were shown pictures of animals and all they had to do was say what the animal was.[17] We might think that this is something that happens instantaneously, but that is not the case.

What happens is that you see the picture with your eyes and that information goes down the optic nerves to the occipital lobe. From there, you have connections going to various places in the visual network, all involved in recognizing the horse as such and activating its corresponding concept. Further connections link the conceptual representation to the phonological image /hors/ in Wernicke's area (in the temporal lobe), and then activation proceeds to the frontal lobe, where movements of the speech production mechanism are organized. All this complex array of connections must be activated just to say the word *horse*. That's what the theory predicts. In the experiment I'm discussing, they use a brain imaging technique called magnetoencephalography, which can measure the time course of activation of different parts of the brain, and the results verified that this is exactly what happens. The interesting thing is that it takes six-tenths of a second – i.e., 600 milliseconds – from the time the subjects see the picture until they actually articulate the word. What appears to be instantaneous is actually a very complex process.

III Relational Network Theory: Applications, Limitations, and Prospects

25. RNT is far from being a mainstream theory of language. It certainly does not enjoy the popularity of other theories, such as Generative Grammar or Systemic-Functional Linguistics, to name but a few examples. Why do you think it has not become more popular?

Well, there are many reasons that we can point to. For one thing, if you think about Generative Grammar as a very popular theory, you will find that Chomsky is a very prolific writer. He's been writing ever since he was in his twenties, and he has a huge volume of literature. I remember one night I heard from a colleague of his, Morris Halle, that Chomsky had come across a paper criticizing his approach to phonology, and he was so incensed that he stayed up that night and by the morning he had a finished paper [*laughs*]. Halliday is a very prolific writer, too. I, on the other hand, did not publish much of anything. In 1966, I published *Outline of Stratificational Grammar*, and it was not until 1999 that I published another book. Of course, I wrote a lot of articles in between, but nowhere near the volume of Chomsky and Halliday. That's one of the main factors. If you want to be known, you have to publish a lot.

26. In order to work within RNT you need to reject many of the tenets upheld by the mainstream linguistic theories. Do you believe that, in a

way, it has become dangerous for linguists to subscribe to your theory? Have you been 'blacklisted' somehow?

To some extent, that is the case. Back in the early days, when I was known to be opposed to Chomsky's ideas … there were various tricks being used to keep alternative views out of the public eye. Not so much in these days, though.

If you want to write a Ph.D. thesis from a relational network perspective, nowadays, there are no options available. As an Emeritus Professor, I am no longer allowed to supervise theses anymore, and I'm practically the only one working within this framework. My students, over the years, have been interested in more practical things than neurocognitive linguistics. Something similar happened to Hjelmslev. He didn't leave any student who worked with him closely to carry on his work. His writings, though, influenced many people, including Halliday and myself.

27. Would it be possible (and, if so, useful) for RNT to incorporate neurological evidence at a smaller scale than it has so far (e.g., different types of neurotransmitters, neuroreceptors, etc.)?

Yes, in neurocognitive linguistics we have an interface between cognitive linguistics and neuroscience, and there are no boundaries. Of course, it's hard to try to foresee anything. But, for example, in addition to local neurotransmitters, there are global transmitters, like dopamine and serotonin, which influence the operation of the brain globally. We can sort of tell when a person gets tired or intoxicated that there's a deficiency in certain global neurotransmitters – maybe an increase in norepinephrine – which leads to more excitation or inhibition of the overall processing. It would be possible to look into that, but of course you need a solid training in neuroscience.

28. Could RNT be used to model non-linguistic aspects of cognition, such as vision, somatosensory perception, or motor action?

Yes, it can and should. I'm just waiting for somebody to do it.

29. How can RNT contribute to foreign language teaching? Are there any pedagogical or didactic applications of the theory?

Well, there can be, but the interesting thing is that good foreign language teachers have really good intuition about how to teach foreign languages, and they've already been doing it the right way. We can show from neurocognitive evidence *why* they're doing it the right way. They have intuitively already found the way to do it well, for example, by using constant repetition – drills – giving students frames in which you substitute words, applying real-life contexts … all these things make the learning process easier in the brain, but teachers already know that.

More and more evidence shows that it's easier for younger brains, which have greater plasticity, and therefore it's easier for them to make new connections and to strengthen existing connections. Yet, people already knew that the earlier you start instruction in a foreign language, the easier it will be for a child to learn the language. Whatever insight you might get from neurocognitive linguistics has already been picked up by language teachers from other sources – sometimes, just from their experience.

There's a very interesting experiment that was done by Susan Ervin at the University of California, Berkeley when I was teaching there. They decided to test different methods of language teaching. They used three different methods, and they had several different language teachers – some were graduate students in linguistics. The teachers had to teach different groups for a period of about eight to twelve weeks, using these different methods. At the end of the experiment, the researchers found that the teaching methods made no significant difference in the students' results, but when they correlated the results with the teachers, they found that good teachers were getting good results no matter which method they used. It was the teacher who made the difference.

30. What are the limitations of RNT? What can it not explain?

The more we learn, the more we realize what we don't know. There's a lot about syntax that remains to be explained in relational terms. We are now at the doorstep of explaining how syntax really works in the brain. The most basic part of syntax is the relationship between verbs and the nouns which co-occur with them. For most action verbs, there needs to be an Actor – corresponding with the subject in the ordinary situation – and in many cases there's also a Goal that realizes the object. By relating this to brain structure we can begin to see how that kind of things works. We can see that syntax is tagged on to ordinary behavior. When you learn a word like *eat*, you know that there has to be an EATER and an EATEE (the eating entity and the food). This is also true in the actual process, quite apart from the linguistic representation. The process of EATING is known by children and used by them from the very first day they are born. When they eat, there is activation going on in the motor cortex controlling the muscles which are used for eating, and they also see and touch the item of food that they are eating – say, a cracker. That brings about activation in the posterior part of the brain – the visual part and the somatosensory part. All that information is connected to the concept CRACKER, in the posterior part of his cortex. The motor representations take place in the frontal lobe, so there are connections established between the frontal and the posterior part of the brain, completely independent from language. The frontal lobe represents the process of EATING and the posterior areas represent the object of EATING. Later on, the child can attach these to linguistic representations. Very close to the location in the frontal lobe where the process of EATING is represented you have the linguistic representation *eat*. The object being eaten, let's say the cracker, will be connected to a phonological representation, /kræker/, in Wernicke's area. There are connections already present going from the morpheme *eat* to the morpheme *cracker*. They're just, as it were, slight additions to what is already there at the conceptual level. This needs to be pursued and developed from that very beginning that I'm just playing around with now.

31. Let me make sure that I understand your point here. Are you saying that the semotactics determines the lexotactics?

Yes, that's correct. That's exactly what I'm saying. And the lexotactics is not something that has to independently be formed in the learning process of language. It's just a few additional connections to the semotactics that is already there. The baby is dealing with combinations of processes and their participants way before he develops his linguistic system. Those patterns, I believe, are used when the baby is learning syntax.

32. Is there any other aspect that needs further development in relational-network terms?

There's also work to be done regarding the given/new distinction that Halliday has worked so much on – information structure.[18] Neither he nor anyone else has ever studied how that works in the brain. That needs to be done, and we haven't done it.

The given/new distinction is one of Michael Halliday's greatest contributions in linguistics. Most linguistics deals with only one of the three functions that he identifies – the ideational function of language. Now, in the given/new distinction, you have the given and the new. Relational network grammar can actually explain what's going on and why that is an important distinction. Remember, we are looking at language in relation to the information system in the brain. First, you have to realize that when two people are talking, each of them has his own information system, in the form of a network. One of the main reasons why people talk to one another is to exchange information. When a person A says something to a person B it is because A believes that B doesn't know the information he wants to convey. Otherwise, why would A say something that B already knows? Of course, there is the phatic function, but we can skip its discussion here.

When you're exchanging information, of course, there is a given and a new. The function of the given, in network terms, is to identify locations in the network where the new information is to be added. New information consists of new connections, and the given is what it is to be connected to. When you tell somebody 'That cat is named James,' you assume that the listener already knows which cat you're talking about – maybe it's a cat in the room. You also assume that the only thing that the speaker doesn't know is the name of the cat. Furthermore, you suppose that your interlocutor somehow wants to know what the name of that cat is. There's only one new item of information in that whole sentence, namely, the cat's name, James. Everything else is there simply to identify locations in the network. The only new thing is the connection to the name: the phonological form /ʒemz/ and the lexicogrammatical form *James* are already there, so the only thing added is the connection proper.

The given will always be represented in terms of dedicated connections, and the new will always involve a latent connection. Sometimes a latent nection needs to be added, sometimes only just a connection between two existing nections. When this happens, the latent connection becomes an established connection. By recognizing this, one is able to make sense of these things that Halliday has been talking about.

33. And what about the description of particular languages?

That's a good point, because it raises a big question: is it appropriate to use relational networks to describe languages, for practical purposes – e.g., writing a grammar of Chinese using relational networks? I'm not so sure that we should. You have to look at the reason for writing a grammar. If your reason is to write a grammar for learning Chinese, then it's better to do it with symbols. Relational networks account for what happens inside your brains. If you want to learn about the description of a language, you have to use your eyes, and eyes are really good at reading symbols. For such a grammar it's better to do it in words. That's another reason why RNT has not become more popular in linguistics, because linguists are mostly interested in languages, as you might expect. But relational networks are actually about how the brain works and how language actually works. What linguists are interested in, surprisingly, is not how language actually works. They want to know how you can do things with languages.

Lockwood offered a relational description of Czech[19] a few decades ago, and I myself described parts of English grammar throughout my career.[20] But even if you constructed a full network of, say, Chinese, nobody would be able to read it. Even somebody who knows relational networks would find it difficult to read. That's because relational networks are describing what's going on in the brain, but when you want to understand something by reading, you should use symbols, for practical purposes. Now, the same consideration applies to systemic-functional networks and Generative Grammar. I believe you will find that any of these generative grammars of Italian or English are not very useful. They don't tell you very much about Italian that you can use. These theories are not really suited for language description. It doesn't mean they are useless, though – however, I must say that a use for Generative Grammar has yet to be found. Systemic-functional grammars, for instance, have proven very useful to provide insights about language structure and how languages work.

34. Still, when we think of the systemic networks with which Halliday characterizes English, for example, we find some details which seem to be exclusive of just English – or, at least, not applicable to the description of just any language. For instance, in English, the relative arrangement of the subject and the operator determines whether the clause is a declarative or an interrogative, irrespective of the intonation we apply on it. Spanish, on the other hand, works in an entirely different way.[21] What about these descriptive differences?

These differences you're talking about can be described in any of many ways, and they have been described many times before Halliday ever came along. Any of those descriptions is just as good, just as meaningful. Going back to the key point in the previous question, relational networks seek to characterize language in the brain and explore its connections with the rest of human cognition. This is where RNT makes its contribution.

35. In 2011, *Pathways of the Brain* was translated into Spanish. Last year, Gordon Tischer released a computer program to design and test relational networks.[22] Also, a symposium was held in 2010 in search of intertheoretical links between your work and that of Halliday and Hasan.[23] Is RNT finally resurfacing, or are these isolated, circumstantial events?

Well, it's impossible to tell. I heard someone was working on an Arabic translation of *Pathways*, and there was supposedly somebody working on a Russian translation, too, but I haven't heard anything about that recently.

Some people have written about my work in Chinese. Other than that, who knows what might happen with the theory? I, for one, don't know.

Syd, thank you very much for your time and insights.

Thank you. It's been a pleasure.

Notes

1. On October 5, 2001, Yale University celebrated the 300th anniversary of its founding in 1701. The occasion was commemorated by a celebration held in Yale Bowl (the university's football stadium). It consisted of a 90-minute stage show with video, orchestra, celebrity hosts, laser show, and a fireworks display. In a section of the program celebrating achievements by Yale graduates, William F. Buckley (an alumnus and a prominent journalist and TV personality) identified, for each of a large number of fields of endeavor, three or four persons who had graduated from Yale during those 300 years. Buckley was reading from a script that had been prepared by a scriptwriter in collaboration with the Tercentennial office at Yale. In speaking about Yale Men of Letters, he said, 'Noah Webster was the class of 1778. We know him as the father of the American dictionary and he was also the publisher of the Blue Backed Speller. Sydney Lamb, 1951, changed the way we understand grammar. William Poole, 1849, was the first publisher of indexed periodical literature, and Sinclair Lewis, 1907, was the first American to be awarded the Nobel Prize for literature.'
2. Most of the references given are based on revised, updated versions of earlier papers by Lamb, as published in the compilation *Language & Reality: Selected Writings of Sydney Lamb* (Webster, 2004).
3. Lamb's critical review of Hjelmslev's *Prolegomena* was first published in 1966 and then published in revised form in Lamb (2004c).
4. A brief reminiscence of Lamb's times as a student under Mary Haas's wing can be found in Lamb (2004g).
5. For an interesting discussion of these exchanges by the two scholars themselves, see Halliday, Lamb, & Regan (1988).
6. The full demonstration can be found in Chapter 4 of *Pathways of the Brain* (Lamb, 1999).
7. Lamb refers here to American structuralism in the Bloomfieldian tradition.
8. For a detailed discussion of Lamb's criticism of descriptive and derivational processes, see Lamb (2004f, 2004k).
9. Lamb's arguments against a definition of language as a socially-shared entity are fully developed in Lamb (2004b).
10. See Lamb (2006).
11. For a neurocognitive contrast between meaning in language and meaning in music, see Lamb (2004l).
12. See, for example, Langacker (1991).
13. The translation in question is titled *Senderos del Cerebro: La Base Neurocognitiva del Lenguaje* (Lamb, 2011).
14. Lamb refers to *Perceptual Neuroscience: The Cerebral Cortex* (Mountcastle, 1998).
15. Not to be confused with a functional web.

16. For an in-depth discussion of the notion of reverberation, see Pulvermüller (2002).
17. Lamb is referring to a study conducted by Levelt *et al.* (1998).
18. See Halliday (1994) and Halliday & Matthiessen (2004).
19. See Lockwood (1972).
20. Some morphological and clausal aspects of English have been described in Lamb (1966a, 1999). A relational account of the basics of English phonotactics can be found in Lamb (1980).
21. See A. García & Gil (2011).
22. The software in question is called Neurocognitive Linguistics Lab and can be freely downloaded at: https://bitbucket.org/kulibali/neurocogling/wiki/Home.
23. Visit http://ctl.cityu.edu.hk/Portal_root/subsites/symposiums/2010/nov/CPLHH/LSS_conference.html for information on the symposium's topics and conclusions.

Glossary of Terms

abstract notation: a notation system for drawing relational networks with bidirectional connections.

activation: the collection of signals traveling across nodes in relational networks; the term also refers to the state of a neural network which has surpassed a critical threshold of excitation.

agrammatism: aphasic condition characterized by loss of grammatical skills.

algebraic notation: variant representation of a relational network where nodes and their connections are presented as formulae.

AND node: a construct in Relational Network Theory expressing a conjunctive relation; it may be upward or downward, ordered or unordered.

archiphoneme: a composite phonological unit postulated as a representation of phonemes whose contrast has been neutralized.

axoaxonic inhibitory connection: type of interneuronal connection through which activity in the afferent neuron is dampened or interrupted by synaptic processes operating on one of its axons.

axosomatic inhibitory connection: type of interneuronal connection through which activity in the afferent neuron is dampened or interrupted by synaptic processes operating on its cell body.

blocking element: relational network mechanism through which activation flow between nodes becomes interrupted.

branching node: a relational network node in narrow notation whose incoming activation spreads out along two or more outgoing lines.

Brodmann areas: regions of the cerebral cortex identified as groupings of specific cell types associated with particular cognitive functions.

characteristics (of a verb): the semantic features of MOOD, TENSE, and ASPECT as realized in Spanish verb morphology.

clitic: a morpheme attached to a host word; it is syntactically similar to an individual word but is phonologically dependent on its host.

cognitive plausibility: the degree to which a theory of language conforms to organizational and functional properties of the human mind.

cohesion: the set of grammatical and lexical linkages which hold a text together and contribute to its integrated meaningfulness.

composite realization: a realizational discrepancy in which a unit of a given stratum gets realized as more than one unit of the immediately lower stratum.

concept: a distributed network integrating information from different perceptual modalities.

confunct: a distributed network integrating information from different perfunctual domains.

cortical minicolumn: a functional unit comprising roughly 100 neurons and proposed to constitute a key processing module in the neocortex.

declension: the inflection of a noun, pronoun, adjective, or article in a particular language.

dedicated (connection): the state achieved by a relational network connection once it becomes stably specialized for processing a specific type of information.

descriptive process: a theoretical operation within analytical linguistics whereby certain linguistic units are derived from other units through mutations or other algorithmic mechanisms.

developmental plausibility: the degree to which a theory of language realistically characterizes the evolution of an individual's linguistic system throughout life.

diamond node: a construct in Relational Network Theory summarizing two unordered AND relationships.

diversification: a realizational discrepancy in which an element in a given stratum is represented by different units on the immediately lower stratum.

downward: direction of information flow leading from a given stratum or level to a lower one.

embodied/conceptual/executive cognition: the collection of neurocognitive systems which ground and coordinate semological information during verbal communication but are neither exclusively nor distinctively linguistic.

eme: any unit belonging to a particular stratum (e.g., phoneme, morpheme, lexeme, sememe).

empty realization: a realizational discrepancy in which units which appear at a given stratum represent nothing on the higher stratum.

established (connection): the state achieved by a relational network connection once it is recruited to process a specific type of information.

excitatory (connection): type of connection through which an efferent node sends positive signals to an afferent node, such that the amount of activation in the latter increases.

feature: a phonetic characteristic of a phoneme, manifested as a hypophoneme in Relational Network Theory.

feature geometry: an approach of Generative Grammar, where distinctive features are represented as a structured hierarchy (represented as a tree) rather than a set, with the goal of reducing the number of features used to distinguish the phonemes of a language.

feedback timing: a mechanism which regulates information flow by sequencing patterns of activation based on a relational network's internal dynamics.

form potential: the whole range of morphological, lexemic, morphotactic, and lexotactic options available in an individual's lexicogrammatical system.

functional web: a widely distributed microsystem of neurons assumed to process specific types of information by virtue of various activity states.

Generative Grammar: a theory of language developed by American linguist Noam Chomsky in the 1950s which models language competence/ knowledge in terms of finite serial rules operating on symbolic objects.

Glossematics: a theory of language proposed by Danish linguist Louis Hjelmslev in the 1930s, whose connectionist and stratificational premises laid the foundation for Relational Network Theory.

graphic notation: variant representation of a relational network as a system of nodes and lines indicating their linkages; it can be implemented through two main sets of conventions known as abstract notation and narrow notation.

hypophoneme: a relation linking phonotactic patterns with phonetic nodes, which subserves specific contrastive features to distinguish between morphemes.

ideonection: a functionally specialized network subserving a specific and contrastive pattern of information in the embodied/conceptual/executive system.

inhibitory (connection): type of connection through which an efferent node sends negative signals to an afferent node, such that activity is reduced or blocked.

introjection: a modeling approach in cognitive science which characterizes the mind as composed of the very objects and operations which populate the physical world around us.

junction node: a relational network node in narrow notation, featuring a hypothetical activation threshold, which integrates signals from two or more efferent nodes.

lexicogrammar: a stratum of the linguistic system composed of logonections, morphonections, lexotactic patterns, and morphotactic patterns which mediate between the semantic and the phonological strata.

lexotactics: the collection of ordering patterns specifying how lexemes may combine in a language.

linearization: the sequencing of units at any level of linguistic or supralinguistic processing.

linguistic paragraph: a portion of discourse characterized by spatio-temporal consistency, internal coherence, and (relative) conceptual autonomy.

logonection: a functionally specialized network subserving a specific and contrastive pattern of lexemic information in the lexicogrammatical stratum.

meaning (of a clitic): any set of semantic features that a clitic explicitly and necessarily expresses in every context of occurrence.

meaning potential: the whole range of possible meanings available in an individual's semantic system.

message (of a clitic): any set of semantic features that a form may implicitly convey in a specific context of occurrence.

morphonection: a functionally specialized network subserving specific patterns of morphological information in the lexicogrammatical stratum.

morphotactics: the collection of ordering patterns specifying how morphemes may combine in a language.

mutable lexeme: a structured lexemic pattern which can consistently evoke distinctive conceptual associations even if one of its lexical constituents is substituted.

narrow notation: a notation system for drawing relational networks with unidirectional connections; relative to abstract notation, it corresponds more precisely to the structure and function of neural networks.

nection: a linkage between two nodes indicated by a single internal line in a relational network; nections at the phonemic, morphemic, lexemic, and sememic strata are called phononections, morphonections, logonections, and semonections, respectively; nections in the embodied/conceptual/executive system are called ideonections.

neocortex: the largest part of the cerebral cortex, covering both cerebral hemispheres.

neurological plausibility: the degree to which a theory of language conforms to organizational and functional properties of the human brain.

neutralization: a realizational discrepancy in which a unit in a lower stratum corresponds to two or more units in an upper stratum.

obstruent: a class of non-sonorant consonants including fricatives, affricates, stops.

onset: the initial portion of a syllable, which may manifest as either a single phoneme or a phoneme cluster.

operational plausibility: the degree to which a theory of language aptly characterizes how people use language in real time given well established processing constraints.

OR node: a construct in Relational Network Theory expressing a disjunctive relation; it may be upward or downward, ordered or unordered.

ordered: a node property specifying sequential order in the emission or reception of activation.

participant: an entity, typically denoted by a noun phrase or a pronoun, with a specific syntactic and semantic role relative to the process realized by its associated verb.

percept: a unimodal perceptual representation.

perfunct: an individual motor representation.

phonology: a stratum of the linguistic system composed of phononections and phonotactic patterns which mediates between the lexicogrammatical and the phonetic systems.

phononection: a functionally specialized network subserving a specific and contrastive pattern of information in the phonological system.

phonotactics: the collection of ordering patterns specifying how phonemes may combine in a language.

phrase structure rule: in the generative tradition, a rewrite rule.

portmanteau realization: a realizational discrepancy in which units on one stratum do not correspond to what their combination yields on an adjacent stratum.

procedural description: a theoretical operation within analytical linguistics whereby linguistic units are adduced and described via deduction or induction.

quantum firing: an account of relational network dynamics which describes how signals are released in a burst from one node to another once the activation level of the firing node is reached.

realization: the relationship between the units of a given stratum and those belonging to the immediately lower one.

recruitment: the process whereby nodes in a relational network or neurons in a neural network become selected to subserve specific functions.

redundancy: specification of the same information in two or more portions of a linguistic unit or its description.

Relational Network Theory: a connectionist theory of language, mainly developed by American linguist Sydney Lamb, that seeks to describe the linguistic system of individuals following the requisites of operational plausibility, developmental plausibility, and neurological plausibility.

relational network: interconnected system of nodes and their linkages conceived to characterize the organization and functional dynamics of an individual's linguistic system.

semantics: a stratum of the linguistic system composed of semonections and semotactic patterns which mediates between embodied/conceptual/executive cognition and the lexicogrammatical system.

semotactics: the collection of ordering patterns specifying how sememes may combine in a language.

speech error (or slip of the tongue): utterance compatible with the speaker's linguistic system but not the intended utterance.

spoonerism: a type of timing error in which linguistic units are transposed.

Stratificational Grammar: a connectionist theory of language developed by Sydney Lamb in the 1960s, which formed the basis for Relational Network Theory.

subcortical structures: brain regions which lie below the cerebral cortex.

substitution error: a speech error in which one linguistic unit (or cognitive unit) is erroneously substituted for another.

syllable: traditionally, a phonological unit including an onset, a nucleus, and a coda.

synapse: a microscopic gap between two neurons through which they exchange chemical or electrical signals.

syntax: in traditional grammar, structural patterns governing the organization of words, groups, phrases, and clauses in a sentence.

Systemic-Functional Linguistics: a theory developed by British linguist Michael Halliday, which conceives of language as a social semiotic.

tactic pattern error (or structural error): an error usually resulting from misordering within a single tactic pattern, such that at least one eme does not occur in the position required by the intended utterance.

threshold: the minimum amount of activation that junction nodes or threshold nodes in relational networks (or neurons in neural networks) must receive in order to fire and send activation to other nodes (or neurons).

threshold node: a type of node which specifies the minimum amount of incoming activation needed for it to fire; this must be distinguished from the threshold of a node.

timing error: a speech error produced by transposition (a spoonerism), anticipation, or perseveration of linguistic units.

underspecification: an approach in Generative Grammar where predictable features are omitted in underlying representations.

unordered: a node property which indicates simultaneity in the emission or reception of activation.

upward: direction of information flow leading from a given stratum or level to a higher one.

zero realization: a realizational discrepancy in which a unit of a given stratum or level has no discernible manifestation at a lower stratum or level.

References

Aijón Oliva, M. A. & Serrano, M. J. (2010). Las bases cognitivas del estilo lingüístico. *Sociolinguistic Studies*, 4 (1), 115–144.

Aissen, J. & Rivas, A. M. (1975). The proper formulation of the spurious *se* rule in Spanish. *Proceedings of the Berkeley Linguistics Society*, 1, 1–15.

Aravena, P., Hurtado, E., Riveros, R., Cardona, J. F., Manes, F., & Ibáñez, A. (2010). Applauding with closed hands: Neural signature of action-sentence compatibility effects. *PLoS ONE*, 5 (7), 1–14.

Arbib, M., Érdi, P., & Szentágothai, J. (1998). *Neural organization: Structure, function, and dynamics.* Cambridge, MA: MIT Press.

Archangeli, D. (1984). *Underspecification in Yawelmani phonology and morphology.* Ph.D. thesis, Massachusetts Institute of Technology.

Ardila, A., Bernal, B., & Rosselli, M. (2015). How localized are language brain areas? A review of Brodmann areas involvement in oral language. *Archives of Clinical Neuropsychology*, 31 (1), 112–122.

Bak, T. H. (2013). The neuroscience of action semantics in neurodegenerative brain diseases. *Current Opinion in Neurology*, 26 (6), 671–677.

Bańko, M. (2004). *Wykłady z polskiej fleksji.* Warsaw: Wydawnictwo Naukowe PWN.

Barsalou, L. W. (1999). Perceptual symbol systems. *Behavioral and Brain Sciences* 22 (4), 577–660.

Baudouin de Courtenay, J. (1972). *A Baudouin de Courtenay reader: The beginnings of structural linguistics* (trans. & ed. E. Stankiewicz). Bloomington, IN: Indiana University Press.

Bello, A. (1980). *Gramática de la lengua castellana.* Madrid: EDAF.

Belloro, V. A. (2007). *Spanish clitic doubling: A study of the syntax-pragmatics interface.* Ann Arbor, MI: ProQuest.

Bennett, D. C. (1975). *Spatial and temporal uses of English prepositions.* London: Longman.

Binkofski, F., Amunts, K., Stephan, K. M., Posse, S., Schormann, T., Freund, H-J., Zilles, K., & Seitz, R. J. (2000). Broca's region subserves imagery of motion: A combined cytoarchitectonic and fMRI study. *Human Brain Mapping*, 11 (4), 273–285.

Bloomfield, L. (1988 [1933]). *Language.* London: George Allen & Unwin Ltd.

Bocanegra, Y., García, A. M., Pineda, D., Buriticá, O., Villegas, A., Lopera, F., Gómez, D., Gómez-Arias, C., Cardona, J. F., Trujillo, N., & Ibáñez, A. (2015). Syntax, action verbs, action semantics, and object semantics in Parkinson's disease: Dissociability, progression, and executive influences. *Cortex*, 69, 237–254.

Bogdan, D. R. & Sullivan, W. J. (2009). *The tense-aspect system of Polish narrative.* Munich: LINCOM Europa.

Bonet, E. (1994). The person-case constraint: A morphological approach. *MIT Working Papers in Linguistics*, 22, 33–52.

Bonet, E. (1995). Feature structure of Romance clitics. *Natural Language and Linguistic Theory*, 13, 607–647.

Braitenberg, V. (1978a). Cell assemblies in the cerebral cortex. In R. Heim & G. Palm (eds.), *Theoretical approaches to complex systems* (pp.171–188). Berlin: Springer.

Braitenberg, V. (1978b). Cortical architectonics: General and areal. In M. Brazier & H. Petsche (eds.), *Architectonics of the cerebral cortex* (pp. 443–465). New York: Raven Press.

Braitenberg, V. & Schüz, A. (1998). *Cortex: Statistics and geometry of neuronal connectivity* (2nd ed.). Berlin: Springer.

Brodmann, K. (1909). *Vergleichende Lokalisationslehre der Grosshirnrinde: In ihren Prinzipien dargestellt auf Grund des Zeelenbaues*. Leipzig: Barth.

Burnod, Y. (1990). *An adaptive neural network: The cerebral cortex*. London: Prentice Hall.

Cardona, J. F., Gershanik, O., Gelormini-Lezama, C., Houck, A. L., Cardona, S., Kargieman, L., Trujillo, N., Arévalo, A., Amoruso, L., Manes, F., & Ibáñez, A. (2013). Action-verb processing in Parkinson's disease: New pathways for motor-language coupling. *Brain Structure and Function*, 218 (6), 1355–1373.

Castel, V. M. (2012). Sobre la visibilidad de significados y mensajes en la relación entre léxico y morfosintaxis. In M. Giammatteo, L. Ferrari, & H. Albano (eds.), *Léxico y sintaxis* (pp. 161–182). Mendoza: Editorial FFyL-UNCuyo y SAL.

Cheng, Q. (1999). An interview with Sydney Lamb. *Foreign Language Teaching and Research*, 2, 61–64.

Chew, P. A. (2003). *A computational phonology of Russian*. Reprint of University of Oxford Ph.D. Dissertation, 1999. Parkland, FL: Dissertation.com.

Chomsky, N. (1957). *Syntactic structures*. The Hague: Mouton.

Chomsky, N. (1964). *Current issues in linguistic theory*. The Hague: Mouton.

Chomsky, N. (1980). *Rules and representations*. New York: Columbia University Press.

Chomsky, N. (1986). *Knowledge of language: Its nature, origin and use*. New York: Praeger.

Chomsky, N. (1995). *The minimalist program*. Cambridge, MA: MIT Press.

Chomsky, N. (2005). Three factors in language design. *Linguistic Inquiry*, 36 (1), 1–22.

Chomsky, N. & Halle, M. (1991 [1968]). *The sound pattern of English*. Boston, MA: MIT Press.

Christiansen, M. H. & Chater, N. (2008). Language as shaped by the brain. *Behavioral and Brain Sciences*, 31, 489–558.

Coleman, D. W. (2009). There are three kinds of abstractions: Abstractions, damned abstractions, and damned lying abstractions. *LACUS Forum*, 35, 109–121.

Dąbrowska, E. (2001). Learning a morphological system without a default: The Polish genitive. *Journal of Child Language*, 28, 545–574.

Deacon, T. (1997). *The symbolic species: The co-evolution of language and the brain*. New York: Norton.

DeFelipe, J. & Farinas, I. (1992). The pyramidal neuron of the cerebral cortex: Morphological and chemical characteristics of the synaptic inputs. *Progress in Neurobiology*, 39 (6), 563–607.

Dell, G. S. (1986). A spreading-activation theory of retrieval in sentence production. *Psychological Review*, 93 (3), 283–321.

Dell, G. S. & Reich, P. A. (1977). A model of slips of the tongue. *LACUS Forum*, 3, 448–455.

Dell, G. S. & Reich, P. A. (1980a). Slips of the tongue: The facts and a stratificational model. In J. Copeland & P. Davis (eds.), *Papers in cognitive-stratificational linguistics* (pp. 19–34). Rice University Studies, 66 (2). Houston, TX: Rice University.

Dell, G. S. & Reich, P. A. (1980b). Toward a unified model of slips of the tongue. In V. A. Fromkin (ed.), *Errors in linguistic performance: Slips of the tongue, ear, pen, and hand* (pp. 273–286). New York: Academic Press.

Eble, C. (2000). Slang and lexicography. In D. G. Lockwood, P. H. Fries, & J. E. Copeland (eds.), *Functional approaches to language, culture, and cognition: Papers in honor of Sydney M. Lamb* (pp. 499–511). Philadelphia, PA: John Benjamins.

Eguren, L. & Fernández Soriano, O. (2004). *Introducción a una sintaxis minimista*. Madrid: Gredos.

Enrique-Arias, A. (2005). When clitics become affixes, where do they come to rest? A case from Spanish. In W. U. Dressler, D. Kastovsky, O. E. Pfeiffer, & F. Rainer (eds.), *Morphology and its demarcations* (pp. 67–79). Amsterdam: John Benjamins.

Estleman, L. D. (2013). *Alive!* New York: Forge/Doherty Associates.

Fawcett, R. P. (2000). *A theory of syntax for systemic functional linguistics*. Amsterdam: John Benjamins.

Fawcett, R. P. (2003). *A generative systemic functional micro-grammar for some central elements of the English clause*. Cardiff: Computational Linguistics Unit, Cardiff University.

Fawcett, R. P. (2011). *Alternative architectures in systemic functional grammar: How do we choose?* London: Equinox.

Fawcett, R. P. (2013). *An integrative architecture of language and its use for systemic functional linguistics and other theories of language*. London: Equinox.

Feldman, J. A. (2006). *From molecule to metaphor: A neural theory of language*. Cambridge, MA: MIT Press.

Fernández Soriano, O. (1999). El pronombre personal: Formas y distribuciones. In I. Bosque & V. Demonte (eds.), *Gramática descriptiva de la lengua española* (pp. 1209–1272). Madrid: Espasa Calpe.

Fillmore, C. J. (1968). The case for case. In E. Bach & R. T. Harms (eds.), *Universals in linguistic theory* (pp. 1–89). New York: Holt, Rinehart and Winston.

Fodor, J. (1983). *The modularity of mind*. Cambridge, MA: MIT Press.

Friederici, A. (2009). Pathways to language: Fiber tracts in the human brain. *Trends in Cognitive Science*, 13 (4), 175–181.

Friston, K. (2002). Functional integration and inference in the brain. *Progress in Neurobiology*, 68 (2), 113–143.

Fromkin, V. A. (1971). The non-anomalous nature of anomalous utterances. *Language*, 47 (1), 27–52.

Fromkin, V. A. (ed.). (1973). *Speech errors as linguistic evidence*. The Hague: Mouton.

Gallese, V. & Lakoff, G. (2005). The brain's concepts: The role of the sensory-motor system in conceptual knowledge. *Cognitive Neuropsychology*, 22 (3), 455–479.

García, A. M. (2013). Relational Network Theory as a bridge between linguistics and neuroscience: An interview with Professor Sydney Lamb. *Linguistics and the Human Sciences*, 8 (1), 3–27.

García, A. M. (2015). A connectionist approach to functional-cognitive linguistics: Spanish pronominal clitics and verb endings in relational-network terms. *Signos*, 48 (88), 197–222.

García, A. M. & Gil, J. M. (2011). Una perspectiva sistémico-funcional del español: Acerca de la multifuncionalidad en la cláusula castellana simple. *Revista de Investigación Lingüística*, 14, 191–214.

García, A. M. & Ibáñez, A. (2014). Words *in* motion: Motor-language coupling in Parkinson's disease. *Translational Neuroscience*, 5 (2), 152–159.

García, A. M. & Ibáñez, A. (2016a). Hands typing what hands do: Action-semantic integration dynamics throughout written verb production. *Cognition*, 149, 56–66.

García, A. M. & Ibáñez, A. (2016b). A touch with words: Dynamic synergies between manual actions and language. *Neuroscience and Biobehavioral Reviews*, 68, 59–95.

García, A. M., Carrillo, F., Orozco-Arroyave, J. R., Trujillo, N., Vargas Bonilla, J. F., Fittipaldi, S., Adolfi, F., Nöth, E., Sigman, M., Fernández Slezak, D., Ibáñez, A., & Cecchi, G. A. (2016). How language flows when movements don't: An automated analysis of spontaneous discourse in Parkinson's disease. *Brain and Language*, 162, 19–28.

García, E. (1975). *The role of theory in linguistic analysis: The Spanish pronoun system*. Amsterdam: North-Holland Publishing Company.

García, E. (2009). *The motivated syntax of arbitrary signs: Cognitive constraints on Spanish clitic clustering*. Amsterdam: John Benjamins.

Gazzaniga, M. (ed.). (2009). *The cognitive neurosciences* (4th ed.). Cambridge, MA: MIT Press.

Gil, J. M. (2013). A neurocognitive interpretation of systemic-functional choice. In L. Fontaine, T. Bartlett, & G. O'Grady (eds.), *Choice: Critical considerations in Systemic Functional Linguistics* (pp. 179–204). Cambridge: Cambridge University Press.

Gil, J. M. & García, A. M. (2010). Transitividad, modo y tema en español: Un primer análisis en términos de la gramática de Cardiff. *Signos*, 43 (72), 71–98.

Gleason, H. A., Jr. (1968). Contrastive analysis in discourse structure. In J. E. Alatis (ed.), *Georgetown University Monograph Series on Languages and Linguistics* (pp. 39–63). Washington, DC: Georgetown University.

Gouskova, M. (2001). Falling sonority onsets, loanwords, and syllable contact. In M. Andronis, C. Ball, H. Elston, & S. Neuvel (eds.), *Papers from the 37th meeting of the Chicago Linguistic Society* (vol. 1) (pp. 175–186). Chicago, IL: CLS.

Grammatical case. Retrieved from: <http://en.wikipedia.org/wiki/Grammatical_ case>. [6 February 2015].

Gribanova, V. (2009). Phonological evidence for a distinction between Russian prepositions and prefixes. In *Workshop on Slavic phonology at FDSL7.* Retrieved from: <http://citeseerx.ist.psu.edu/viewdoc/download?-doi=10.1.1.515.12&rep=rep1&type=pdf>. [24 October 2015].

Grzegorczykowa, R., Laskowski, R., & Wróbel, H. (eds.). (1998). *Gramatyka współczesnego języka polskiego: Morfologia* (2nd ed.) (vols. 1-2). Warsaw: Wydawnictwo Naukowe PWN.

Halle, M. (1959). *The sound pattern of Russian.* The Hague: Mouton.

Halliday, M. A. K. (1967/1968). Notes on transitivity and theme in English. *Journal of Linguistics,* I, 3 (1), 37–81; II, 3 (2), 199–244; III, 4 (2), 179–215.

Halliday, M. A. K. (1994). *An introduction to functional grammar* (2nd ed.). London: Edward Arnold.

Halliday, M. A. K. (2002). *Linguistic studies of text and discourse* (ed. J. J. Webster). New York: Continuum.

Halliday, M. A. K. (2009). *The essential Halliday* (ed. J. J. Webster). New York: Continuum.

Halliday, M. A. K. & Hasan, R. (1976). *Cohesion in English.* New York: Longman.

Halliday, M. A. K., Lamb, S. M., & Regan, J. (1988). In retrospect: Using language and knowing how. In *Twelfth in a series of seminars: Issues in communication.* Claremont, CA: The Claremont Graduate School.

Halliday, M. A. K. & Matthiessen, C. M. I. M. (2004). *An introduction to functional grammar* (3rd ed.). London: Arnold.

Halliday, M. A. K. & Matthiessen, C. M. I. M. (2014). *Halliday's introduction to functional grammar* (4th ed.). New York: Routledge.

Harris, J. (1996). The morphology of Spanish clitics. In H. Campos & P. Kempchinsky (eds.), *Evolution and revolution in linguistic theory: Essays in honor of Carlos Otero* (pp. 168–197). Washington DC: Georgetown University Press.

Harrison, C. J. (2000). *PureNet: A modeling program for neurocognitive linguistics.* Ph.D. thesis, Rice University. Retrieved from: <https://scholarship.rice. edu/handle/1911/19501>. [30 April 2016].

Hasan, R. & Fries, P. H. (1995). *On subject and theme: A discourse and functional perspective.* Amsterdam: John Benjamins.

Haspelmath, M. (2004). Explaining the ditransitive person-role constraint: A usage-based approach. *Constructions,* 2, 1–71.

Hauser, M. D., Chomsky, N., & Fitch, W. T. (2002). The faculty of language: What is it, who has it, and how did it evolve?' *Science,* 298, 1569–1579.

Hauser, M. D., Chomsky, N., & Fitch, W. T. (2005). The evolution of the language faculty: Clarifications and implications. *Cognition,* 97, 179–210.

Hebb, D. (1949). *The organization of behavior: A neuropsychological theory.* New York: Wiley.

Hjelmslev, L. (1961 [1943]). *Prolegomena to a theory of language* (trans. F. J. Whitfield, revised 2nd ed.). Madison, WI: University of Wisconsin Press.

Hochstadt, J., Nakano, H., Lieberman, P., & Friedman, J. (2006). The roles of sequencing and verbal working memory in sentence comprehension deficits in Parkinson's disease. *Brain and Language,* 97 (3), 243–257.

Hockett, C. F. (1947). Problems of morphemic analysis. *Language*, 23 (4), 321–343.

Hockett, C. F. (1954). Two models of grammatical description. *Word*, 10, 210–231.

Hockett, C. F. (1961). Linguistic elements and their relations. *Language*, 37 (1), 29–53.

Hockett, C. F. (1975). A new point d'appui for phonology. *LACUS Forum*, 2, 67–90.

Holtgraves, T. & McNamara, P. (2010). Pragmatic comprehension deficit in Parkinson's disease. *Journal of Clinical and Experimental Neuropsychology*, 32 (4), 388–397.

Howie, S. M. (2014). Formant transitions of Russian palatalized and nonpalatalized syllables. *Indiana University Linguistics Club Working Papers*, 1 (1). Retrieved from: <https://www.indiana.edu/~iulcwp/wp/article/view/01-01/20>. [24 October 2015].

Hubel, D. & Wiesel, T. N. (1962). Receptive fields, binocular interaction and functional architecture in the cat's visual cortex. *Journal of Physiology*, 160, 106–154.

Hubel, D. & Wiesel, T. N. (1977). Functional architecture of macaque monkey visual cortex. *Proceedings of the Royal Society of London, B: Biological Sciences*, 198, 1–59.

Jakobson, R. (1962 [1929]). Remarques sur l'évolution phonologique du russe comparée à celle des autres langues slaves. In *Roman Jakobson: Selected writings* (vol. 1) (pp. 7–116). Berlin: Mouton.

Jakobson, R. (1971a [1958]). Morfologičeskie nabljudenija nad slavjanskim skloneniem. In *Roman Jakobson: Selected writings* (vol. 2) (pp. 154–183). The Hague: Mouton.

Jakobson, R. (1971b [1939]). Signe zero. In *Roman Jakobson: Selected writings* (vol. 2) (pp. 211–219). The Hague: Mouton.

Jakobson, R. (1984 [1936]). Contribution to the general theory of case: General meanings of the Russian cases. In L. Waugh & M. Halle (eds.), *Roman Jakobson: Russian and Slavic grammar studies 1931–1981* (pp. 59–103). New York: Mouton.

Jakobson, R., Cherry, E. C., & Halle, M. (1962 [1953]). Toward the logical description of languages in their phonemic aspect. In *Roman Jakobson: Selected writings* (vol. 1) (pp. 449–463). Berlin: Mouton.

Kandel, E. R. (1991). Cellular mechanisms of learning and the biological basis of individuality. In E. Kandel, J. H. Schwartz, & T. M. Jessell (eds.), *Principles of neural science* (3rd ed.) (pp. 1009-1031). New York: Elsevier.

Kornai, A. (1993). The generative power of feature geometry. *Annals of Mathematics and Artificial Intelligence*, 8, 37–46.

Kulikov, V. (2011). Features, cues, and syllable structure in the acquisition of Russian palatalization by L2 American learners. In M. Wrembel, M. Kul, & K. Dziubalska-Kołaczyk (eds.), *Achievements and perspectives in SLA of speech: New sounds 2010* (vol. 1) (pp. 193–204). Frankfurt: Peter Lang.

Lakoff, G. (1991). Cognitive versus generative linguistics: How commitments influence results. *Language and Communication*, 11 (1–2), 53–62.

Lamb, S. M. (1966a). *Outline of Stratificational Grammar*. Washington, DC: Georgetown University Press.

Lamb, S. M. (1966b). Prolegomena to a theory of phonology. *Language, 42* (2), 536–573.

Lamb, S. M. (1980). A new look at phonotactics. In J. Copeland & P. Davis (eds.), *Papers in cognitive stratificational linguistics* (pp. 1–18). *Rice University Studies, 66* (2). Houston, TX: Rice University.

Lamb, S. M. (1999). *Pathways of the brain: The neurocognitive basis of language.* Amsterdam: John Benjamins.

Lamb, S. M. (2004a). Linguistics to the beat of a different drummer. In J. J. Webster (ed.), *Language & reality: Selected writings of Sydney Lamb* (pp. 12–44). New York: Continuum.

Lamb, S. M. (2004b). What is a language? In J. J. Webster (ed.), *Language & reality: Selected writings of Sydney Lamb* (pp. 394–414). New York: Continuum.

Lamb, S. M. (2004c). Epilegomena to a theory of language. In J. J. Webster (ed.), *Language & reality: Selected writings of Sydney Lamb* (pp. 71–117). New York: Continuum.

Lamb, S. M. (2004d). Language as a network of relationships. In J. J. Webster (ed.), *Language & reality: Selected writings of Sydney Lamb* (pp.133–175). New York Continuum.

Lamb, S. M. (2004e). Some types of ordering. In J. J. Webster (ed.), *Language & reality: Selected writings of Sydney Lamb* (pp. 126–132). New York: Continuum.

Lamb, S. M. (2004f). Mutations and relations. In J. J. Webster (ed.), *Language & reality: Selected writings of Sydney Lamb* (pp. 176–194). New York: Continuum.

Lamb, S. M. (2004g). Mary R. Haas: Lessons in and out of the classroom. In J. J. Webster (ed.), *Language & reality: Selected writings of Sydney Lamb* (pp. 45–47). New York: Continuum.

Lamb, S. M. (2004h). Saussure's error: Objects of study in linguistics and other sciences. In J. J. Webster (ed.), *Language & reality: Selected writings of Sydney Lamb* (pp. 471–487). New York: Continuum.

Lamb, S. M. (2004i). Using language and knowing how. In J. J. Webster (ed.), *Language & reality: Selected writings of Sydney Lamb* (pp. 211–223). New York: Continuum.

Lamb, S. M. (2004j). Questions of evidence in neurocognitive linguistics. In J. J. Webster (ed.), *Language & reality: Selected writings of Sydney Lamb* (pp. 324–351). New York: Continuum.

Lamb, S. M. (2004k). Descriptive process. In J. J. Webster (ed.), *Language & reality: Selected writings of Sydney Lamb* (pp. 195–210). New York: Continuum.

Lamb, S. M. (2004l). Meaning in language and meaning in music. In J. J. Webster (ed.), *Language & reality: Selected writings of Sydney Lamb* (pp. 488–495). New York: Continuum.

Lamb, S. M. (2006). Being realistic, being scientific. *LACUS Forum*, 32, 201–209.

Lamb, S. M. (2011). *Senderos del cerebro: La base neurocognitiva del lenguaje* (J. M. Gil & A. M. García, trans.). Mar del Plata: EUDEM.

Lamb, S. M. (2013). Systemic networks, relational networks, and choice. In L. Fontaine, T. Bartlett, & G. O'Grady (eds.), *Choice: Critical considerations in Systemic Functional Linguistics* (pp. 137–160). Cambridge: Cambridge University Press.

Langacker, R. W. (1991). *Concept, image, and symbol.* New York: Mouton de Gruyter.

Langacker, R. W. (2011). Conceptual semantics, symbolic grammar, and the 'day after day' construction. *LACUS Forum*, 36, 3–24.

Levelt, W. J. M., Praamstra, P., Meyer, A. S., Helenius, P., & Salmelin, R. (1998). An MEG study of picture naming. *Journal of Cognitive Neuroscience*, 10 (5), 553–567.

Lieberman, P., Kako, E., Friedman, J., Tajchman, G., Feldman, L. S., & Jiminez, E. B. (1992). Speech production, syntax comprehension, and cognitive deficits in Parkinson's disease. *Brain and Language*, 43 (2), 169–189.

Lockwood, D. G. (1969). Markedness in stratificational phonology. *Language,* 45 (2), 300–308.

Lockwood, D. G. (1972). *Introduction to stratificational linguistics.* New York: Harcourt Brace Jovanovich.

Lockwood, D. G. (1977). Anatactic relations in grammar and phonology. In *Papers from the annual meeting of the Michigan Linguistic Society.* Ann Arbor, MI: University of Michigan Papers in Linguistics.

Lombardi, L. (2003). Second language data and constraints on manner: Explaining substitutions for the English interdentals. *Second Language Research*, 19 (3), 225–250.

Longacre, R. E. (1976). *An anatomy of speech notions.* Lisse: Peter de Ridder Press.

Loritz, D. (1999). *How the brain evolved language.* Oxford: Oxford University Press.

Makkai, A. & Lockwood, D. G. (eds.), (1973). *Readings in Stratificational Linguistics.* Tuscaloosa, AL: University of Alabama Press.

Martínez, A. (2010). De España a América: Recategorización y desplazamientos en el sistema de clíticos. *Olivar: Revista de literatura y cultura españolas,* 14, 149–162.

Mayberry, R. I. (1993). First-language acquisition after childhood differs from second-language acquisition: The case of American Sign Language. *Journal of Speech, Language, and Hearing Research*, 36 (6), 1258–1270.

McCulloch, W. S. & Pitts, W. H. (1943). A logical calculus of the ideas immanent in nervous activity. *Bulletin of Mathematical Biophysics*, 5, 115–133.

Mendikoetxea, A. (1999). Construcciones con *se*: Medias, pasivas e impersonales. In I. Bosque & V. Demonte (eds.), *Gramática descriptiva de la lengua española* (pp. 1631–1722). Madrid: Espasa Calpe.

Menn, L. & MacWhinney, B. (1984). The repeated morph constraint: Toward an explanation. *Language,* 60, 519–541.

Meyer, C. F. (1991). 'What shall we talk about next?': Cognitive topic in the production and interpretation of conversation. *LACUS Forum*, 17, 85–98.

Meyer, C. F. (1992). Twice-told tales: Aspects of storage and expression of personal experience. *LACUS Forum*, 18, 63–74.

Meyer, C. F. (2000). Cognitive networks in conversation. In D. G. Lockwood, P. H. Fries, & J. E. Copeland (eds.), *Functional approaches to language, culture, and cognition.* Philadelphia, PA: John Benjamins.

Miceli, G., Silveri, M. C., Romani, C., & Caramazza, A. (1989). Variation in the pattern of omissions and substitutions of grammatical morphemes in the spontaneous speech of so-called agrammatic patients. *Brain and Language*, 36 (3), 447–492.

Monetta, L. & Pell, M. D. (2007). Effects of verbal working memory deficits on metaphor comprehension in patients with Parkinson's disease. *Brain and Language*, 101 (1), 80–89.

Mountcastle, V. (1998). *Perceptual neuroscience: The cerebral cortex*. Cambridge, MA: Harvard University Press.

Müller, E.-A. (2000). Valence and phraseology in Stratificational Linguistics. In D. G. Lockwood, P. H. Fries, & J. E. Copeland (eds.), *Functional approaches to language, culture, and cognition: Papers in honor of Sydney M. Lamb* (pp. 3–21). Philadelphia, PA: John Benjamins.

Ostapenko, O. (2005). The optimal L2 Russian syllable onset. *LSO Working Papers in Linguistics 5: Proceedings of WIGL 2005*, pp. 140–151.

Pandya, D. N. & Yeterian, E. H. (1985). Architecture and connections of cortical association areas. In A. Peters & E. G. Jones (eds.), *Cerebral cortex: Vol. 4: Association and auditory cortices* (pp. 3–61). London: Plenum Press.

Parsons, L. M., Fox, P. T., Downs, J. H., Glass, T., Hirsch, T. B., Martin, C. C., Jerabek, P. A., & Lancaster, J. L. (1995). Use of implicit motor imagery for visual shape discrimination as revealed by PET. *Nature*, 375 (6526), 54–58.

Patterson, K., Nestor, P. J., & Rogers, T. T. (2007). Where do you know what you know? The representation of semantic knowledge in the human brain. *Nature Reviews Neuroscience*, 8 (12), 976–987.

Peeters, B. (2001). Does cognitive linguistics live up to its name? In R. Dirven, B. Hawkins, & E. Sandikcioglu (eds.), *Language and ideology: Volume 1: Theoretical cognitive approaches* (pp. 83–106). Amsterdam: John Benjamins.

Piera, C. & Varela, S. (1999). Relaciones entre morfología y sintaxis. In I. Bosque & V. Demonte (eds.), *Gramática descriptiva de la lengua española* (pp. 4367–4422). Madrid. Espasa Calpe

Pinker, S. & Jackendoff, R. (2005). The faculty of language: What's special about it? *Cognition*, 95, 201–236.

Poeppel, D. & Embick, D. (2005). Defining the relation between linguistics and neuroscience. In A. Cutler (ed.), *Twenty-first century psycholinguistics: Four cornerstones* (pp. 103–118). Mahwah, NJ: Lawrence Erlbaum.

Pulvermüller, F. (2002). *The neuroscience of language: On brain circuits of words and serial order*. New York: Cambridge University Press.

Pulvermüller, F. (2005). Brain mechanisms linking language and action. *Nature Reviews Neuroscience*, 6 (7), 576–582.

Quian Quiroga, R., Reddy, L., Kreiman, G., Koch, C., & Fried, I. (2005). Invariant visual representation by single neurons in the human brain. *Nature*, 435, 1102–1107.

Raskin, S. A., Sliwinski, M., & Borod, J. C. (1992). Clustering strategies on tasks of verbal fluency in Parkinson's disease. *Neuropsychologia*, 30 (1), 95–99.

Real Academia Española. *CREA: Corpus de referencia del español actual*. Retrieved from: <http://www.rae.es>. [24 January 2015].

Reich, P. A. (1985). Unintended puns. *LACUS Forum*, 11, 314–322.

Reich, P. A. (1973). Competence, performance, and relational networks. In A. Makkai & D. G. Lockwood (eds.), *Readings in Stratificational Linguistics* (pp. 84-91). Tuscaloosa, AL: University of Alabama.

Roca, I. (1994). *Generative phonology*. New York: Routledge.

Sampson, G. (1975). On the need for a phonological base. In D. L. Goyvaerts & G. K. Pullum (eds.) *Essays on the sound pattern of English* (pp. 439–474). Philadelphia, PA: John Benjamins.

Schenker, A. M. (1964). *Polish declension: A descriptive analysis*. The Hague: Mouton.

Schenker, A. M. (1973). *Beginning Polish* (vols. 1–2). New Haven, CT: Yale University Press.

Sharp, R. (2005). A unified treatment of Spanish *se*. In A. Branco, T. McEnery, & R. Mitkov (eds.), *Anaphora processing* (pp. 113–136). Amsterdam: John Benjamins.

Smith, D. J. (2010). *Speech errors, speech production models, and speech pathology*. Retrieved from: <http://www.smithsrisca.co.uk/speech-errors.html>. [25 March 2016].

Springer, J. A., Binder, J. R., Hammeke, T. A., Swanson, S. J., Frost, J. A., Bellgowan, P. S. F., Brewer, C. C., Perry, H. M., Morris, G. L., & Mueller, W. M. (1999). Language dominance in neurologically normal and epilepsy subjects: A functional MRI study. *Brain*, 122, 2033–2046.

Strutyński, J. (1997). *Gramatyka polska*. Kraków: Wydawnictwo Janusz Strutyński.

Sullivan, W. J. (1969). *A stratificational description of the phonology and inflectional morphology of Russian*. Ph.D. thesis, Yale University.

Sullivan, W. J. (1974). The archiphoneme in stratificational description. In L. Heilmann (ed.), *Proceedings of the XIth International Conference of Linguists* (pp. 287–299). Bologna: Società editrice il Mulino.

Sullivan, W. J. (1977). The archiphonemes of Russian: A stratificational view. In A. Makkai, V. Becker Makkai, & L. Heilmann (eds.), *Linguistics at the crossroads* (pp. 451–484). Padova: Liviana Editrice.

Sullivan, W. J. (1980). Syntax and linguistic semantics in stratificational theory. In E. A. Moravesik & J. R. Wirth (eds.), *Syntax and semantics: Current approaches to syntax* (vol. 13) (pp. 301–327). Leiden: Brill.

Sullivan, W. J. (1992). Constraints in Universal Grammar: Consequences and objections. *LACUS Forum*, 18, 198–208.

Sullivan, W. J. (1994). Binarity, phonetic reality and the Bulgarian vowel. *LACUS Forum*, 21, 130–142.

Sullivan, W. J. (1998a). Underspecification and feature geometry: Theorems of a reticular theory of language. *LACUS Forum*, 24, 53–65.

Sullivan, W. J. (1998b). *Space and time in Russian*. Munich: LINCOM Europa.

Sullivan, W. J. (2000). The logic of anataxis. In D. G. Lockwood, P. H. Fries, & J. E. Copeland (eds.), *Functional approaches to language, culture, and cognition: Papers in honor of Sydney M. Lamb* (pp. 81–104). Philadelphia, PA: John Benjamins.

Sullivan, W. J. (2002). A plausible contradiction. *LACUS Forum*, 28, 125–132.

Sullivan, W. J. (2004). Participant realization in English narrative. In H. Kardela, W. J. Sullivan, & A. Głaz (eds.), *Perspectives on language: Papers from the 11th annual PASE Conference, 2001* (pp. 273–280). Lublin: Wydawnictwo UMCS.

Sullivan, W. J. (2005). The persistence of a fiction: The segmental phoneme. *LACUS Forum*, 31, 169–180.

Sullivan, W. J. (2010). Order. In P. Stalmaszczyk (ed.), *Philosophy of language & linguistics* (vol. 1). Heusenstamm: Ontos Verlag.

Sullivan, W. J. (2011). Input, output, and (de)linearization: What we owe to Sydney M. Lamb. *LACUS Forum*, 36, 279–289.

Sullivan, W. J. & Bogdan, D. R. (in press). Fatal Russian eggs. *LACUS Forum*, 38.

Sullivan, W. J. & Tsiang, S. (2011). Speech errors and the ontological status of the morpheme. *Kwartalnik Neofilologiczny*, 58 (3), 357–373.

Sullivan, W. J. & Tsiang, S. (2012). Conceptual chunking, speech errors, and linguistic architecture. In K. Kosecki & J. Badio (eds.), *Cognitive processes in language* (pp. 121–135). Frankfurt: Peter Lang.

Sullivan, W. J. & Tsiang, S. (in press a). Classifying unclassified speech errors: An examination of the unexamined. *LACUS Forum*, 41.

Sullivan, W. J. & Tsiang, S. (in press b). Tactic pattern errors and the architecture of stratificational theory. *LACUS Forum*, 37.

Sullivan, W. J. & Tsiang, S. (in press c). 'It's *deja vu* all over again!': Are redundancies speech errors? *LACUS Forum*, 39.

Sullivan, W. J. & Tsiang, S. (in press d). Substitution errors and the architecture of the linguistic system. *LACUS Forum*, 40.

Swan, O. E. (2002). *Grammar of contemporary Polish*. Bloomington, IN: Slavica.

Tokarski, J. (2001). *Fleksja polska*. Warsaw: Wydawnictwo Naukowe PWN.

Trager, G. L. (1934). The phonemes of Russian. *Language*, 10 (4), 334–344.

Tsiang, S. & Sullivan, W. J. (in press). Unintended blends and the stratification of language. *LACUS Forum*, 38.

Tsumoto, T. (1992). Long-term potentiation and long-term depression in the neocortex. *Progress in Neurobiology*, 39, 209–228.

Ullman, M. T. (2004). Contributions of memory circuits to language: The declarative/procedural model. *Cognition*, 92 (1–2), 231–270.

Visser, M., Jefferies, E., & Lambon Ralph, M. A. (2010). Semantic processing in the anterior temporal lobes: A meta-analysis of the functional neuroimaging literature. *Journal of Cognitive Neuroscience*, 22 (6), 1083–1094.

Webster, J. J. (ed.) (2004). *Language & reality: Selected writings of Sydney Lamb*. New York: Continuum.

Whorf, B. L. (1956 [1940]). Science and linguistics. In J. B. Carroll (ed.), *Language, thought and reality: Selected writings of Benjamin Lee Whorf* (pp. 207–219). Cambridge, MA: MIT Press.

Wickens, J. R. (1993). *A theory of the striatum*. Oxford: Pergamon Press.

Wróbel, H. (2001). *Gramatyka języka polskiego*. Kraków: Spółka Wydawnicza 'OD NOWA'.

Young, M. P., Scannell, J. W., & Burns, G. (1995). *The analysis of cortical connectivity*. Heidelberg: Springer.

Zeldes, A. (2007). Abstracting suffixes: A morphophonemic approach to Polish morphological analysis. *Zeitschrift für Sprachwissenschaft*, 26, 347–370.

Zillmer, A. & Spiers, M. V. (2001). *Principles of neuropsychology*. Belmont, CA: Wadsworth/Thomson Learning.

Indexes

Index of key terms

abstract notation 27, 30–32, 34, 36, 41, 69–70, 75, 83, 86, 108, 130, 134

activation 20–21, 23, 25–29, 31–34, 36, 38, 41, 46–49, 51–53, 57, 65–74, 82–83, 112, 114–115, 126, 128, 130–131, 152–153, 157–158, 160, 162, 171, 173, 176, 192–194, 196, 198

agrammatism 169

algebraic notation 30

AND node xvii, 20, 23, 27, 31–32, 34, 36, 38–39, 42, 46, 85, 96, 111, 113, 126–127, 130–131, 134, 150, 162, 191, 193

archiphoneme 85, 88, 90, 93, 98, 100

axoaxonic inhibitory connection 65, 73, 194

axosomatic inhibitory connection 65, 73

blocking element 32–33, 195

branching node 31, 34, 73

Brodmann areas 57, 62

characteristics (of a verb) 117, 127–128, 130, 145

clitic 6, 117–119, 121, 123–124, 126–129, 130–134, 149, 175

cognitive plausibility 119, 130, 132

cohesion 136–138, 140, 146, 154–155

composite realization 17

concept (see also confunct) 43, 45

confunct 43, 45

cortical minicolumn 66–69, 192–193

declension 105, 108, 113–114

dedicated (connection) 47, 51–52, 71, 200

descriptive process 11, 13–14

developmental plausibility 3, 24, 47, 56–57

diamond node 27, 38–39, 41, 96, 108

diversification 17, 110, 132–133

downward 20, 29–31, 35, 37–38, 52, 55, 73, 100, 108–109, 111–112, 121, 126–128, 130–131

embodied/conceptual/executive cognition 16, 25, 30, 41, 157

eme 35, 39, 41–42

empty realization 17

established (connection) 44, 47–48, 51–52, 65, 71–72, 199–200

excitatory (connection) 32–33, 49, 65–66, 72–74, 177, 180, 195

feature geometry v, 82, 94, 96, 98–101

feature 41

feedback timing 34

form potential 132

functional web 6, 57, 66–69, 192–194

Generative Grammar 1, 4, 7, 175–176, 178, 184, 196, 201

Glossematics 14, 18

graphic notation 31

hypophoneme 35, 94–96, 98, 100–101, 168, 171

ideonection 30, 41, 46, 51–53

inhibitory (connection) 32–34, 49, 65–66, 71–74, 177, 180, 194–195

introjection 3, 4

junction node 31, 34, 72–73

lexicogrammar 15, 17
lexotactics 17, 36–37, 39, 41, 109,
    112, 114–115, 148–150, 152–154,
    159, 162, 199
linearization v, 157–159, 164
linguistic paragraph 138–141, 159
logonection 30, 51–52

meaning potential xvii
morphonection 30, 34, 52
morphotactics 17, 112–114, 127,
    130–131, 152, 159, 166
mutable lexeme 53–55

narrow notation 6, 27, 30–34, 68–70,
    75, 134, 195
nection 21–23, 27–32, 39, 42–43,
    46–53, 56–57, 68–71, 155, 192,
    200
neocortex 1, 58–61, 65–66, 74
neurological plausibility 3–4, 50,
    56–57, 132, 175
neutralization 12, 17, 25, 85, 93, 105,
    109, 132

obstruent 6, 79–81, 83–86, 88, 90–93,
    95, 98, 100–102, 149
onset 6, 30, 79, 81–83, 86–95, 98,
    100–101, 149, 164, 166
operational plausibility 3, 27–28, 56
OR node xvii, 19–20, 23, 25, 27,
    31–33, 36–38, 41, 46, 91, 93, 100,
    109–114, 121, 126, 128, 130–131,
    134, 152, 162, 191
ordered 12, 20, 23, 31–34, 36–38, 41,
    55, 79, 87, 95, 114–115, 121, 126–
    128, 130–131, 152, 162, 177, 193

participant v, 6
percept 43, 46–49, 51, 67, 69, 71
perfunct 43
phonology 4, 6, 14–16, 20, 25,
    44–45, 75, 79, 81–83, 93–95,
    98–101, 114, 159, 175, 178, 183,
    185, 187–188, 196
phononection 30, 50–52, 98, 140

phonotactics 17, 27, 84, 86, 95, 98,
    100, 159, 164, 203
phrase structure rule 82, 90, 176
portmanteau realization 17, 33, 36
procedural description 12

quantum firing 27–29, 82

realization 7, 17–19, 33, 36, 38, 41,
    82, 90, 100, 112–113, 126, 131–
    132, 141, 146, 148–150, 152, 154–
    155, 157–158, 163, 166, 171–172,
    183, 187, 195
recruitment 50–51, 56
redundancy 48, 52, 119, 131, 135
Relational Network Theory v, xiii–
    xvii, 1–8, 11–14, 18, 20–21, 23–25,
    27–28, 30–31, 34–36, 38, 42–43,
    47, 50–51, 53, 55–58, 68–75, 79,
    82–83, 85–86, 98, 103, 106, 108–
    109, 112, 114–115, 117, 121, 127,
    131–137, 146, 148, 154, 157, 159,
    162, 172, 175–182, 187–189, 191,
    194, 196, 197, 198, 200, 201
relational network v, xiii, xvi–xvii,
    4–7, 11–12, 18, 20, 22–23, 25,
    27–31, 37, 48, 52–53, 56–57, 68,
    70, 72, 74–75, 81, 83, 85–86, 90,
    95–96, 98, 100–101, 104, 115,
    118–119, 127, 130–131, 133,
    147–149, 153–154, 157, 160–162,
    173, 179–180, 182–183, 186–189,
    191–193, 195, 197, 199–201

semantics 4, 44, 59, 105, 114, 131,
    184–185, 187, 190–191
semotactics 17, 38, 41, 109, 112, 140,
    149–150, 152–155, 162, 172, 199
speech error (or slip of the tongue) v,
    7, 39, 75, 157–163, 173, 175, 177,
    179
spoonerism 157, 161, 163–164, 173
Stratificational Grammar xvi, 1, 5,
    14–15, 18, 20, 35, 188–189, 196
subcortical structures 58–59, 74
substitution error v

syllable 6, 12, 16, 25, 30, 39, 50, 79, 81–83, 89, 94, 100–101, 149, 159, 164–166, 171, 193, 210
synapse 6, 57, 63–66, 69, 72, 192
syntax 7, 17, 27, 36–37, 56, 59, 75, 81, 87, 103, 105, 108, 110, 112–115, 131, 136, 147–148, 152, 162, 176–177, 179, 188, 191, 198–199
Systemic-Functional Linguistics 155, 178–179, 196

tactic pattern error (or structural error) v, 7, 102, 157, 160–161, 164
threshold 31–34, 46–49, 52–53, 65, 71–74, 191

threshold node 19, 26, 46
timing error 7, 157, 160, 163–164, 172

underspecification v, 94, 96, 98–101
unordered 20, 31, 36, 38, 42, 55, 79, 95, 121, 126, 128, 130–131, 157, 162, 177
upward 12, 20, 23, 25, 29–31, 34–35, 48, 55–56, 91, 93, 100, 108–109, 111, 112–113, 126, 128, 130–131, 134

zero realization 17, 42, 146

Index of names

Aijón Oliva, M.A. 118, 213
Aissen, J. 133, 213
Aravena, P. 69, 213
Arbib, M. 66, 213
Archangeli, D. 94, 99, 100, 213
Ardila, A. 60, 61, 213

Bak, T.H. 59, 213
Bańko, M. 104, 213
Barsalou, L.W. 104, 213
Baudouin de Courtenay, J. xiii, 5. 11, 12, 25, 213
Bello, A. 118, 213
Belloro, V.A. 118, 213
Bennett, D.C. xiii, 26, 115, 213
Binkofski, F. 118, 213
Bloomfield, L. 31, 80, 85, 103, 202, 213
Bocanegra, Y. 59, 213
Bogdan, D.R. xiv, 135, 172, 179, 213, 223
Bonet, E. 118, 133, 213, 214
Braitenberg, V. 66, 72, 213
Brodmann, K. 62, 214
Burnod, Y. 66, 214

Cardona, J.F. 59, 213

Castel, V.M. xiii, 119–123, 130, 131, 214
Cheng, Q. 181, 213
Chew, P.A. 82, 213
Chomsky, N. xiv, 1, 2, 7, 14, 17, 30, 81–83, 98–100, 103, 133, 137, 147, 159, 160, 172, 176, 178, 183, 184, 191, 196, 197, 207, 214, 217
Christiansen, M.H. 7, 214
Coleman, D.W. xiv, 30, 214
Costello, P. xiv

Dąbrowska, E. 104, 214
Deacon, T. 7, 214
DeFelipe, J. 64, 215
Dell, G.S. 53, 160, 173, 215

Eble, C. 53, 215
Eguren, L. 175, 215
Enrique-Arias, A. 118, 215
Estleman, L.D. 139, 145, 147, 149, 215

Fawcett, R.P. 119, 132, 215
Feldman, J.A. 1, 178, 215, 220
Fernández Soriano, O. 117, 133, 175, 215

Fillmore, C.J. 103, 115, 184, 215
Fodor, J. 176, 215
Friederici, A. 69, 215
Friston, K. 69, 215
Fromkin, V.A. 159, 160, 215, 216

Gallese, V. 25, 216
García, A.M. v, xiv, 5, 13, 25, 59,
    134, 181, 203, 213, 216, 219
García, E. 117, 118, 119, 121, 123,
    133, 134, 216
Gazzaniga, M. 132, 216
Głaz, A. v, 223
Gleason, H.A., Jr. xiii, xvi, 19, 26,
    135–137, 140, 146, 154, 155, 216
Gouskova, M. 81, 216
Gribanova, V. 81, 217
Grzegorczykowa, R. 104, 217

Halle, M. 12, 18, 52, 79, 81–84, 99,
    101, 118, 137, 196, 214, 217, 218
Halliday, M.A.K. xiii, 11, 15, 18, 25,
    26, 28, 41, 103, 135–137, 155, 179,
    183, 196, 197, 199–203, 212, 217
Harris, J. 118, 133, 217
Harrison, C.J. 179, 217
Hasan, R. xiii, xv, 136, 155, 201, 217
Haspelmath, M. 118, 217
Hauser, M.D. 176, 178, 217
Hebb, D. 66, 71, 217
Hjelmslev, L. xiii, xiv, 5, 11–15, 18,
    19, 23, 25, 175, 182, 183, 197, 202,
    208, 217
Hochstadt, J. 59, 217
Hock, H.H. xiv
Hockensmith, J.S. xiv
Hockett, C.F. xiii, xvi, 11, 14, 25, 83,
    182–184, 218
Holtgraves, T. 59, 218
Howie, S.M. 82, 218
Hubel, D. 67, 218

Ibáñez, A. xiii, 25, 59, 213, 214, 216

Jakobson, R. xiii, 5, 11, 12, 25, 79,
    81, 103–105, 115, 178, 218

Kandel, E.R. 66, 218
Kardela, H. v, xiv, 223
Kornai, A. 82, 218
Kulikov, V. 82, 218

Lakoff, G. 7, 25, 184, 191, 216,
Lamb, S.M. v, vi, xiii, xv, xviii, 1–5,
    7, 11, 13–20, 23–26, 28, 37–39,
    43–45, 47, 49–54, 68, 74, 83, 130,
    175, 179, 181, 188, 192, 202, 203,
    211, 214–219, 221–223
Langacker, R.W. 137, 190, 191, 202,
    220
Levelt, W.J.M. 203, 220
Lieberman, P. 59, 217, 220
Lockwood, D.G. xiii, 26, 38, 173,
    179, 201, 203, 215, 220–222
Lombardi, L. 169, 220
Longacre, R.E. 136, 220
Loritz, D. 7, 220

Makkai, A. 220, 222
Martínez, A. 118, 220
Mayberry, R.I. 169, 220
McCulloch, W. S. 191, 220
Mendikoetxea, A. 191, 220
Menn, L. 133, 220
Meyer, C.F. 53, 220
Miceli, G. 169,22
Monetta, L. 59, 221
Mountcastle, V. 1, 66, 67, 192, 202,
    221
Müller, E.-A. 52, 221

Ostapenko, O. 82, 221

Pandya, D.N. 84, 221
Paradis, M. xiii
Parsons, L.M. 25, 221
Patterson, K. 25, 221
Peeters, B. 190, 221
Piera, C. 118, 221
Pinker, S. 176, 192, 221
Poeppel, D. 177, 221
Pulvermüller, F. 7, 25, 66, 67, 69,
    192, 203, 221

Quian Quiroga, R. 67, 221

Raskin, S.A. 59, 221
Reich, P.A. xiii, 26, 29, 53, 56, 101,
    160, 178, 180, 189, 215, 221, 222
Roca, I. 99, 222

Sampson, G. 82, 222
Schenker, A.M. xi, 104, 105, 115,
    222
Sharp, R. 133, 222
Smith, D.J. 173, 222
Springer, J.A. 60, 222
Starčević, K. xiv, 173
Strutyński, J. 104, 222
Sullivan, Mary xiv, 171, 173
Sullivan, W.J. v, vi, xiv, 11, 12, 24,
    25, 26, 38, 39, 41, 56, 80, 81, 83,
    84, 89, 90, 98, 99, 101, 102, 103,
    115, 135, 137, 155, 160, 161, 162,
    171, 172, 173, 174, 177, 178, 179,
    180, 213, 222, 223

Swan, O.E. 104, 223

Tokarski, J. 104, 223
Trager, G.L. x, 79, 80, 223
Tsiang, S. v, xiv, 160, 161, 173, 195,
    197, 223
Tsumoto, T. 66, 223

Ullman, M.T. 59, 60

Visser, M. 25, 223

Webster, J.J. v, xv, 155, 179, 181,
    202, 217, 219, 223
Whorf, B.L. 3, 5, 223
Wickens, J.R. 74, 224
Wróbel, H. 104, 217, 224

Young, M.P. 66, 224

Zeldes, A. 105, 224
Zillmer, A. 25, 224

Index of languages

Bulgarian 179

Chinese xv, 148, 155, 200, 201
Czech 179, 201

English 4, 6–7, 16, 17, 36–38, 41, 56,
    75, 135ff., 157ff., 175, 179, 180,
    183, 185, 190, 201, 203
English, American 138

German 185

Iroquoian 182
Italian 201

Monachi xv, 14

Polish 4, 6, 16, 42, 75, 101, 103ff.,
    135, 148, 152, 157ff., 175, 179
Polynesian-type 101

Russian xv, 4, 6, 14, 16, 75, 79ff.,
    105, 115, 149, 161–162, 164, 173,
    175, 178, 179

Slavic 89
Spanish 4, 6, 75, 117ff., 149, 175,
    185, 201, 205

Ukrainian 80, 101

CPSIA information can be obtained
at www.ICGtesting.com
Printed in the USA
BVOW08*1647140517

483389BV00003B/13/P